THE DAILY STUDY BIBLE SERIES
REVISED EDITION

THE GOSPEL OF
JOHN

Volume 2

THE GOSPEL OF
JOHN

Volume 2
(Chapters 8 to 21)

REVISED EDITION

Translated
with an Introduction and Interpretation
by
WILLIAM BARCLAY

THE WESTMINSTER PRESS
PHILADELPHIA

Revised Edition
Copyright © 1975 William Barclay

First published by The Saint Andrew Press
Edinburgh, Scotland

First Edition, September, 1955

Second Edition, November, 1956

Published by The Westminster Press ®
Philadelphia, Pennsylvania

PRINTED IN THE UNITED STATES OF AMERICA

Third printing, 1977   ·

Library of Congress Cataloging in Publication Data

Bible. N.T. John. English. Barclay. 1975.
  The Gospel of John.

  (The Daily study Bible series. — Rev. ed.)
  1. Bible. N.T. John — Commentaries. I. Barclay,
William, lecturer in the University of Glasgow, ed.
II. Title. III. Series.
BS2613   1975   226'.5'077   74-30031
ISBN 0-664-21305-7 (v. 2)
ISBN 0-664-24105-0 (v. 2) pbk.

GENERAL INTRODUCTION

The Daily Study Bible series has always had one aim—to convey the results of scholarship to the ordinary reader. A. S. Peake delighted in the saying that he was a " theological middleman ", and I would be happy if the same could be said of me in regard to these volumes. And yet the primary aim of the series has never been academic. It could be summed up in the famous words of Richard of Chichester's prayer—to enable men and women " to know Jesus Christ more clearly, to love him more dearly, and to follow him more nearly ".

It is all of twenty years since the first volume of *The Daily Study Bible* was published. The series was the brain-child of the late Rev. Andrew McCosh, M.A., S.T.M., the then Secretary and Manager of the Committee on Publications of the Church of Scotland, and of the late Rev. R. G. Macdonald, O.B.E., M.A., D.D., its Convener.

It is a great joy to me to know that all through the years *The Daily Study Bible* has been used at home and abroad, by minister, by missionary, by student and by layman, and that it has been translated into many different languages. Now, after so many printings, it has become necessary to renew the printer's type and the opportunity has been taken to restyle the books, to correct some errors in the text and to remove some references which have become outdated. At the same time, the Biblical quotations within the text have been changed to use the Revised Standard Version, but my own original translation of the New Testament passages has been retained at the beginning of each daily section.

There is one debt which I would be sadly lacking in courtesy if I did not acknowledge. The work of revision and correction has been done entirely by the Rev. James Martin, M.A., B.D., Minister of High Carntyne Church, Glasgow. Had it not been for him this task would never have been undertaken, and it is impossible for me to thank him enough for the selfless toil he has put into the revision of these books.

It is my prayer that God may continue to use *The Daily Study Bible* to enable men better to understand His word.

Glasgow   WILLIAM BARCLAY

CONTENTS

viii

CONTENTS

JOHN

WRETCHEDNESS AND PITY

John 7: 53–8: 11

And each of them went to his own house; but Jesus went to the Mount of Olives. Early in the morning he was again in the Temple precincts, and all the people came to him. He sat down and went on teaching them. The scribes and Pharisees brought a woman arrested for adultery. They set her in the midst and said to him: " Teacher, this woman was arrested as she was committing adultery—in the very act. In the law Moses enjoined us to stone women like this. What do *you* say about her? " They were testing him when they said this, so that they might have some ground on which to accuse him. Jesus stooped down and wrote with his finger on the ground. When they went on asking him their question, he straightened himself and said to them: " Let the man among you who is without sin be the first to cast a stone at her." And again he bent down and wrote with his finger on the ground. One by one those who had heard what he said went out, beginning from the eldest down to the youngest. So Jesus was left alone, and the woman was still there in the midst. Jesus straightened himself and said to her: " Woman, where are they? Has no one condemned you? " She said: " No one, sir." Jesus said: " I am not going to pass judgment on you either. Go, and from now on, sin no more."

[This incident is not included in all the ancient manuscripts and appears only in a footnote in the Revised Standard Version; see the Note on pp. 290–292]

THE scribes and Pharisees were out to get some charge on which they could discredit Jesus; and here they thought they had impaled him inescapably on the horns of a dilemma. When a difficult legal question arose, the natural and routine thing was to take it to a Rabbi for a decision. So the scribes and

Pharisees approached Jesus as a Rabbi with a woman taken in adultery.

In the eyes of the Jewish law adultery was a serious crime. The Rabbis said: " Every Jew must die before he will commit idolatry, murder or adultery." Adultery was, in fact one of the three gravest sins and it was punishable by· death, although there were certain differences in respect of the way in which the death penalty was to be carried out. *Leviticus* 20: 10 lays it down: " If a man commits adultery with the wife of his neighbour, both the adulterer and the adulteress shall be put to death." There the method of death is not specified. *Deuteronomy* 22: 13–24 lays down the penalty in the case of a girl who is already betrothed. In a case like that she and the man who seduced her are to be brought outside the city gates, " and you shall stone them to death with stones." The *Mishnah*, that is, the Jewish codified law, states that the penalty for adultery is strangulation, and even the method of strangulation is laid down. " The man is to be enclosed in dung up to his knees, and a soft towel set within a rough towel is to be placed around his neck (in order that no mark may be made, for the punishment is God's punishment). Then one man draws in one direction and another in the other direction, until he be dead." The *Mishnah* reiterates that death by stoning is the penalty for a girl who is betrothed and who then commits adultery. From the purely legal point of view the scribes and Pharisees were perfectly correct. This woman was liable to death by stoning.

The dilemma into which they sought to put Jesus was this. If he said that the woman ought to be stoned to death, two things followed. First, he would lose the name he had gained for love and for mercy and never again would be called the friend of sinners. Second, he would come into collision with the Roman law, for the Jews had no power to pass or carry out the death sentence on anyone. If he said that the woman should be pardoned, it could immediately be said that he was teaching men to break the law of Moses, and that he was condoning and even encouraging people to commit adultery. That was the trap in which the scribes and Pharisees sought to entrap Jesus. But he turned their attack in such a way that it recoiled against themselves.

At first Jesus stooped down and wrote with his finger on the ground. Why did he do that? There may be four possible reasons.

(i) He may quite simply have wished to gain time and not be rushed into a decision. In that brief moment he may have been both thinking the thing out and taking it to God.

(ii) Certain manuscripts add, " As though he did not hear them." Jesus may well have deliberately forced the scribes and Pharisees to repeat their charges, so that, in repeating them, they might possibly realize the sadistic cruelty which lay behind them.

(iii) Seeley in *Ecce Homo* makes an interesting suggestion. " Jesus was seized with an intolerable sense of shame. He could not meet the eye of the crowd, or of the accusers, and perhaps at that moment least of all of the woman. . . . In his burning embarrassment and confusion he stooped down so as to hide his face, and began writing with his fingers upon the ground." It may well be that the leering, lustful look on the faces of the scribes and Pharisees, the bleak cruelty in their eyes, the prurient curiosity of the crowd, the shame of the woman, all combined to twist the very heart of Jesus in agony and pity, so that he hid his eyes.

(iv) By far the most interesting suggestion emerges from certain of the later manuscripts. The Armenian translates the passage this way: " He himself, bowing his head, was writing with his finger on the earth to declare their sins; and they were seeing their several sins on the stones." The suggestion is that Jesus was writing in the dust the sins of the very men who were accusing the woman. There may be something in that. The normal Greek word for *to write* is *graphein*; but here the word used is *katagraphein*, which can mean *to write down a record against someone*. (One of the meanings of *kata* is *against*). So in *Job* 13: 26 Job says: " Thou *writest* (*katagraphein*) bitter things against me." It may be that Jesus was confronting those self-confident sadists with the record of their own sins.

However that may be, the scribes and Pharisees continued to insist on an answer—and they got it. Jesus said in effect: " All right! Stone her! But let the man that is without sin be the first to cast a stone." It may well be that the word for *without sin* (*anamartētos*) means not only *without sin*, but even *without a sinful desire*. Jesus was saying: " Yes, you may stone her—but only if you never wanted to do the same thing yourselves." There was a silence—and then slowly the accusers drifted away.

So Jesus and the woman were left alone. As Augustine put it: " There remained a great misery (*miseria*) and a great pity (*misericordia*)." Jesus said to the woman: " Has no one condemned you? " " No one, sir," she said. Jesus said: " I am not for the moment going to pass judgment on you either. Go, and make a new start, and don't sin any more."

WRETCHEDNESS AND PITY

John 7: 53–8: 11 (*continued*)

THIS passage shows us two things about the attitude of the scribes and the Pharisees.

(i) It shows us their *conception of authority*. The scribes and the Pharisees were the legal experts of the day; to them problems were taken for decision. It is clear that to them authority was characteristically critical, censorious and condemnatory. That authority should be based on sympathy, that its aim should be to reclaim the criminal and the sinner, never entered their heads. They conceived of their function as giving them the right to stand over others like grim invigilators, to watch for every mistake and every deviation from the law, and to descend on them with savage and unforgiving punishment; they never dreamed that it might lay upon them the obligation to cure the wrongdoer.

There are still those who regard a position of authority as giving them the right to condemn and the duty to punish. They think that such authority as they have has given them the right to be moral watch-dogs trained to tear the sinner to pieces; but all true authority is founded on sympathy. When George Whitefield saw the criminal on the way to the gallows, he uttered the famous sentence: " There, but for the grace of God, go I."

The first duty of authority is to try to understand the force of the temptations which drove the sinner to sin and the seductiveness of the circumstances in which sin became so attractive. No man can pass judgment on another unless he at least tries to understand what the other has come through. The second duty of authority is to seek to reclaim the wrongdoer. Any authority which is solely concerned with punishment is wrong; any authority, which, in its exercise, drives a wrongdoer either to despair or to resentment, is a failure. The function of authority is not to banish the sinner from all decent society, still less to wipe him out; it is to make him into a good man. The man set in authority must be like a wise physician; his one desire must be to heal.

(ii) This incident shows vividly and cruelly *the attitude of the scribes and Pharisees to people.* They were not looking on this woman as a person at all; they were looking on her only as a thing, an instrument whereby they could formulate a charge against Jesus. They were using her, as a man might use a tool, for their own purposes. To them she had no name, no personality, no feelings; she was simply a pawn in the game whereby they sought to destroy Jesus.

It is always wrong to regard people as things; it is always unchristian to regard people as cases. It was said of Beatrice Webb, afterwards Lady Passfield, the famous economist, that " she saw men as specimens walking." Dr Paul Tournier in *A Doctor's Casebook* talks of what he calls " the personalism of the Bible." He points out how fond the Bible is of names. God says to Moses: " I know you by name " (*Exodus* 33: 17). God said to Cyrus; " It is I, the God of Israel, who call you by your name " (*Isaiah* 45: 3). There are whole pages of names in the Bible. Dr Tournier insists that this is proof that the Bible thinks of people first and foremost, not as fractions of the mass, or abstractions, or ideas, or cases, but as persons. " The proper name," Dr Tournier writes, " is the symbol of the person. If I forget my patients' names, if I say to myself, ' Ah! There's that gall-bladder type or that consumptive that I saw the other day,' I am interesting myself more in their gall-bladders or in their lungs than in themselves as persons." He insists that a patient must be always a person, and never a case.

It is extremely unlikely that the scribes and the Pharisees even knew this woman's name. To them she was nothing but a case of shameless adultery that could now be used as an instrument to suit their purposes. The minute people become things the spirit of Christianity is dead.

God uses his authority to love men into goodness; to God no person ever becomes a thing. We must use such authority as we have always to understand and always at least to try to mend the person who has made the mistake; and we will never even begin to do that unless we remember that every man and woman is a person, not a thing.

WRETCHEDNESS AND PITY

John 7: 53–8: 11 (*continued*)

FURTHER, this incident tells us a great deal about Jesus and his attitude to the sinner.

(i) It was a first principle of Jesus that only the man who himself is without fault has the right to express judgment on the fault of others. " Judge not," said Jesus, " that you be not judged " (*Matthew* 7: 1). He said that the man who attempted to judge his brother was like a man with a plank in his own eye trying to take a speck of dust out of someone else's eye (*Matthew* 7: 3–5). One of the commonest faults in life is that so many of us demand standards from others that we never even try to meet ourselves; and so many of us condemn faults in others which are glaringly obvious in our own lives. The qualification for

judging is not knowledge—we all possess that; it is achievement in goodness—none of us is perfect there. The very facts
of the human situation mean that only God has the right to
judge, for the simple reason that no man is good enough to
judge any other.

(ii) It was also a first principle with Jesus that our first
emotion towards anyone who has made a mistake should be
pity. It has been said that the duty of the doctor is " sometimes
to heal, often to afford relief and always to bring consolation."
When a person suffering from some ailment is brought to a
doctor, he does not regard him with loathing even if he is
suffering from a loathsome disease. In fact the physical revul-
sion which is sometimes inevitable is swallowed up by the great
desire to help and to heal. When we are confronted with
someone who has made a mistake, our first feeling ought to be,
not, " I'll have nothing more to do with someone who could act
like that," but, " What can I do to help? What can I do to undo
the consequences of this mistake? " Quite simply, we must
always extend to others the same compassionate pity we would
wish to be extended to ourselves if we were involved in a like
situation.

(iii) It is very important that we should understand just how
Jesus did treat this woman. It is easy to draw the wrong lesson
altogether and to gain the impression that Jesus forgave lightly
and easily, as if the sin did not matter. What he said was: " I
am not going to condemn you just now; *go, and sin no more*."
In effect what he was doing was not to abandon judgment and
say, " Don't worry; it's quite all right." What he did was, as it
were, *to defer sentence*. He said, " I am not going to pass a final
judgment *now*; go and prove that you can do better. You have
sinned; go and sin no more and I'll help you all the time. At the
end of the day we will see how you have lived." Jesus's attitude
to the sinner involved a number of things.

(*a*) It involved *the second chance*. It is as if Jesus said to the
woman: " I know you have made a mess of things; but life is
not finished yet; I am giving you another chance, the chance to
redeem yourself." Someone has written the lines:

> " How I wish that there was some wonderful place
>   Called the Land of Beginning Again,
>   Where all our mistakes and all our heartaches
>   And all our poor selfish grief
>   Could be dropped like a shabby old coat at the door,
>   And never put on again."

In Jesus there is the gospel of the second chance. He was always intensely interested, not only in what a person had been, but also in what a person could be. He did not say that what they had done did not matter; broken laws and broken hearts always matter; but he was sure that every man has a future as well as a past.

(*b*) It involved *pity*. The basic difference between Jesus and the scribes and Pharisees was that they wished to condemn; he wished to forgive. If we read between the lines of this story it is quite clear that they wished to stone this woman to death and were going to take pleasure in doing so. They knew the thrill of exercising the power to condemn; Jesus knew the thrill of exercising the power to forgive. Jesus regarded the sinner with pity born of love; the scribes and Pharisees regarded him with disgust born of self-righteousness.

(*c*) It involved *challenge*. Jesus confronted this woman with the challenge of the sinless life. He did not say: " It's all right; don't worry; just go on as you are doing." He said: " It's all wrong; go out and fight; change your life from top to bottom; go, and sin no more." Here was no easy forgiveness; here was a challenge which pointed a sinner to heights of goodness of which she had never dreamed. Jesus confronts the bad life with the challenge of the good.

(*d*) It involved *belief in human nature*. When we come to think of it, it is a staggering thing that Jesus should say to a woman of loose morals: " Go, and sin no more." The amazing, heart-uplifting thing about him was his belief in men and women. When he was confronted with someone who had gone wrong, he did not say: " You are a wretched and a hopeless creature." He said: " Go, and sin no more." He believed that with his help the sinner has it in him to become the saint. His method was not to blast men with the knowledge—which they already possessed—that they were miserable sinners, but to inspire them with the unglimpsed discovery that they were potential saints.

(*e*) It involved *warning*, clearly unspoken but implied. Here we are face to face with the eternal choice. Jesus confronted the woman with a choice that day—either to go back to her old ways or to reach out to the new way with him. This story is unfinished, for every life is unfinished until it stands before God.

[As we noted at the beginning, this story does not appear in all the ancient manuscripts. A discussion of the textual questions involved will be found at the end of this book.]

THE LIGHT MEN FAILED TO RECOGNIZE

John 8: 12–20

So Jesus again continued to speak to them. " I am the Light of the World," he said. " He who follows me will not walk in darkness, but he will have the light of life." So the Pharisees said to him: " You are bearing witness about yourself. Your witness is not true." Jesus answered: " Even if I do bear witness about myself, my witness is true, because I know where I came from and where I am going to. You do not know where I came from and where I am going to. You form your judgments on purely human grounds. I do not judge anyone. But if I do form a judgment, my judgment is true, because I am not alone in my judgment, but I and the Father who sent me join in such a judgment. It stands written in your law, that the witness of two persons is to be accepted as true. It is I who witness about myself, and the Father who sent me also witnesses about me." They said to him: " Where is your Father? " Jesus answered: " You know neither me nor my Father. If you had known me you would know my Father too." He spoke these words in the treasury while he was teaching in the Temple precincts; and no one laid violent hands upon him, because his hour had not yet come.

THE scene of this argument with the Jewish authorities was in the Temple treasury, which was in the Court of the Women. The first Temple court was the Court of the Gentiles; the second was the Court of the Women. It was so called because women might not pass beyond it unless they were actually about to offer sacrifice on the altar which was in the Court of the Priests. Round the Court of the Women there was a colonnade or porch; and, in that porch, set against the wall, there were thirteen treasure chests into which people dropped their offerings. These were called *The Trumpets* because they were shaped like trumpets, narrow at the top and swelling out towards the foot.

The thirteen treasure chests all had their allotted offering. Into the first two were dropped the half shekels which every Jew had to pay towards the upkeep of the Temple. Into the third and fourth were dropped sums which would purchase the two pigeons which a woman had to offer for her purification after the birth of a child (*Leviticus* 12: 8). Into the fifth were put contributions towards the cost of the wood which was needed to keep the altar fire alight. Into the sixth were dropped contributions towards the cost of the incense which was used at the Temple services. Into the seventh went contributions towards the upkeep of the golden vessels which were used at these services. Sometimes a man or a family set apart a certain sum to make some trespass- or thank-offering; into the remaining six trumpets people dropped any money which remained after such an offering had been made, or anything extra which they wished to offer.

Clearly the Temple treasury would be a busy place, with a constant flow of worshippers coming and going. There would be no better place to collect an audience of devout people and to teach them than the Temple treasury.

In this passage Jesus makes the great claim: "I am the Light of the World." It is very likely that the background against which he made it made it doubly vivid and impressive. The festival with which John connects these discourses is the Festival of Tabernacles (*John* 7: 2). We have already seen (*John*

7: 37) how its ceremonies lent drama to Jesus's claim to give to
men the living water. But there was another ceremony connected with this festival.

On the evening of its first day there was a ceremony called
The Illumination of the Temple. It took place in the Court of the
Women. The court was surrounded with deep galleries, erected
to hold the spectators. In the centre four great candelabra were
prepared. When the dark came the four great candelabra were
lit and, it was said, they sent such a blaze of light throughout
Jerusalem that every courtyard was lit up with their brilliance.
Then all night long, until cock-crow the next morning, the
greatest and the wisest and the holiest men in Israel danced
before the Lord and sang psalms of joy and praise while the
people watched. Jesus is saying: " You have seen the blaze of
the Temple illuminations piercing the darkness of the night. *I
am the Light of the World*, and, for the man who follows me
there will be light, not only for one exciting night, but for all the
pathway of his life. The light in the Temple is a brilliant light,
but in the end it flickers and dies. I am the Light which lasts for
ever."

THE LIGHT MEN FAILED TO RECOGNIZE

John 8: 12–20 (*continued*)

JESUS said: " He who follows me will not walk in darkness, but
will have the light of life." *The light of life* means two things.
The Greek can mean either the light which issues from the
source of life or the light which gives life. In this passage it
means both. Jesus is the very light of God come among men;
and he is the light which gives men life. Just as the flower can
never blossom when it never sees the sunlight, so our lives can
never flower with the grace and beauty they ought to have until
they are irradiated with the light of the presence of Jesus.

In this passage Jesus talks of *following* himself. We often
speak of following Jesus; we often urge men to do so. What do

we mean? The Greek for *to follow* is *akolouthein*; and its meanings combine to shed a flood of light on what it means *to follow* Jesus. *Akolouthein* has five different but closely connected meanings.

(i) It is often used of a soldier following his captain. On the long route marches, into battle, in campaigns in strange lands, the soldier follows wherever the captain may lead. The Christian is the soldier whose commander is Christ.

(ii) It is often used of a slave accompanying his master. Wherever the master goes the slave is in attendance upon him, always ready to spring to his service and to carry out the tasks he gives him to do. He is literally at his master's beck and call. The Christian is the slave whose joy it is always to serve Christ.

(iii) It is often used of accepting a wise counsellor's opinion. When a man is in doubt he goes to the expert, and if he is wise he accepts the judgment he receives. The Christian is the man who guides his life and conduct by the counsel of Christ.

(iv) It is often used of giving obedience to the laws of a city or a state. If a man is to be a useful member of any society or citizen of any community, he must agree to abide by its laws. The Christian, being a citizen of the kingdom of heaven, accepts the law of the kingdom and of Christ as the law which governs his life.

(v) It is often used of following a teacher's line of argument, or of following the gist of someone's speech. The Christian is the man who has understood the meaning of the teaching of Christ. He has not listened in dull incomprehension or with slack inattention. He takes the message into his mind and understands, receives the words into his memory and remembers, and hides them in his heart and obeys.

To be a follower of Christ is to give oneself body, soul and spirit into the obedience of the Master; and to enter upon that following is to walk in the light. When we walk alone we are bound to stumble and grope, for so many of life's problems are beyond our solution. When we walk alone we are bound to take the wrong way, because we have no secure map of life. We need the heavenly wisdom to walk the earthly way. The man who has

a sure guide and an accurate map is the man who is bound to
come in safety to his journey's end. Jesus Christ is that guide;
he alone possesses the map to life. To follow him is to walk in
safety through life and afterwards to enter into glory.

THE LIGHT MEN FAILED TO RECOGNIZE

John 8: 12–20 (*continued*)

WHEN Jesus made his claim to be the Light of the World the
scribes and Pharisees reacted with hostility. That claim would
sound even more astonishing to them than to us. To them it
would sound like a claim—as indeed it was—to be the
Messiah, and, even more, to do the work that only God could
do. The word *light* was specially associated in Jewish thought
and language with God. " The Lord is my *light* " (*Psalm* 27: 1).
" The Lord will be your everlasting *light* " (*Isaiah* 60: 19). " By
his *light* I walked through darkness " (*Job* 29: 3). " When I sit
in darkness the Lord will be a *light* to me " (*Micah* 7: 8). The
Rabbis declared that the name of the Messiah was Light. When
Jesus claimed to be the Light of the World, he was making a
claim than which none could possibly be higher.

The argument of this passage is difficult and complicated,
but it involves three strands.

(i) The Jews first insisted that a statement such as Jesus made
could not be regarded as accurate because it was backed by
insufficient witness. It was, as they saw it, backed by his word
alone; and it was Jewish law that any statement must be
founded on the evidence of two witnesses before it could be
regarded as true. " A single witness shall not prevail against a
man for any crime or for any wrong in connection with any
offence that he has committed; only on the evidence of two
witnesses, or of three witnesses, shall a charge be sustained "
(*Deuteronomy* 19: 15). " On the evidence of two witnesses or of
three witnesses he that is to die shall be put to death; a person
shall not be put to death on the evidence of one witness "

(*Deuteronomy* 17: 6). " No person shall be put to death on the testimony of one witness" (*Numbers* 35: 30). Jesus's answer was twofold.

First, he answered that his own witness was enough. He was so conscious of his own authority that no other witness was necessary. This was not pride or self-confidence. It was simply the supreme instance of the kind of thing which happens every day. A great surgeon is confident in his own verdict; he does not need anyone to support him; his witness is his own skill. A great lawyer or judge is sure of his own interpretation and application of the law. It is not that he is proud of his own knowledge; it is simply that he knows that he knows. Jesus was so aware of his closeness to God that he needed no other authority for his claims than his own relationship to God.

Second, Jesus said that in point of fact he *had* a second witness, and *that second witness was God.* How does God bear witness to the supreme authority of Jesus? (*a*) The witness of God is in Jesus's *words*. No man could speak with such wisdom unless God had given him knowledge. (*b*) The witness of God is in Jesus's *deeds*. No man could do such things unless God was acting through him. (*c*) The witness of God is in *the effect of Jesus upon men.* He works changes in men which are obviously beyond human power to work. The very fact that Jesus can make bad men good is proof that his power is not simply a man's power, but God's. (*d*) The witness of God is in *the reaction of men to Jesus.* Wherever and whenever Jesus has been full displayed, wherever and whenever the Cross has been preached in all its grandeur and its splendour, there has been an immediate and overwhelming response in the hearts of men. That response is the Holy Spirit of God working and witnessing in the hearts of men. It is God in our hearts who enables us to see God in Jesus.

Jesus dealt in this way with the argument of the scribes and Pharisees that his words could not be accepted because of inadequate witness. His words were in fact backed by a double witness, that of his own consciousness of authority and that of God.

(ii) Second, Jesus dealt with his right to judge. His coming into the world was not primarily for judgment; it was for love. At the same time a man's reaction to Jesus is in itself a judgment; if he sees no beauty in him, he condemns himself. Here Jesus draws a contrast between two kinds of judgment.

(*a*) There is the judgment that is based on human knowledge and human standards and which never sees below the surface. That was the judgment of the scribes and Pharisees; and, in the last analysis, that is any human judgment, for in the nature of things men can never see below the surface of things.

(*b*) There is the judgment that is based on knowledge of *all* the facts, even the hidden facts, and that can belong only to God. Jesus claims that any judgment he passes is not a human one; it is God's—because he is so one with God. Therein lies at once our comfort and our warning. Only Jesus knows all the facts. That makes him merciful as none other can ever be; but it also enables him to see the sins in us which are hidden from the eyes of men. The judgment of Jesus is perfect because it is made with the knowledge which belongs to God.

(iii) Lastly, Jesus bluntly told the scribes and Pharisees that they had no real knowledge of God. The fact that they did not recognize him for who and what he was was the proof that they did not. The tragedy was that the whole history of Israel had been designed so that the Jews should recognize the Son of God when he came; but they had become so involved with their own ideas, so intent on their own way, so sure of their own conception of what religion was that they had become blind to God.

THE FATAL INCOMPREHENSION

John 8: 21–30

So he said to them again: " I am going away, and you will search for me, and you will die in your sin. You cannot come where I am going." So the Jews said: " Surely he is not going to kill himself, because he is saying: ' You cannot come where I am going '? " He said to them: " You are from below, but I am from above. You belong to this world, but I do not belong to this world. I said to you that you will die in your sins. For if you will not believe that I am who I am, you will die in your sins." They said to him: " Who are you? " Jesus said to them: " Anything I am saying to you is only the beginning. I have many things to say about you, and many judgments to deliver on you; but he who sent me is true, and I speak to the world what I have heard from him." They did not know that it was about the Father that he was speaking to them. So Jesus said to them: " When you lift up the Son of Man, then you will know that I am who I am, and that I do nothing on my own authority, but that I speak these things as the Father has taught me. And he who sent me is with me. He has not left me alone, because I always do the things that are pleasing to him." As he said these things, many believed in him.

THIS is one of the passages of argument and debate so characteristic of the Fourth Gospel and so difficult to elucidate and to understand. In it various strands of argument are all woven together.

Jesus begins by telling his opponents that he is going away; and that, after he is gone, they will realize what they have missed, and will search for him and not find him. This is the true prophetic note. It reminds us of three things. (i) There are certain opportunities which come and which do not return. To every man is given the opportunity to accept Christ as Saviour and Lord; but that opportunity can be refused and lost. (ii) Implicit in this argument is the truth that life and time are limited. It is within an allotted span that we must make our decision for Christ. The time we have to make that decision is limited—and none of us knows what his limit is. There is therefore every reason for making it now. (iii) Just because there is opportunity in life there is also judgment. The greater the opportunity, the more clearly it beckons, the oftener it comes, the greater the judgment if it be refused or missed. This passage brings us face to face with the glory of our opportunity, and the limitation of time in which to seize it.

When Jesus spoke about going away, he was speaking about

his return to his Father and to his glory. That was precisely
where his opponents could not follow him, because by their
continuous disobedience and their refusal to accept him, they
had shut themselves off from God. His opponents met his
words with a grim and mocking jest. Jesus said that they could
not follow where he went; and they suggested that perhaps he
was going to kill himself. The point is that, according to Jewish
thought, the depths of hell were reserved for those who took
their own lives. With a kind of grim blasphemy, they were
saying: " Maybe he will take his own life; maybe he is on the
way to the depths of Hell; it is true that we cannot and will not
follow him there.

Jesus said that if they continued to refuse him they would *die
in their sins*. That is a prophetic phrase (cp. *Ezekiel* 3: 18; 18:
18). There are two things involved there. (i) The word for sin is
hamartia, which originally had to do with shooting and literally
means *a missing of the target*. The man who refuses to accept
Jesus as Saviour and Lord has missed the target in life. He dies
with life unrealized; and he therefore dies unfitted to enter into
the higher life with God. (ii) The essence of sin is that it
separates a man from God. When Adam, in the old story,
committed the first sin, his first instinct was to hide himself
from God (*Genesis* 3: 8–10). The man who dies in sin dies at
enmity with God; the man who accepts Christ already walks
with God, and death only opens the way to a closer walk. To
refuse Christ is to be a stranger to God; to accept him is to be
the friend of God, and in that friendship the fear of death is for
ever banished.

THE FATAL INCOMPREHENSION

John 8: 21–30 (*continued*)

JESUS goes on to draw a series of contrasts. His opponents
belong to earth, he is from heaven; they are of the world; he is
not of the world.

John frequently talks about the world; the word in Greek is *kosmos*. He uses it in a way that is all his own.

(i) The *kosmos* is the opposite of heaven. Jesus came from heaven into the world (*John* 1: 9). He was sent by God into the world (*John* 3: 17). He is not of the world; his opponents are of the world (*John* 8: 23). The *kosmos* is the changing, transient life that we live; it is all that is human as opposed to all that is divine.

(ii) Yet the *kosmos* is not separated from God. First and foremost, it is God's creation (*John* 1: 10). It was through God's word that his world was made. Different as the world is from heaven, there is yet no unbridgeable gulf between them.

(iii) More than that, the *kosmos* is the object of God's love. God so loved the world that he sent his Son (*John* 3: 16). However different it may be from all that is divine, God has never abandoned it; it is the object of his love and the recipient of his greatest gift.

(iv) But at the same time there is something wrong with the *kosmos*. There is a *blindness* in it; when the Creator came into the world, it did not recognize him (*John* 1: 10). The world cannot receive the Spirit of truth (*John* 14: 17). The world does not know God (*John* 17: 25). There is, too, an hostility to God in the *kosmos* and to his people. The world hates Christ and hates his followers (*John* 15: 18, 19). In its hostility Christ's followers can look only for trouble and tribulation (*John* 16: 33).

(v) Here we have a strange sequence of facts. The world is separate from God; and yet between it and God there is no gulf which cannot be spanned. God created the world; God loves it; God sent his Son into it. And yet in it, there is this blindness and hostility to him.

There is only one possible conclusion. G. K. Chesterton once said that there was only one thing certain about man—that man is not what he was meant to be. There is only one thing certain about the *kosmos*, it is not what it was meant to be. Something has gone wrong. That something is sin. It is sin which separated the world from God; it is sin which blinds it to

God; it is sin which is fundamentally hostile to God.

Into this world which has gone wrong comes Christ; and Christ comes with the cure. He brings forgiveness; he brings cleansing; he brings strength and grace to live as man ought and to make the world what it ought to be. But a man can refuse a cure. A doctor may tell a patient that a certain treatment is able to restore him to health; he may actually tell him that if he does not accept the treatment, death is inevitable. That is precisely what Jesus is saying: " If you will not believe that I am who I am you will die in your sins."

There is something wrong with the world—anyone can see that. Only recognition of Jesus Christ as the Son of God, obedience to his perfect wisdom and acceptance of him as Saviour and Lord can cure the individual soul and cure the world.

We are only too well aware of the disease which haunts and wrecks the world; the cure lies before us. The responsibility is ours if we refuse to accept it.

THE TRAGIC INCOMPREHENSION

John 8: 21–30 (*continued*)

THERE is no verse in all the New Testament more difficult to translate than *John* 8: 25. No one can really be sure what the Greek means. It could mean: " Even what I have told you from the beginning," which is the meaning the Revised Standard Version takes. Other suggested translations are: " Primarily, essentially, I am what I am telling you." " I declare to you that I am the beginning." " How is it that I even speak to you at all? " which is the translation of Moffatt. It is suggested in our translation that it may mean: " Everything I am saying to you now is only a beginning." If we take it like that, the passage goes on to say that men will see the real meaning of Christ in three ways.

(i) They will see it in the Cross. It is when Christ is lifted up that we really see what he is. It is there we see the love that will never let men go and which loves them to the end.

(ii) They will see it in the Judgment. He has many judgments still to pass. At the moment he might look like the outlawed carpenter of Nazareth; but the day will come when they will see him as judge and know what he is.

(iii) When that happens they will see in him the embodied will of God. " I *always* do the things that are pleasing to him," Jesus said. Other men however good are spasmodic in their obedience. The obedience of Jesus is continuous, perfect and complete. The day must come when men see that in him is the very mind of God.

THE TRUE DISCIPLESHIP

John 8: 31–32

> So Jesus said to the Jews who had come to believe in him:
> " If you remain in my word, you are truly my disciples: and
> you will know the truth: and the truth will make you free."

FEW New Testament passages have such a complete picture of discipleship as this.

(i) *Discipleship begins with belief.* Its beginning is the moment when a man accepts what Jesus says as true, all that he says about the love of God, all that he says about the terror of sin, all that he says about the real meaning of life.

(ii) *Discipleship means constantly remaining in the word of Jesus* and that involves four things.

(*a*) It involves constant *listening* to the word of Jesus. It was said of John Brown of Haddington that when he preached he paused every now and then as if listening for a voice. The Christian is the man who all his life listens for the voice of Jesus and will take no decision until he has first heard what he has to say.

(*b*) It involves constant *learning* from Jesus. The disciple (*mathētēs*) is literally *the learner*, for that is what the Greek word means. All his life a Christian should be learning more and more about Jesus. The shut mind is the end of discipleship.

(c) It involves constant *penetrating* into the truth which the words of Jesus bear. No one can hear or read the words of Jesus once and then say that he understands their full meaning. The difference between a great book and an ephemeral one lies in the fact that we read an ephemeral book once and never wish to go back to it; whereas we read a great book many times. To remain in the word of Jesus means constantly to study and think about what he said until more and more of its meaning becomes ours.

(d) It involves constant *obeying* of the word of Jesus. We study it not simply for academic satisfaction or for intellectual appreciation, but in order to find out what God wishes us to do. The disciple is the learner who learns in order to do. The truth which Jesus brought is designed for action.

(iii) *Discipleship issues in knowledge of the truth.* To learn from Jesus is to learn the truth. " You will know the truth," said Jesus. What is that truth? There are many possible answers to that question but the most comprehensive way to put it is that the truth which Jesus brings shows us the real values of life. The fundamental question to which every man has consciously or unconsciously to give an answer is: " To what am I to give my life? To a career? To the amassing of material possessions? To pleasure? To the service of God? " In the truth of Jesus we see what things are really important and what are not.

(iv) *Discipleship results in freedom.* " The truth will make you free." " In his service is perfect freedom." Discipleship brings us four freedoms. (a) It brings us freedom from *fear*. The man who is a disciple never again has to walk alone. He walks for ever in the company of Jesus, and in that company fear is gone. (b) It brings freedom from *self*. Many a man fully recognizes that his greatest handicap is his own self. And he may in despair cry out: " I cannot change myself. I have tried, but it is impossible." But the power and presence of Jesus can re-create a man until he is altogether new. (c) It brings freedom from *other people*. There are many whose lives are dominated by the fear of what other people may think and say. H. G. Wells once said that the voice of our neighbours sounds louder in our ears than the voice of God. The disciple is the man who has ceased to care what people say, because he thinks only of what God says. (*d*) It brings freedom from *sin*. Many a man has come to the stage when he sins, not because he wants to, but because he cannot help it. His sins have so mastered him that, try as he will, he cannot break away from them. Discipleship breaks the chains which bind us to them and enables us to be the persons we know we ought to be.

> " O that a man may arise in me
>   That the man I am may cease to be "—

that is the very prayer which the disciple of Christ will find answered.

FREEDOM AND SLAVERY

John 8: 33–36

> They answered him: " We are the descendants of Abraham and we have never been slaves to any man. How do you say: ' You will become free '? " Jesus answered them: " This is the truth I tell you—everyone who commits sin is the slave of sin. The slave is not a permanent resident in the house; the son is a permanent resident. If the son shall make you free you will be really free."

JESUS'S talk of freedom annoyed the Jews. They claimed that they had never been slaves to any man. Obviously there was a sense in which this was simply not true. They had been captives in exile in Babylon; and at the moment they were subjects of the Romans. But the Jews set a tremendous value on freedom which they held to be the birthright of every Jew. In the Law it was laid down that no Jew, however poor, must descend to the level of being a slave. " And if your brother becomes poor beside you, ànd sells himself to you, you shall not make him serve as a slave: ... For they are my servants, whom I brought

forth out of the land of Egypt; they shall not be sold as slaves "
(*Leviticus* 25: 39–42). Again and again Jewish rebellions flared
up because some fiery leader arose who insisted that the Jews
could obey no earthly ruler because God was their only King.

Josephus writes of the followers of Judas of Galilee who led a
famous revolt against the Romans: " They have an inviolable
attachment to liberty, and they say that God is to be their only
Ruler and Lord " (Josephus, *Antiquities of the Jews*, 18: 1, 6).
When the Jews said that they had been no man's slaves they
were saying something which was a fundamental article of their
creed of life. And even if it was true that there had been times
when they were subject to other nations, even if it was true that
at that very moment they were subject to Rome, it was also true
that even in servitude they maintained an independence of spirit
which meant that they might be slaves in body but never in
soul. Cyril of Jerusalem wrote of Joseph: " Joseph was sold to
be a bond slave, yet he was free, all radiant in the nobility of his
soul." Even to suggest to a Jew that he might be regarded as a
slave was a deadly insult.

But it was another slavery of which Jesus was speaking.
" Everyone," he said, " who commits sin is the slave of sin."
Jesus was reiterating a principle which the wise Greeks had
stated again and again. The Stoics said: " Only the wise man is
free; the foolish man is a slave." Socrates had demanded:
" How can you call a man free when his pleasures rule over
him? " Paul later was to thank God that the Christian was freed
from slavery to sin (*Romans* 6: 17–20).

There is something very interesting and very suggestive here.
Sometimes when a man is rebuked for doing something wrong
or warned against such a thing, his answer is: " Surely I can do
what I like with my own life." But the point is that the man who
sins does *not* do what he likes; he does what sin likes. A man
can let a habit get such a grip of him that he cannot break it. He
can allow a pleasure to master him so completely that he cannot
do without it. He can let some self-indulgence so dominate him
that he is powerless to break away from it. He can get into such
a state that in the end, as Seneca said, he hates and loves his

sins at one and the same time. So far from doing what he likes, the sinner has lost the power to do what he likes. He is a slave to the habits, the self-indulgences, the wrong pleasures which have mastered him. This is precisely Jesus's point. No man who sins can ever be said to be free.

Then Jesus makes a veiled threat, but one which the listening Jews would well understand. The word *slave* reminds him that in any household there is a difference between the slave and the son. The son is a permanent dweller in the household, but the slave can be ejected at any time. In effect Jesus is saying to the Jews: " You think that you are sons in God's house and that nothing, therefore, can ever banish you from God. Have a care; by your conduct you are making yourselves slaves, and the slave can be ejected from the master's presence at any time." Here is a threat. It is a terrible thing to trade on the mercy of God—and that is what the Jews were doing. There is warning here for more than the Jews.

REAL SONSHIP

John 8: 37–41

" I know that you are the descendants of Abraham, but you are trying to find a way to kill me, because there is no room in you for my word. I speak what I have seen in the presence of the Father. So you must do what you have heard from the Father." " Our father is Abraham," they answered. " If," answered Jesus, " you are the children of Abraham, act as Abraham acted. But, as it is, you are trying to find a way to kill me, a man who has spoken the truth to you, truth which I heard from God. That Abraham did not do. As for you, you do the works of your father."

IN this passage Jesus is dealing a death-blow to a claim which to the Jews was all-important. For the Jew Abraham was the greatest figure in all religious history; and the Jew considered himself safe and secure in the favour of God simply because he was a descendant of Abraham. The psalmist could address the

people as : " O offspring of Abraham his servant, sons of
Jacob, his chosen ones! " (*Psalm* 105: 6). Isaiah said to the
people: " But you, Israel, (are) my servant, Jacob, whom I have
chosen, the offspring of Abraham, my friend " (*Isaiah* 41: 8).
The admiration which the Jews gave to Abraham was perfectly
legitimate, for he is a giant in the religious history of mankind,
but the deductions they drew from his greatness were quite
misguided. They believed that Abraham had gained such merit
from his goodness that this merit was sufficient, not only for
himself, but for all his descendants also. Justin Martyr had a
discussion with Trypho the Jew about Jewish religion and the
conclusion was that, " the eternal kingdom will be given to
those who are the seed of Abraham according to the flesh, even
though they be sinners and unbelievers and disobedient to
God " (Justin Martyr, *The Dialogue with Trypho*, 140). Quite
literally the Jew believed that he was safe because he was a
descendant of Abraham.

The attitude of the Jews is not without parallel in modern life.

(*a*) There are still those who try to live on a *pedigree and a
name*. At some time in the history of their family someone
performed some really outstanding service to church or state,
and ever since they have claimed a special place because of
that. But a great name should never be an excuse for comfort-
able inaction; it should always be an inspiration to new effort.

(*b*) There are those who try to live on *a history and a
tradition*. Many a church has a quite undue sense of its own
importance because at one time it had a famous ministry. There
is many a congregation living on the spiritual capital of the
past; but if capital be always drawn upon and never built up
anew, the day inevitably comes when it is exhausted.

No man or church or nation can live on the achievements of
the past. That is what the Jews were trying to do.

Jesus is quite blunt about this. He declares in effect that the
real descendant of Abraham is the man who acts in the way in
which Abraham acted. That is exactly what John the Baptist
had said before. He had told the people plainly that the day of
judgment was on the way and that it was no good pleading that

they were descendants of Abraham, for God could raise up descendants to Abraham from the very stones, if he chose to do so (*Matthew* 3: 9; *Luke* 3: 8). It was the argument which again and again Paul was to use. It was not flesh and blood which made a man a descendant of Abraham; it was moral quality and spiritual fidelity.

In this particular matter Jesus ties it down to one thing. They are seeking a way to kill him; that is precisely the opposite of what Abraham did. When a messenger from God came to him, Abraham welcomed him with all eagerness and reverence (*Genesis* 18: 1–8). Abraham had welcomed God's messenger; the Jews of the present were trying to kill God's messenger. How could they dare call themselves descendants of Abraham, when their conduct was so very different?

By calling to mind the old story in *Genesis* 18, Jesus is implying that he too is the messenger of God. Then he makes the claim explicit: " I speak what I have seen in the presence of the Father." The fundamental thing about Jesus is that he brought to men, not his own opinions, but a message from God. He was not simply a man telling other men what he thought about things; he was the Son of God telling men what God thought. He told men the truth as God sees it.

At the end of this passage comes a shattering statement. " You," said Jesus, " do the works of your father." He has just said that Abraham is *not* their father. Who then is their father? For a moment the full impact is held back. It comes in verse 44—their father is the devil. Those who had gloried in the claim that they are the children of Abraham are devastatingly confronted with the charge that they are children of the devil. Their works had revealed their true sonship, for man can prove his kinship to God only by his conduct.

CHILDREN OF THE DEVIL

John 8: 41–45

> They said to him: " We were born of no adulterous union. We
> have one Father—God." " If God was your Father," said Jesus,
> " you would love me. For it was from God that I came forth and
> have come here. I had nothing to do with my own coming, but it
> was he who sent me. Why do you not understand what I am
> saying? The reason is that you are unable to hear my word. You
> belong to your father, the devil, and it is the evil desires of your
> father that you wish to do. He was a murderer from the very
> beginning, and he never took his stand in the truth, because the
> truth is not in him. When he speaks falsehood it is his charac-
> teristic way of speaking, because he is a liar and the father of
> falsehood. But because I speak the truth, you do not believe in
> me."

JESUS had just told the Jews that by their life and conduct and
by their reaction to him they had made it clear that they were
no real children of Abraham. Their reaction was to make an
even greater claim. They claimed that God was their Father. All
over the Old Testament there is repeated the fact that God was
in a special way the Father of his people Israel. God commanded Moses to say to Pharaoh: " Thus saith the Lord, Israel
is my firstborn son " (*Exodus* 4: 22). When Moses was chiding
the people for their disobedience, his appeal was: " Do you thus
requite the Lord, you foolish and senseless people? Is not he
your Father who created you? " (*Deuteronomy* 32: 6). Isaiah
speaks of his trust in God: " For thou art our Father, though
Abraham does not know us and Israel does not acknowledge
us; thou, O Lord, art our Father, our Redeemer from of old is
thy name " (*Isaiah* 63: ·16). " Yet, O Lord, thou art our
Father " (*Isaiah* 64: 8). " Have we not all one Father? "
demanded Malachi. " Has not one God created us? " (*Malachi*
2: 10). So the Jews claimed that God was their Father.

" We," they said proudly, " were born of no adulterous
union." There may be two things there. In the Old Testament

one of the loveliest descriptions of the nation of Israel is that which sees in her the Bride of God. Because of that when Israel forsook God, she was said to go awhoring after strange gods; her infidelity was spiritual adultery. When the nation was thus faithless, the apostate people were said to be " children of harlotry " (*Hosea* 2: 4). So when the Jews said to Jesus that they were not the children of any adulterous union, they meant that they did not belong to a nation of idolaters but they had always worshipped the true God. It was a claim that they had never gone astray from God—a claim that only a people steeped in self-righteousness would ever have dared make.

But when the Jews spoke like this, there may have been something much more personal in it. It is certainly true in later times that the Jews spread abroad a most malicious slander against Jesus. The Christians very early preached the miraculous birth of Jesus. The Jews put it about that Mary had been unfaithful to Joseph; that her paramour had been a Roman soldier called Panthera; and that Jesus was the child of that adulterous union. It is just possible that the Jews were flinging at Jesus even then an insult over his birth, as if to say: " What right have you to speak to the like of us as you do? "

Jesus's answer to the claim of the Jews is that it is false; and the proof is that if God was really their Father, they would have loved and welcomed him. Here again is the key thought of the Fourth Gospel; the test of a man is his reaction to Jesus. To be confronted with Jesus is to be confronted with judgment; he is the touchstone of God by which all men are judged.

Jesus's closeknit indictment goes on. He asks " Why do you not understand what I am saying? " The answer is terrible—not that they are intellectually stupid, but that they are spiritually deaf. They refuse to hear and they refuse to understand. A man can stop his ears to any warning; if he goes on doing that long enough, he becomes spiritually deaf. In the last analysis, a man will only hear what he wishes to hear; and if for long enough he attunes his ears to his own desires and to the wrong voices, in the end he will be unable to tune in at all to the wavelength of God. That is what the Jews had done.

Then comes the scarifying accusation. The real father of the Jews is the devil. Jesus chooses two characteristics of him.

(i) The devil is characteristically a murderer. There may be two things in Jesus's mind. He may be thinking back to the old Cain and Abel story. Cain was the first murderer and he was inspired by the devil. He may be thinking of something even more serious than that. It was the devil who first tempted man in the old *Genesis* story. Through the devil sin entered into the world; and through sin came death (*Romans* 5: 13). If there had been no temptation, there would have been no sin; and, if there had been no sin, there would have been no death; and therefore, in a sense, the devil is the murderer of the whole human race.

But, even apart from the old stories, the fact remains that Christ leads to life and the devil to death. The devil murders goodness, chastity, honour, honesty, beauty, all that makes life lovely; he murders peace of mind and happiness and even love. Evil characteristically destroys; Christ characteristically brings life. At that very moment the Jews were plotting how to kill Christ; they were taking the devil's way.

(ii) The devil characteristically loves falsehood. Every lie is inspired by the devil and does the devil's work. Falsehood always hates the truth, and always tries to destroy it. When the Jews and Jesus met, the false way met the true, and inevitably the false tried to destroy the true.

Jesus indicted the Jews as children of the devil because their thoughts were bent on the destruction of the good and the maintaining of the false. Every man who tries to destroy the truth is doing the devil's work.

THE GREAT INDICTMENT AND THE SHINING FAITH

John 8: 46–50

" Who of you can convict me of sin? If I speak the truth, why do you not believe in me? He who is from God hears God's words. That is why you do not hear, because you are not from God." The

Jews answered: " Are we not right in saying that you are a
Samaritan, and that you have a devil? " Jesus answered: " It is
not I who have a devil. I honour my Father, but you dishonour
me. I do not seek my own glory. There is One who seeks and
judges."

WE must try to see this scene happening before our eyes. There
is drama here, and it is not only in the words, but in the pauses
between them. Jesus began with a tremendous claim. " Is there
anyone here," he demanded, " who can point the finger at any
evil in my life? " Then must have followed a silence during
which the eyes of Jesus ranged round the crowd waiting for
anyone to accept the extraordinary challenge that he had
thrown down. The silence went on. Search as they like, none
could formulate a charge against him. When he had given them
their chance, Jesus spoke again. " You admit," he said, " that
you can find no charge against me. Then why do you not accept
what I say? " Again there was an uncomfortable silence. Then
Jesus answered his own question. " You do not accept my
words," he said, " because you are not from God."

What did Jesus mean? Think of it this way. No experience
can enter into a man's mind and heart unless there is something
there to answer to it; and a man may lack the something
essential which will enable him to have the experience. A man
who is tone deaf cannot experience the thrill of music. A
man who is colour blind cannot fully appreciate a picture. A
man with no sense of time and rhythm cannot fully appreciate
ballet or dancing.

Now the Jews had a very wonderful way of thinking of the
Spirit of God. They believed that he had two great functions.
He revealed God's truth to men; and he enabled men to
recognize and grasp that truth when they saw it. That quite
clearly means that unless the Spirit of God is in a man's heart
he *cannot* recognize God's truth when he sees it. And it also
means that if a man shuts the door of his heart against the
Spirit of God, then, even when the truth is full displayed before
his eyes, he is quite unable to see it and recognize it and grasp it
and make it his.

Jesus was saying to the Jews: " You have gone your own way and followed your own ideas; the Spirit of God has been unable to gain an entry into your hearts; that is why you cannot recognize me and that is why you will not accept my words." The Jews believed they were religious people; but because they had clung to their idea of religion instead of to God's idea, they had in the end drifted so far from God that they had become godless. They were in the terrible position of men who were godlessly serving God.

To be told that they were strangers to God stung the Jews to the quick. They hurled their invective against Jesus. As our present form of the words has it they accused him of being a Samaritan and of being mad. What did they mean by calling him a Samaritan? They meant that he was a foe of Israel, for there was deadly enmity between the Jews and the Samaritans, that he was a law breaker because he did not observe the law, and above all that he was a heretic, for Samaritan and heretic had become synonymous. It would be extraordinary that the Son of God should be branded as a heretic. And beyond a doubt it would happen to him again if he returned to this world and its churches.

But it is just possible that the word Samaritan is really a corruption of something else. To begin with, we note that Jesus replied to the charge that he was mad, but did not reply to the charge that he was a Samaritan. That makes us wonder if we have the charge of the Jews rightly stated. In the original Aramaic the word for Samaritan would be *Shomeroni*. *Shomeron* was also a title for the prince of the devils, otherwise called Ashmedai and Sammael and Satan. In point of fact the *Koran*, the Mohammedan bible, actually says that the Jews were seduced into idolatry by Shomeron, the prince of the devils. So the word *Shomeroni* could quite well mean *a child of the devil*. It is very likely that what the Jews said to Jesus was: " You are a child of the devil; you have a devil; you are mad with the madness of the Evil One."

His answer was that, so far from being a servant of the devil, his one aim was to honour God, while the conduct of the Jews was a continual dishonouring of God. He says in effect: " It is not *I* who have a devil; it is *you*."

Then comes the radiance of the supreme faith of Jesus. He says: " I am not looking for honour in this world: I know that I will be insulted and rejected and dishonoured and crucified. But there is One who will one day assess things at their true value and assign to men their true honour; and he will give me the honour which is real because it is his." Of one thing Jesus was sure—ultimately God will protect the honour of his own. In time Jesus saw nothing but pain and dishonour and rejection; in eternity he saw only the glory which he who is obedient to God will some day receive. In *Paracelsus* Browning wrote:

> " If I stoop
> Into a dark tremendous sea of cloud,
> It is but for a time; I press God's lamp
> Close to my breast; its splendour, soon or late,
> Will pierce the gloom: I shall emerge one day."

Jesus had the supreme optimism born of supreme faith, the optimism which is rooted in God.

THE LIFE AND THE GLORY

John 8: 51–55

" This is the truth I tell you—if anyone keeps my word, he will not see death for ever." The Jews said to him: " Now we are certain that you are mad. Abraham died and so did the prophets, yet you are saying: ' If anyone keeps my word, he will not taste of death for ever.' Surely you are not greater than our father Abraham who did die? And the prophets died too. Who are you making yourself out to be? " Jesus answered: " It is my Father who glorifies me, that Father, who, you claim, is your God, and yet you know nothing about him. But I know him. If I were to say that I do not know him, I would be a liar, like you. But I know him and I keep his word."

THIS chapter passes from lightning flash to lightning flash of astonishment. Jesus makes claim after claim, each more tremendous than the one which went before. Here he makes the claim that if anyone keeps his words, he will never know death. It shocked the Jews. Zechariah had said: " Your fathers, where are they? And the prophets, do they live for ever? " (*Zechariah* 1: 5). Abraham was dead; the prophets were dead; and had they not, in their day and generation, kept the word of God? Who is Jesus to set himself above the great ones of the faith? It is the literalmindedness of the Jews which blocks their intelligence. It is not physical life and physical death of which Jesus is thinking. He means that, for the man who fully accepts him, death has lost its finality; he has entered into a relationship with God which neither time nor eternity can sever. He goes, not from life to death, but from life to life; death is only the introduction to the nearer presence of God.

From that Jesus goes on to make a great statement—*all true honour must come from God*. It is not difficult to honour oneself; it is easy enough—in fact, fatally easy—to bask in the sunshine of one's own approval. It is not over difficult to win honour from men; the world honours the successful man. But the real honour is the honour which only eternity can reveal; and the verdicts of eternity are not the verdicts of time.

Then Jesus makes the two claims which are the very foundation of his life.

(i) He claims *unique knowledge of God*. He claims to know him as no one else ever has known him or ever will. Nor will he lower that claim, for to do so would be a lie. The only way to full knowledge of the heart and mind of God is through Jesus Christ. With our own minds we can reach fragments of knowledge about God; but only in Jesus Christ is the full orb of truth, for only in him do we see what God is like.

(ii) He claims *unique obedience to God*. To look at Jesus is to be able to say; " This is how God wishes me to live." To look at his life is to say: " This is serving God."

In Jesus alone we see what God wants us to know and what God wants us to be.

THE TREMENDOUS CLAIM

John 8: 56–59

" Abraham your father rejoiced to see my day; and he saw it and
was glad." The Jews said to him: " You are not yet fifty years old,
and have you seen Abraham? " Jesus said to them: " This is the
truth I tell you—before Abraham was I am." So they lifted stones
to throw them at him, but Jesus slipped out of their sight, and
went out of the Temple precincts.

ALL the previous lightning flashes pale into significance before
the blaze of this passage. When Jesus said to the Jews that
Abraham rejoiced to see his day, he was talking language that
they could understand. The Jews had many beliefs about
Abraham which would enable them to see what Jesus was
implying. There were altogether five different ways in which
they would interpret this passage.

(*a*) Abraham was living in Paradise and able to see what was
happening on earth. Jesus used that idea in the Parable of Dives
and Lazarus (*Luke* 16: 22–31). That is the simplest way to
interpret this saying.

(*b*) But that is not the correct interpretation. Jesus said
Abraham *rejoiced* to see my day, the past tense. The Jews
interpreted many passages of scripture in a way that explains
this. They took the great promise to Abraham in *Genesis* 12: 3:
" By you all the families of the earth shall bless themselves,"
and said that when that promise was made, Abraham knew that
it meant that the Messiah of God was to come from his line and
rejoiced at the magnificence of the promise.

(*c*)' Some of the Rabbis held that in *Genesis* 15: 8–21
Abraham was given a vision of the whole future of the nation of
Israel and therefore had a vision beforehand of the time when
the Messiah would come.

(*d*) Some of the Rabbis took *Genesis* 17: 17, which tells how
Abraham laughed when he heard that a son would be born to
him, not as a laugh of unbelief, but as a laugh of sheer joy that
from him the Messiah would come.

(*e*) Some of the Rabbis had a fanciful interpretation of *Genesis* 24: 1. There the Revised Standard Version has it that Abraham was " well advanced in years." The margin of the Authorised Version tells us that the Hebrew literally means that Abraham had " gone into days." Some of the Rabbis held that to mean that in a vision given by God Abraham had *entered into the days which lay ahead*, and had seen the whole history of the people and the coming of the Messiah.

From all this we see clearly that the Jews did believe that somehow Abraham, while he was still alive, had a vision of the history of Israel and the coming of the Messiah. So when Jesus said that Abraham had seen his day, he was making a deliberate claim that he was the Messiah. He was really saying: " I am the Messiah Abraham saw in his vision."

Immediately Jesus goes on to say of Abraham: " He saw it (my day) and was glad." Some of the early Christians had a very fanciful interpretation of that. In 1 *Peter* 3: 18–22 and 4: 6 we have the two passages which are the basis of that doctrine which became imbedded in the creed in the phrase, " He descended into Hell." It is to be noted that the word *Hell* gives the wrong idea; it ought to be *Hades*. The idea is not that Jesus went to the place of the tortured and the damned, as the word Hell suggests. Hades was the land of the shadows where all the dead, good and bad alike, went; in which the Jews believed before the full belief in immortality came to them. The apocryphal work called the Gospel of Nicodemus or the Acts of Pilate has a passage which runs: " O Lord Jesus Christ, the resurrection and the life of the world, give us grace that we may tell of thy resurrection and of thy marvellous works, which thou didst in Hades. We, then, were in Hades together with all them that have fallen asleep since the beginning. And at the hour of midnight there rose upon those dark places as it were the light of the sun, and shined, and all we were enlightened and beheld one another. And straightway our father Abraham, together with the patriarchs and the prophets, were at once filled with joy and said to one another: ' This light cometh of the great lightening.' " The dead saw Jesus and were given the chance to believe and to repent; and at that sight Abraham rejoiced.

To us these ideas are strange; to a Jew they were quite normal, for he believed that Abraham had already seen the day when the Messiah would come.

The Jews, although they knew better, chose to take this literally. " How," they demanded, " can you have seen Abraham when you are not yet fifty? " Why fifty? That was the age at which the Levites retired from their service (*Numbers* 4: 3). The Jews were saying to Jesus: " You are a young man, still in the prime of life, not even old enough to retire from service. How can you possibly have seen Abraham? This is mad talk." It was then that Jesus made that most staggering statement: " Before Abraham was, I am." We must note carefully that Jesus did not say: " Before Abraham was, I *was*," but, " Before Abraham was, I *am*." Here is the claim that Jesus is *timeless*. There never was a time when he came into being; there never will be a time when he is not in being.

What did he mean? Obviously he did not mean that he, the human figure Jesus, had always existed. We know that Jesus was born into this world at Bethlehem; there is more than that here. Think of it this way. There is only one person in the universe who is timeless; *and that one person is God*. What Jesus is saying here is nothing less than that the life in him is the life of God; he is saying, as the writer of the Hebrews put it more simply, that he is the same yesterday, today and forever. In Jesus we see, not simply a man who came and lived and died; we see the timeless God, who was the God of Abraham and of Isaac and of Jacob, who was before time and who will be after time, who always *is*. In Jesus the eternal God showed himself to men.

LIGHT FOR THE BLIND EYES

John 9: 1–5

> As Jesus was passing by, he saw a man who was blind from the day of his birth. " Rabbi," his disciples said to him, " who was it who sinned that he was born blind—this man or his parents? " " It was neither he nor his parents who sinned," answered Jesus, " but it happened that in him there might be a demonstration of what God can do. We must do the works of him who sent me while day lasts; the night is coming when no man is able to work. So long as I am in the world, I am the light of the world."

THIS is the only miracle in the gospels in which the sufferer is said to have been afflicted from his birth. In *Acts* we twice hear of people who had been helpless from their birth (the lame man at the Beautiful Gate of the Temple in *Acts* 3: 2, and the cripple at Lystra in *Acts* 14: 8), but this is the only man in the gospel story who had been so afflicted. He must have been a well-known character, for the disciples knew all about him.

When they saw him, they used the opportunity to put to Jesus a problem with which Jewish thought had always been deeply concerned, and which is still a problem. The Jews connected suffering and sin. They worked on the assumption that wherever there was suffering, somewhere there was sin. So they asked Jesus their question. " This man," they said, " is blind. Is his blindness due to his own sin, or to the sin of his parents? "

How could the blindness possibly be due to his own sin, when he had been blind *from his birth*? To that question the Jewish theologians gave two answers.

(i) Some of them had the strange notion of prenatal sin. They actually believed that a man could begin to sin while still in his mother's womb. In the imaginary conversations between Antoninus and Rabbi Judah the Patriarch, Antoninus asks: " From what time does the evil influence bear sway over a man, from the formation of the embryo in the womb or from the moment of birth? " The Rabbi first answered: " From the formation of the embryo." Antoninus disagreed and convinced Judah by his arguments, for Judah admitted that, if the evil impulse began with the formation of the embryo, then the child would kick in the womb and break his way out. Judah found a text to support this view. He took the saying in *Genesis* 4: 7: " Sin is couching at the door." And he put the meaning into it that sin awaited man at the door of the womb, as soon as he was born. But the argument does show us that the idea of pre-natal sin was known.

(ii) In the time of Jesus the Jews believed in the pre-existence of the soul. They really got that idea from Plato and the Greeks. They believed that all souls existed before the creation of the world in the garden of Eden, or that they were in the seventh heaven, or in a certain chamber, waiting to enter into a body. The Greeks had believed that such souls were good, and that it was the entry into the body which contaminated them; but there were certain Jews who believed that these souls were already good and bad. The writer of *The Book of Wisdom* says: " Now I was a child good by nature, and a good soul fell to my lot " (*Wisdom* 8: 19).

In the time of Jesus certain Jews did believe that a man's affliction, even if it be from birth, might come from sin that he had committed before he was born. It is a strange idea, and it may seem to us almost fantastic; but at its heart lies the idea of a sin-infected universe.

The alternative was that the man's affliction was due to the sin of his parents. The idea that children inherit the consequences of their parents' sin is woven into the thought of the Old Testament. " I the Lord your God am a jealous God, visiting the iniquity of the fathers upon the children to the third and the fourth generation " (*Exodus* 20: 5: cp. *Exodus* 34: 7, *Numbers* 14: 18). Of the wicked man the psalmist says: " May the iniquity of his fathers be remembered before the Lord; and let not the sin of his mother be blotted out " (*Psalm* 109: 14). Isaiah talks about their iniquities and the " iniquities of their fathers," and goes on to say: " I will measure into their bosom payment for their former doings " (*Isaiah* 65: 6, 7). One of the keynotes of the Old Testament is that the sins of the fathers are always visited upon the children. It must never be forgotten that no man lives to himself and no man dies to himself. When a man sins, he sets in motion a train of consequences which has no end.

LIGHT FOR THE BLIND EYES

John 9: 1–5 (*continued*)

IN this passage there are two great eternal principles.

(i) Jesus does not try to follow out or to explain the connection of sin and suffering. He says that this man's affliction came to him to give an opportunity of showing what God can do. There are two senses in which that is true.

(*a*) For John the miracles are always a sign of the glory and the power of God. The writers of the other gospels had a different point of view; and regarded them as a demonstration of the compassion of Jesus. When Jesus looked on the hungry crowd he had *compassion* on them, because they were as sheep not having a shepherd (*Mark* 6: 34). When the leper came with his desperate request for cleansing Jesus was *moved with compassion* (*Mark* 1: 41). It is often urged that in this the Fourth Gospel is quite different from the others. Surely there is no real contradiction here. It is simply two ways of looking at the same thing. At its heart is the supreme truth that the glory of God lies in his compassion, and that he never so fully reveals his glory as when he reveals his pity.

(*b*) But there is another sense in which the man's suffering shows what God can do. Affliction, sorrow, pain, disappointment, loss always are opportunities for displaying God's grace. First, it enables the sufferer to show God in action. When trouble and disaster fall upon a man who does not know God, that man may well collapse; but when they fall on a man who walks with God they bring out the strength and the beauty, and the endurance and the nobility, which are within a man's heart when God is there. It is told that when an old saint was dying in an agony of pain, he sent for his family, saying: " Come and see how a Christian can die." It is when life hits us a terrible blow that we can show the world how a Christian can live, and, if need be, die. Any kind of suffering is an opportunity to demonstrate the glory of God in our own lives. Second, by helping those who are in trouble or in pain, we can demonstrate to others the glory of God. Frank Laubach has the great thought that when Christ, who is the Way, enters into us " we become part of the Way. God's highway runs straight through us." When we spend ourselves to help those in trouble, in distress, in pain, in sorrow, in affliction, God is using us as the highway by which he sends his help into the lives of his people. To help a fellow-man in need is to manifest the glory of God, for it is to show what God is like.

Jesus goes on to say that he and all his followers must do God's work while there is time to do it. God gave men the day for work and the night for rest; the day comes to an end and the time for work is also ended. For Jesus it was true that he had to press on with God's work in the day for the night of the Cross lay close ahead. But it is true for every man. We are given only so much time. Whatever we are to do must be done within it. There is in Glasgow a sundial with the motto: " Tak' tent of time ere time be tint." " Take thought of time before time is ended." We should never put things off until another time, for another time may never come. The Christian's duty is to fill the time he has—and no man knows how much that will be—with the service of God and of his fellow-men. There is no more poignant sorrow than the tragic discovery that it is too late to do something which we might have done.

But there is another opportunity we may miss. Jesus said: " So long as I am in the world I am the light of the world." When Jesus said that, he did not mean that the time of his life and work were limited but that our opportunity of laying hold on him is limited. There comes to every man a chance to accept Christ as his Saviour, his Master and his Lord; and if that opportunity is not seized it may well never come back. E. D.

Starbuck in *The Psychology of Religion* has some interesting
and warning statistics about the age at which conversion
normally occurs. It can occur as early as seven or eight; it
increases gradually to the age of ten or eleven; it increases
rapidly to the age of sixteen; it declines steeply up to the age of
twenty; and after thirty it is very rare. God is always saying to
us: " *Now* is the time." It is not that the power of Jesus grows
less, or that his light grows dim; it is that if we put off the great
decision we become ever less able to take it as the years go on.
Work must be done, decisions must be taken, while it is day,
before the night comes down.

THE METHOD OF A MIRACLE

John 9: 6–12

> When he had said this he spat on the ground, and made clay from
> the spittle, and he smeared the clay on his eyes and said to him:
> " Go, wash in the Pool of Siloam." (The word " Siloam " means
> " sent.") So he went away and washed, and he came able to see.
> So the neighbours and those who formerly knew him by sight and
> knew that he was a beggar, said: " Is this not the man who sat
> begging? " Some said:." It is he." Others said: " It is not he, but it
> is someone like him." The man himself said: " I am he." " How
> then," they said to him, " have your eyes been opened? " " The
> man they call Jesus made clay," he said, " and smeared it on my
> eyes, and said to me: ' Go to the Pool of Siloam and wash.' So I
> went and washed, and sight came to me." They said to him:
> " Where is this man you are talking about? " He said: " I don't
> know."

THIS is one of two miracles i which Jesus is said to have used
spittle to effect a cure. The other is the miracle of the deaf
stammerer (*Mark* 7: 33). The use of spittle seems to us strange
and repulsive and unhygienic; but in the ancient world it was
quite common. Spittle, and especially the spittle of some
distinguished person, was believed to possess certain curative
qualities. Tacitus tells how, when Vespasian visited Alexandria,

there came to him two men, one with diseased eyes and one with a diseased hand, who said that they had been advised by their god to come to him. The man with the diseased eyes wished Vespasian " to moisten his eye-balls with spittle "; the man with the diseased hand wished Vespasian " to trample on his hand with the sole of his foot." Vespasian was very unwilling to do so but was finally persuaded to do as the men asked. " The hand immediately recovered its power; the blind man saw once more. Both facts are attested to this day, when falsehood can bring no reward, by those who were present on the occasion " (Tacitus, *Histories* 4: 81).

Pliny, the famous Roman collector of what was then called scientific information, has a whole chapter on the use of spittle. He says that it is a sovereign preservative against the poison of serpents; a protection against epilepsy; that lichens and leprous spots can be cured by the application of fasting spittle; that ophthalmia can be cured by anointing the eyes every morning with fasting spittle; that carcinomata and crick in the neck can be cured by the use of spittle. Spittle was held to be very effective in averting the evil eye. Persius tells how the aunt or the grandmother, who fears the gods and is skilled in averting the evil eye, will lift the baby from his cradle and " with her middle finger apply the lustrous spittle to his forehead and slobbering lips." The use of spittle was very common in the ancient world. To this day, if we burn a finger our first instinct is to put it into our mouth; and there are many who believe that warts can be cured by licking them with fasting spittle.

The fact is that Jesus took the methods and customs of his time and used them. He was a wise physician; he had to gain the confidence of his patient. It was not that he believed in these things, but he kindled expectation by doing what the patient would expect a doctor to do. After all, to this day the efficacy of any medicine or treatment depends at least as much on the patient's faith in it as in the treatment or the drug itself.

After anointing the man's eyes with spittle, Jesus sent him to wash in the Pool of Siloam. The Pool of Siloam was one of the landmarks of Jerusalem; and it was the result of one of the great engineering feats of the ancient world. The water supply of Jerusalem had always been precarious in the event of a siege. It came mainly from the Virgin's Fountain or the Spring Gihon, which was situated in the Kidron Valley. A staircase of thirty-three rock-cut steps led down to it; and there, from a stone basin, people drew the water. But the spring was completely exposed and, in the event of a siege, could be completely cut off, with disastrous consequences.

When Hezekiah realized that Sennacherib was about to invade Palestine he determined to cut through the solid rock a tunner or conduit from the spring into the city (2 *Chronicles* 32: 2–8, 30; *Isaiah* 22: 9–11; 2 *Kings* 20: 20). If the engineers had cut straight it would have been a distance of 366 yards; but because they cut in a zig-zag, either because they were following a fissure in the rock, or to avoid sacred sites, the conduit is actually 583 yards. The tunnel is at places only about two feet wide, but its average height is about six feet. The engineers began their cutting from both ends and met in the middle—a truly amazing feat for the equipment of the time.

In 1880 a tablet was discovered commemorating the completion of the conduit. It was accidently discovered by two boys who were wading in the pool. It runs like this: " The boring through is completed. Now is the story of the boring through. While the workmen were still lifting pick to pick, each towards his neighbour, and while three cubits remained to be cut through, each heard the voice of the other who called his neighbour, since there was a crevice in the rock on the right side. And on the day of the boring through the stonecutters struck, each to meet his fellow, pick to pick; and there flowed the waters to the pool for a thousand and two hundred cubits, and a hundred cubits was the height of the rock above the heads of the stone-cutters."

The Pool of Siloam was the place where the conduit from the Virgin's Fountain issued in the city. It was an open air basin twenty by thirty feet. That is how the pool got its name. It was called *Siloam*, which, it was said, meant *sent*, because the water in it had been *sent* through the conduit into the city.

Jesus sent this man to wash in this pool; and the man washed and saw.

Having been cured, he had some difficulty in persuading the people that a real cure had been effected. But he stoutly maintained the miracle which Jesus had wrought. Jesus is still doing things which seem to the unbeliever far too good and far too wonderful to be true.

PREJUDICE AND CONVICTION

John 9: 13–16

> They brought him, the man who had been blind, to the Pharisees. The day on which Jesus had made the clay and opened his eyes was the Sabbath day. So the Pharisees asked him again how sight had come to him. He said to them: " He put clay on my eyes; and I washed; and now I can see." So some of the Pharisees said: " This man is not from God, because he does not observe the Sabbath." But others said: " How can a man who is a sinner perform such signs? " And there was a division of opinion among them. So they said to the blind man: " What is your opinion about him, in view of the fact that he opened your eyes? " He said: " He is a prophet."

Now comes the inevitable trouble. It was the Sabbath day on which Jesus had made the clay and healed the man. Undoubtedly Jesus had broken the Sabbath law, as the scribes had worked it out, and done so in fact in three different ways.

(i) By making clay he had been guilty of working on the Sabbath when even the simplest acts constituted work. Here are some of the things which were forbidden on the Sabbath. " A man may not fill a dish with oil and put it beside a lamp and put the end of the wick in it." " If a man extinguishes a lamp on the Sabbath to spare the lamp or the oil or the wick, he is culpable." " A man may not go out on the Sabbath with sandals shod with nails." (The weight of the nails would have constituted a burden, and to carry a burden was to break the Sabbath.) A man might not cut his finger nails or pull out a hair of his head or his beard. Obviously in the eyes of such a law to make clay was to work and so to break the Sabbath.

(ii) It was forbidden to heal on the Sabbath. Medical attention could be given only if life was in actual danger. Even then it must be only such as to keep the patient from getting worse, not to make him any better. For instance, a man with toothache might not suck vinegar through his teeth. It was forbidden to set a broken limb. " If a man's hand or foot is dislocated he may not pour cold water over it." Clearly the man who was born blind was in no danger of his life; therefore Jesus broke the Sabbath when he healed him.

(iii) It was quite definitely laid down: " As to fasting spittle, it is not lawful to put it so much as upon the eyelids."

The Pharisees are typical of the people in every generation who condemn anyone whose idea of religion is not theirs. They thought that theirs was the only way of serving God. But some of them thought otherwise and declared that no one who did the things Jesus did could be a sinner.

They brought the man and examined him. When he was asked his opinion of Jesus, he gave it without hesitation. He said that Jesus was a prophet. In the Old Testament a prophet was often tested by the signs he could produce. Moses guaranteed to Pharaoh that he really was God's messenger by the signs and wonders which he performed (*Exodus* 4: 1–17). Elijah proved that he was the prophet of the real God by doing things the prophets of Baal could not do (1 *Kings* 18). No doubt the man's thoughts were running on these things when he said that in his opinion Jesus was a prophet.

Whatever else, this was a brave man. He knew quite well what the Pharisees thought of Jesus. He knew quite well that if he came out on Jesus's side he was certain to be excommunicated. But he made his statement and took his stand. It was as if he said: " I am bound to believe in him, I am bound to stand by him because of all that he has done for me." Therein he is our great example.

THE PHARISEES DEFIED

John 9: 17–35

Now the Jews refused to believe that he had been blind and had
become able to see, until they called the parents of the man who
had become able to see, and asked them: " Is this your son? And
do you say that he was born blind? How, then, can he now see? "
His parents answered: " We know that this is our son; and we
know that he was born blind; how he has now come to see we do
not know; or who it was who opened his eyes we do not know.
Ask himself. He is of age. He can answer his own questions." His
parents said this because they were afraid of the Jews; for the
Jews had already agreed that if anyone acknowledged Jesus to be
the Anointed One of God, he should be excommunicated from the
synagogue. That is why his parents said: " He is of age. Ask
him." A second time they called the man who used to be blind.
" Give the glory to God," they said. " We know that this man is a
sinner." " Whether he is a sinner or not," the man answered, " I
do not know. One thing I do know—I used to be blind and now I
can see." " What did he do to you? " they said. " How did he
open your eyes? " " I have already told you," the man said, " and
you did not listen. Why do you want to hear the story all over
again? Surely you can't want to become his disciples? " They
heaped abuse on him. " It is you who are his disciple," they said.
" We are Moses's disciples. We know that God spoke to Moses;
but, as for this man, we do not know where he comes from." The
man answered: " It is an astonishing thing that you do not know
where he comes from, when he opened my eyes. It is a fact known
to all of us that God does not listen to sinners. But if a man is a
reverent man and does his will, God hears him. Since time began
no one has ever heard of anyone who opened the eyes of a man
born blind. If this man was not from God, he could not have done
anything." " You were altogether born in sins," they said to him,
" and are you trying to teach us? " And they ordered him to get
out.

THERE is no more vivid character drawing in all literature than
this. With deft and revealing touches John causes the people
involved to live before us.

(i) There was the blind man himself. He began by being irritated at the persistence of the Pharisees. " Say what you like," he said, " about this man; I don't know anything about him except that he made me able to see." It is the simple fact of Christian experience that many a man may not be able to put into theologically correct language what he believes Jesus to be, but in spite of that he can witness to what Jesus has done for his soul. Even when a man cannot understand with his intellect, he can still feel with his heart. It is better to love Jesus than to love theories about him.

(ii) There were the man's parents. They were obviously unco-operative, but at the same time they were afraid. The synagogue authorities had a powerful weapon, the weapon of excommunication, whereby a man was shut off from the congregation of God's people. Away back in the days of Ezra we read of a decree that whosoever did not obey the command of the authorities " his property should be forfeited and he himself banned from the congregation " (*Ezra* 10: 8). Jesus warned his disciples that their name would be cast out for evil (*Luke* 6: 22). He told them that they would be put out of the synagogues (*John* 16: 2). Many of the rulers in Jerusalem really believed in Jesus, but were afraid to say so " lest they should be put out of the synagogue " (*John* 12: 42).

There were two kinds of excommunication. There was the ban, the *cherem*, by which a man was banished from the synagogue for life. In such a case he was publicly anathematized. He was cursed in the presence of the people, and he was cut off from God and from man. There was sentence of temporary excommunication which might last for a month, or for some other fixed period. The terror of such a situation was that a Jew would regard it as shutting him out, not only from the synagogue but from God. That is why the man's parents answered that their son was quite old enough to be a legal witness and to answer his own questions. The Pharisees were so venomously embittered against Jesus that they were prepared to do what ecclesiastics at their worst have sometimes done—to use ecclesiastical procedure to further their own ends.

(iii) There were the Pharisees. They did not believe at first that the man had been blind. That is to say, they suspected that this was a miracle faked between Jesus and him. Further, they were well aware that the law recognized that a false prophet could produce false miracles for his own false purposes (*Deuteronomy* 13: 1–5 warns against the false prophet who produces false signs in order to lead people away after strange gods). So the Pharisees began with suspicion. They went on to try to browbeat the man. " Give the glory to God," they said. " We know that this man is a sinner." " Give the glory to God," was a phrase used in cross-examination which really meant: " Speak the truth in the presence and the name of God." When Joshua was cross-examining Achan about the sin which had brought disaster to Israel, he said to him: " Give glory to the Lord God of Israel, and render praise to him; and tell me now what you have done; do not hide it from me " (*Joshua* 7: 19).

They were annoyed because they could not meet the man's argument which was based on scripture It was: " Jesus has done a very wonderful thing; the fact that he has done it means that God hears him; now God never hears the prayers of a bad man; therefore Jesus cannot be a bad man." The fact that God did not hear the prayer of a bad man is a basic thought of the Old Testament. When Job is speaking of the hypocrite, he says: " Will God hear his cry when trouble comes upon him? " (*Job* 27: 9). The psalmist says: " If I had cherished iniquity in my heart, the Lord would not have listened." (*Psalm* 66: 18). Isaiah hears God say to the sinning people: " When you spread forth your hands (the Jews prayed with the hands stretched out, palms upwards), I will hide my eyes from you; even though you make many prayers, I will not listen; your hands are full of blood " (*Isaiah* 1: 15). Ezekiel says of the disobedient people: " Though they cry in my ears with a loud voice, I will not hear them " (*Ezekiel* 8: 18). Conversely they believed that the prayer of a good man was always heard. " The eyes of the Lord are toward the righteous, and his ears toward their cry " (*Psalm* 34: 15). " He fulfils the desire of all who fear him, he also hears their cry, and saves them. " (*Psalm* 145: 19). " The Lord is far

from the wicked; but he hears the prayer of the righteous "
(*Proverbs* 15: 29). The man who had been blind presented the
Pharisees with an argument which they could not answer.

When they were confronted with such an argument, see what
they did. First, they resorted to *abuse*. " They heaped abuse on
him." Second, they resorted to *insult*. They accused the man of
being born in sin. That is to say, they accused him of pre-natal
sin. Third, they resorted to *threatened force*. They ordered him
out of their presence.

Often we have our differences with people, and it is well that
it should be so. But the moment insult and abuse and threat
enter into an argument, it ceases to be an argument and
becomes a contest in bitterness. If we become angry and resort
to wild words and hot threats, all we prove is that our case is
disturbingly weak.

REVELATION AND CONDEMNATION

John 9: 35–41

> Jesus heard that they had put him out, so he found him and said
> to him: " Do you believe in the Son of God? " " But who is he,
> sir," he answered him, " that I might believe in him? " Jesus said
> to him: " You have both seen him, and he who is talking with you
> is he." " Lord," he said, " I believe." And he knelt before him.
> Jesus said: " It was for judgment that I came into this world that
> those who do not see might see, and that those who see might
> become blind." Some of the Pharisees who were with him heard
> this. " Surely," they said, " *we* are not blind? " Jesus said to them:
> " If you were blind, you would not have sin. As it is, your claim is,
> ' We see.' Your sin remains."

THIS section begins with two great spiritual truths.

(i) Jesus looked for the man. As Chrysostom put it: " The
Jews cast him out of the Temple; the Lord of the Temple found
him." If any man's Christian witness separates him from his
fellow-men, it brings him nearer to Jesus Christ. Jesus is always
true to the man who is true to him.

(ii) To this man there was made the great revelation that Jesus was the Son of God. Loyalty always brings revelation; it is to the man who is true to him that Jesus most fully reveals himself. The penalty of loyalty may well be persecution and ostracism at the hands of men; its reward is a closer walk with Christ, and an increasing knowledge of his wonder.

John finishes this story with two of his favourite thoughts.

(i) Jesus came into this world for judgment. Whenever a man is confronted with Jesus, that man at once passes a judgment on himself. If he sees in Jesus nothing to desire, nothing to admire, nothing to love, then he has condemned himself. If he sees in Jesus something to wonder at, something to respond to, something to reach out to, then he is on the way to God. The man who is conscious of his own blindness, and who longs to see better and to know more, is the man whose eyes can be opened and who can be led more and more deeply into the truth. The man who thinks he knows it all, the man who does not realize that he cannot see, is the man who is truly blind and beyond hope and help. Only the man who realizes his own weakness can become strong. Only the man who realizes his own blindness can learn to see. Only the man who realizes his own sin can be forgiven.

(ii) The more knowledge a man has the more he is to be condemned if he does not recognize the good when he sees it. If the Pharisees had been brought up in ignorance, they could not have been condemned. Their condemnation lay in the fact that they knew so much and claimed to see so well, and yet failed to recognize God's Son when he came. The law that responsibility is the other side of privilege is written into life.

GREATER AND GREATER

John 9

BEFORE we leave this very wonderful chapter we would do well to read it again, this time straight through from start to finish. If we do so read it with care and attention, we will see the loveliest progression in the blind man's idea of Jesus. It goes through three stages, each one higher than the last.

(i) He began by calling Jesus a *man*. " A man that is called Jesus opened mine eyes " (verse 11). He began by thinking of Jesus as a wonderful man. He had never met anone who could do the kind of things Jesus did; and he began by thinking of Jesus as supreme among men.

We do well sometimes to think of the sheer magnificence of the manhood of Jesus. In any gallery of the world's heroes he must find a place. In any anthology of the loveliest lives ever lived, his would have to be included. In any collection of the world's greatest literature his parables would have to be listed. Shakespeare makes Mark Antony say of Julius Caesar:

> " His life was gentle, and the elements
> So mix'd in him that Nature might stand up
> And say to all the world, ' This was a man! ' "

Whatever else is in doubt, there is never any doubt that Jesus was a man among men.

(ii) He went on to call Jesus a *prophet*. When asked his opinion of Jesus in view of the fact that he had given him his sight, his answer was: " He is a prophet " (verse 17). Now a prophet is a man who brings God's message to men. " Surely the Lord God does nothing," said Amos, " without revealing his secret to his servants the prophets " (*Amos* 3: 7). A prophet is a man who lives close to God and has penetrated into his inner councils. When we read the wisdom of the words of Jesus, we are bound to say: " This is a prophet! " Whatever else may be in doubt, this is true—if men, followed the teachings of Jesus, all personal, all social, all national, all international problems would be solved. If ever any man had the right to be called a prophet, Jesus has.

(iii) Finally the blind man came to confess that Jesus was the *Son of God*. He came to see that human categories were not adequate to describe him. Napoleon was once in a company in which a number of clever sceptics were discussing Jesus. They dismissed him as a very great man and nothing more. " Gentlemen," said Napoleon, " I know men, and Jesus Christ was more than a man."

> " If Jesus Christ is a man
>   And only a man—I say
> That of all mankind I cleave to him
>   And to him will I cleave alway.
>
> If Jesus Christ is a god—
>   And the only God—I swear
> I will follow him through heaven and hell,
>   The earth, the sea, and the air! "

It is a tremendous thing about Jesus that the more we know him the greater he becomes. The trouble with human relationships is that often the better we know a person the more we know his weaknesses and his failings; but the more we know Jesus, the greater the wonder becomes; and that will be true, not only in time, but also in eternity.

THE SHEPHERD AND HIS SHEEP

John 10: 1–6

> Jesus said: " This is the truth I tell you; he who does not enter the sheepfold through the door, but climbs in some other way, is a thief and a robber. But he who comes in through the door is the shepherd of the sheep. The keeper of the door opens the door to him; and the sheep hear his voice; and he calls his own sheep by name and leads them out. Whenever he puts his own sheep out, he walks in front of them; and the sheep follow him, because they know his voice. But they will not follow a stranger, but they will run away from him, because they do not know the voice of strangers." Jesus spoke this parable to them, but they did not know what he was saying to them.

THERE is no better loved picture of Jesus than the Good Shepherd. The picture of the shpherd is woven into the language and imagery of the Bible. It could not be otherwise. The main part of Judaea was a central plateau, stretching from Bethel to Hebron for a distance of about 35 miles and varying from 14 to 17 miles across. The ground, for most part, was rough and stony. Judaea was, much more a pastoral than an agricultural country and was, therefore, inevitable that the most familiar figure of the Judaean uplands was the shepherd.

His life was very hard. No flock ever grazed without a shepherd, and he was never off duty. There being little grass, the sheep were bound to wander, and since there were no protecting walls, the sheep had constantly to be watched. On either side of the narrow plateau the ground dipped sharply down to the craggy deserts and the sheep were always liable to stray away and get lost. The shepherd's task was not only constant but dangerous, for, in addition, he had to guard the flock against wild animals, especially against wolves, and there were always thieves and robbers ready to steal the sheep. Sir George Adam Smith, who travelled in Palestine, writes: " On some high moor, across which at night the hyaenas howl, when you meet him, sleepless, far-sighted, weather-beaten, leaning on his staff, and looking out over his scattered sheep, every one of them on his heart, you understand why the shepherd of Judaea sprang to the front in his people's history; why they gave his name to their king, and made him the symbol of providence; why Christ took him as the type of self-sacrifice." Constant vigilance, fearless courage, patient love for his flock, were the necessary characteristics of the shepherd.

In the Old Testament God is often pictured as the shepherd, and the people as his flock. " The Lord is my shepherd: I shall not want " (*Psalm* 23: 1). " Thou didst lead thy people like a flock by the hand of Moses and Aaron " (*Psalm* 77: 20). " We thy people, the flock of thy pasture, will give thanks to thee for ever " (*Psalm* 79: 13). " Give ear, O Shepherd of Israel, thou who leadest Joseph like a flock " (*Psalm* 80: 1). " He is our God, and we are the people of his pasture, and the sheep of his hand " (*Psalm* 95: 7). " We are his people, and the sheep of his pasture " (*Psalm* 100: 3). God's Anointed One, the Messiah, is also pictured as the shepherd of the sheep. " He will feed his

flock like a shepherd: he will gather the lambs in his arms, and
will carry them in his bosom, and gently lead those that are with
young " (*Isaiah* 40: 11). " He will be shepherding the flock of
the Lord faithfully and righteously, and will suffer none of them
to stumble in their pasture. He will lead them all aright "
(*Psalms of Solomon* 17: 45). The leaders of the people are
described as the shepherds of God's people and nation. " Woe
to the shepherds who destroy and scatter the sheep of my
pasture! " (*Jeremiah* 23: 1–4). Ezekiel has a tremendous indictment of the false leaders who seek their own good rather than
the good of the flock. " Woe be to the shepherds of Israel who
have been themselves! Should not shepherds feed the sheep? "
(*Ezekiel* 34).

This picture passes over into the New Testament. Jesus is the
Good Shepherd. He is the shepherd who will risk his life to seek
and to save the one straying sheep (*Matthew* 18: 12; *Luke* 15:
4). He has pity upon the people because they are as sheep
without a shepherd (*Matthew* 9: 36; *Mark* 6: 34). His disciples
are his little flock (*Luke* 12: 32). When he, the shepherd, is
smitten the sheep are scattered (*Mark* 14: 27; *Matthew* 26: 31).
He is the shepherd of the souls of men (I *Peter* 2: 25), and the
great shepherd of the sheep (*Hebrews* 13: 20).

Just as in the Old Testament picture, the leaders of the
Church are the shepherds and the people are the flock. It is
the duty of the leader to feed the flock of God, to accept the
oversight willingly and not by constraint, to do it eagerly and
not for love of money, not to use the position for the exercise of
power and to be an example to the flock (1 *Peter* 5: 2, 3). Paul
urges the elders of Ephesus to take heed to all the flock over
which the Holy Spirit had made them overseers (*Acts* 20: 28). It
is Jesus's last command to Peter that he should feed his lambs
and his sheep (*John* 21: 15–19). The very word *pastor* (*Ephesians* 4: 11) is the Latin word for *shepherd*.

The Jews had a lovely legend to explain why God chose
Moses to be the leader of his people. " When Moses was feeding
the sheep of his father-in-law in the wilderness, a young kid ran
away. Moses followed it until it reached a ravine, where it found

a well to drink from. When Moses got up to it he said: ' I did
not know that you ran away because you were thirsty. Now
you must be weary.' He took the kid on his shoulders and
carried it back. Then God said: ' Because you have shown pity
in leading back one of a flock belonging to a man, you shall lead
my flock Israel.' "

The word shepherd should paint a picture to us of the
unceasing vigilance and patience of the love of God; and it
should remind us of our duty towards our fellow-men, especially if we hold any kind of office in the Church of Christ.

THE SHEPHERD AND HIS SHEEP

John 10: 1–6 (*continued*)

THE Palestinian shepherd had different ways of doing things
from the shepherds of our country; and, to get the full meaning
of this picture, we must look at the shepherd and the way in
which he worked.

His equipment was very simple. He had his *scrip*, a bag
made of the skin of an animal, in which he carried his food. In it
he would have no more than bread, dried fruit, some olives and
cheese. He had his *sling*. The skill of many of the men of
Palestine was such that they " could sling a stone at a hair and
not miss " (*Judges* 20: 16). The shepherd used his sling as a
weapon of offence and defence; but he made one curious use of
it. There were no sheep dogs in Palestine, and, when the
shepherd wished to call back a sheep which was straying away,
he fitted a stone into his sling and landed it just in front of the
straying sheep's nose as a warning to turn back. He had his
staff, a short wooden club which had a lump of wood at the end
often studded with nails. It usually had a slit in the handle at the
top, through which a thong passed; and by the thong the staff
swung at the shepherd's belt. His staff was the weapon with
which he defended himself and his flock àgainst marauding
beasts and robbers. He had his *rod*, which was like the

shepherd's crook. With it he could catch and pull back any sheep which was moving to stray away. At the end of the day, when the sheep were going into the fold, the shepherd held his rod across the entrance, quite close to the ground; and every sheep had to pass under it (*Ezekiel* 20: 37; *Leviticus* 27: 32); and, as each sheep passed under, the shepherd quickly examined it to see if it had received any kind of injury throughout the day.

The relationship between sheep and shepherd is quite different in Palestine. In Britain the sheep are largely kept for killing; but in Palestine largely for their wool. It thus happens that in Palestine the sheep are often with the shepherd for years and often they have names by which the shepherd calls them. Usually these names are descriptive, for instance, " Brown-leg," " Black-ear." In Palestine the shepherd went in front and the sheep followed. The shepherd went first to see that the path was safe, and sometimes the sheep had to be encouraged to follow. A traveller tells how he saw a shepherd leading his flock come to a ford across a stream. The sheep were unwilling to cross. The shepherd finally solved the problem by carrying one of the lambs across. When its mother saw her lamb on the other side she crossed too, and soon all the rest of the flock had followed her.

It is strictly true that the sheep know and understand the eastern shepherd's voice; and that they will never answer to the voice of a stranger. H. V. Morton has a wonderful description of the way in which the shepherd talks to the sheep. " Sometimes he talks to them in a loud sing-song voice, using a weird language unlike anything I have ever heard in my life. The first time I heard this sheep and goat language I was on the hills at the back of Jericho. A goat-herd had descended into a valley and was mounting the slope of an opposite hill, when turning round, he saw his goats had remained behind to devour a rich patch of scrub. Lifting his voice, he spoke to the goats in a language that Pan must have spoken on the mountains of Greece. It was uncanny because there was nothing human about it. The words were animal sounds arranged in a kind of order. No sooner had he spoken than an answering bleat shivered over the herd, and one or two of the animals turned their heads in his direction. But they did not obey him. The goat-herd then called out one word, and gave a laughing kind of whinny. Immediately a goat with a bell round his neck stopped eating, and, leaving the herd, trotted down the hill, across the valley, and up the opposite slopes. The man, accompanied by this animal, walked on and disappeared round a ledge of rock. Very soon a panic spread among the herd. They forgot to eat. They looked up for the shepherd. He was not to be seen. They became conscious that the leader with the bell at his neck was no longer with them. From the distance came the strange laughing call of the shepherd, and at the sound of it the entire herd stampeded into the hollow and leapt up the hill after him " (H. V. Morton, *In the Steps of the Master*, pp. 154, 155). W. M. Thomson in *The Land and the Book* has the same story to tell. " The shepherd calls sharply from time to time, to remind them of his presence. They know his voice, and follow on; but, if a stranger call, they stop short, lift up their heads in alarm, and if it is repeated, they turn and flee, because they know not the voice of a stranger. I have made the experiment repeatedly." That is exactly John's picture.

H. V. Morton tells of a scene that he saw in a cave near Bethlehem. Two shepherds had sheltered their flocks in the cave during the night. How were the flocks to be sorted out? One of the shepherds stood some distance away and gave his peculiar call which only his own sheep knew, and soon his whole flock had run to him, because they knew his voice. They would have come for no one else, but they knew the call of their own shepherd. An eighteenth century traveller actually tells how Palestinian sheep could be made to dance, quick or slow, to the peculiar whistle or the peculiar tune on the flute of their own shepherd.

Every detail of the shepherd's life lights up the picture of the Good Shepherd whose sheep hear his voice and whose constant care is for his flock.

THE DOOR TO LIFE

John 10: 7–10

> So Jesus said to them again: " This is the truth I tell you—I am
> the door of the sheep. All who came before me are thieves and
> robbers, but the sheep did not listen to them. I am the door. If any
> man enter in through me, he will be saved, and he will go in and
> out, and he will find pasture. The thief comes only to kill and to
> steal and to destroy; I am come that they might have life, and that
> they might have it more abundantly."

THE Jews did not understand the meaning of the story of the
Good Shepherd. So Jesus, plainly and without concealment,
applied it to himself.

He began by saying: " I am the door." In this parable Jesus
spoke about two kinds of sheep-folds. In the villages and towns
themselves there were communal sheep-folds where all the
village flocks were sheltered when they returned home at night.
These folds were protected by a strong door of which only the
guardian of the door held the key. It was to that kind of fold
Jesus referred in verses 2 and 3. But when the sheep were out on
the hills in the warm season and did not return at night to the
village at all, they were collected into sheep-folds on the hillside.
These hillside sheep-folds were just open spaces enclosed by a
wall. In them there was an opening by which the sheep came in
and went out; but there was no door of any kind. What
happened was that at night the shepherd himself lay down
across the opening and no sheep could get out or in except over
his body. In the most literal sense the shepherd was the door.

That is what Jesus was thinking of when he said: " I am the
door." Through him, and through him alone, men find access to
God. " Through him," said Paul, " we have access to the
Father " (*Ephesians* 2: 18). " He," said the writer to the
Hebrews, " is the new and living way " (*Hebrews* 10: 20). Jesus
opens the way to God. Until Jesus came men could think of
God only as, at best, a stranger and as, at worst, an enemy. But
Jesus came to show men what God is like, and to open the way

to him. He is the door through whom alone entrance to God becomes possible for men.

To describe something of what that entrance to God means, Jesus uses a well-known Hebrew phrase. He says that through him *we can go in and come out*. To be able to come and go unmolested was the Jewish way of describing a life that is absolutely secure and safe. When a man can go in and out without fear, it means that his country is at peace, that the forces of law and order are supreme, and that he enjoys perfect security. The leader of the nation is to be one who can bring them out and lead them in (*Numbers* 27: 17). Of the man who is obedient to God it is said that he is blessed when he comes in and blessed when he goes out (*Deuteronomy* 28: 6). A child is one who is not yet able by himself to go out and to come in (1 *Kings* 3: 7). The Psalmist is certain that God will keep him in his going out and in his coming in (*Psalm* 121: 8). Once a man discovers, through Jesus Christ, what God is like, a new sense of safety and of security enters into life. If life is known to be in the hands of a God like that, the worries and the fears are gone.

Jesus said that those who came before him were thieves and robbers. He was of course not referring to the great succession of the prophets and the heroes, but to these adventurers who were continually arising in Palestine and promising that, if people would follow them, they would bring in the golden age. All these claimants were insurrectionists. They believed that men would have to wade through blood to the golden age. At this very time Josephus speaks of there being ten thousand disorders in Judaea, tumults caused by men of war. He speaks of men like the Zealots who did not mind dying themselves and who did not mind slaughtering their own loved ones, if their hopes of conquest could be achieved. Jesus is saying: " There have been men who claimed that they were leaders sent to you from God. They believed in war, murder, assassination. Their way only leads for ever farther and farther away from God. My way is the way of peace and love and life; and if you will only take it, it leads ever closer and closer to God." There have been, and still are, those who believe that the golden age must be brought in with violence, class warfare, bitterness, destruction. It is the message of Jesus that the only way that leads to God in heaven and to the golden age on earth is the way of love.

Jesus claims that he came that men might have life and might have it more abundantly. The Greek phrase used for *having it more abundantly* means to have *a superabundance of a thing*. To be a follower of Jesus, to know who he is and what he means, is to have a superabundance of life. A Roman soldier came to Julius Caesar with a request for permission to commit suicide. He was a wretched dispirited creature with no vitality. Caesar looked at him. " Man," he said, " were you ever really alive? " When we try to live our own lives, life is a dull, dispirited thing. When we walk with Jesus, there comes a new vitality, a superabundance of life. It is only when we live with Christ that life becomes really worth living and we begin to live in the real sense of the word

THE TRUE AND THE FALSE SHEPHERD

John 10: 11–15

> " I am the good shepherd; the good shepherd gives his life for the sheep. The hireling, who is not a real shepherd, and to whom the sheep do not really belong, sees the wolf coming, and leaves the sheep, and runs away; and the wolf seizes them and scatters them. He abandons the sheep because he is a hireling, and the sheep are nothing to him. I am the good shepherd, and I know my own sheep, and my own sheep know me, just as the Father knows me and I know the Father. And I lay down my life for the sheep.

THIS passage draws the contrast between the good and the bad, the faithful and the unfaithful shepherd. The shepherd was absolutely responsible for the sheep. If anything happened to a sheep, he had to produce some kind of proof that it was not his fault. Amos speaks about the shepherd rescuing two legs or a piece of an ear out of a lion's mouth (*Amos* 3: 12). The law laid it down: " If it is torn by beasts, let him bring it as evidence "

(*Exodus* 22: 13). The idea is that the shepherd must bring home proof that the sheep had died, and that he had been unable to prevent the death. David tells Saul how when he was keeping his father's sheep, he had the battle with the lion and the bear (1 *Samuel* 17: 34–36). Isaiah speaks of the crowd of shepherds being called out to deal with the lion (*Isaiah* 31: 4). To the shepherd it was the most natural thing to risk his life in defence of his flock. Sometimes the shepherd had to do more than risk his life: sometimes he had to lay it down, perhaps when thieves and robbers came to despoil the flock. Dr W. M. Thomson in *The Land and the Book* writes: " I have listened with intense interest to their graphic descriptions of downright and desperate fights with these savage beasts. And when the thief and the robber come (and come they do), the faithful shepherd has often to put his life in his hand to defend his flock. I have known more than one case where he had literally to lay it down in the contest. A poor faithful fellow last spring, between Tiberias and Tabor, instead of fleeing, actually fought three Bedawin robbers until he was hacked to pieces with their khanjars, and died among the sheep he was defending." The true shepherd never hesitated to risk, and even to lay down, his life for his sheep.

But, on the other hand, there was the unfaithful shepherd. The difference was this. A real shepherd was born to his task. He was sent out with the flock as soon as he was old enough to go; the sheep became his friends and his companions; and it became second nature to think of them before he thought of himself. But the false shepherd came into the job, not as a calling, but as a means of making money. He was in it simply and solely for the pay he could get. He might even be a man who had taken to the hills because the town was too hot to hold him. He had no sense of the height and the responsibility of his task; he was only a hireling.

Wolves were a threat to a flock. Jesus said of his disciples that he was sending them out as sheep in the midst of wolves (*Matthew* 10: 16); Paul warned the elders of Ephesus that grievous wolves would come, not sparing the flock (*Acts* 20: 29). If these wolves attacked, the hireling shepherd forgot everything but the saving of his own life and ran away. Zechariah marks it as the characteristic of a false shepherd that he made no attempt to gather together the scattered sheep (*Zechariah* 11: 16). Carlyle's father once took this imagery caustically to his speech. In Ecclefechan they were having trouble with their minister; and it was the worst of all kinds of such trouble—it was about money. Carlyle's father rose and said bitingly: " Give the hireling his wages and let him go."

Jesus's point is that the man who works only for reward thinks chiefly of the money; the man who works for love thinks chiefly of the people he is trying to serve. Jesus was the good shepherd who so loved his sheep that for their safety he would risk, and one day give, his life.

We may note two further points before we leave this passage. Jesus describes himself as the *good* shepherd. Now in Greek, there are two words for good. There is *agathos* which simply describes the moral quality of a thing; there is *kalos* which means that in the goodness there is a quality of winsomeness which makes it lovely. When Jesus is described as the *good* shepherd, the word is *kalos*. In him there is more than efficiency and more than fidelity; there is loveliness. Sometimes in a village or town people speak about *the good doctor*. They are not thinking only of the doctor's efficiency and skill as a physician; they are thinking of the sympathy and the kindness and the graciousness which he brought with him and which made him the friend of all. In the picture of Jesus as the Good Shepherd there is loveliness as well as strength and power.

The second point is this. In the parable the flock is the Church of Christ; and it suffers from a double danger. It is always liable to attack from outside, from the wolves and the robbers and the marauders. It is always liable to trouble from the inside, from the false shepherd. The Church runs a double danger. It is always under attack from outside and often suffers from the tragedy of bad leadership, from the disaster of shepherds who see their calling as a career and not as a means of service. The second danger is by far the worse; because, if the shepherd is faithful and good, there is a strong defence from the attack from outside; but if the shepherd is faithless and a hireling, the foes from outside can penetrate into and destroy the flock. The Church's first essential is a leadership based on the example of Jesus Christ.

THE ULTIMATE UNITY

John 10: 16

> " But I have other sheep which are not of this fold. These too I must bring in, and they will hear my voice; and they will become one flock, and there will be one shepherd."

ONE of the hardest things in the world to unlearn is exclusiveness. Once a people, or a section of a people, gets the idea that they are specially privileged, it is very difficult for them to accept that the privileges which they believed belonged to them and to them only are in fact open to all men. That is what the Jews never learned. They believed that they were God's chosen people and that God had no use for any other nation. They believed that, at the best, other nations were designed to be their slaves, and, at the worst, that they were destined for elimination from the scheme of things. But here Jesus is saying that there will come a day when all men will know him as their shepherd.

Even the Old Testament is not without its glimpses of that day. Isaiah had that very dream. It was his conviction that God had given Israel for *a light to the nations* (*Isaiah* 42: 6; 49: 6; 56: 8) and always there had been some lonely voices which insisted that God was not the exclusive property of Israel, but that her destiny was to make him known to all men.

At first sight it might seem that the New Testament speaks with two voices on this subject; and some passages of the New Testament may well trouble and perplex us a little. As Matthew tells the story, when Jesus sent out his disciples, he said to them: " Go nowhere among the Gentiles, and enter no town of the Samaritans, but go rather to the lost sheep of the house of Israel " (*Matthew* 10: 5, 6). When the Syro-Phoenician woman appealed to Jesus for help, his first answer was that he was sent only to the lost sheep of the house of Israel (*Matthew* 15: 24). But there is much to be set on the other side. Jesus himself stayed and taught in Samaria (*John* 4: 40); he declared that descent from Abraham was no guarantee of entry into the kingdom (*John* 8: 39). It was of a Roman centurion that Jesus said that he had never seen such faith in Israel (*Matthew* 8: 10); it was a Samaritan leper who alone returned to give thanks (*Luke* 17: 18, 19); it was the Samaritan traveller who showed the kindness that all men must copy (*Luke* 10: 37); many would come from the east and the west and the north and the south to sit down in the Kingdom of God (*Matthew* 8: 11; *Luke* 13: 29); the command in the end was to go out and to preach the gospel to all nations (*Mark* 16: 15; *Matthew* 28: 19); Jesus was, not the light of the Jews, but the light of the world (*John* 8: 12).

What is the explanation of the sayings which seem to limit the work of Jesus to the Jews? The explanation is in reality very simple. The *ultimate* aim of Jesus was the world for God. But any great commander knows that he must in the first instance limit his objectives. If he tries to attack on too wide a front, he only scatters his forces, diffuses his strength, and gains success nowhere. In order to win an ultimately complete victory he must begin by concentrating his forces at certain limited objectives. That is what Jesus did. Had he gone here, there and everywhere, had he sent his disciples out with no limitation to their sphere of work, nothing would have been achieved. At the moment he deliberately concentrated on the Jewish nation, but his ultimate aim was the gathering of the whole world into his love.

There are three great truths in this passage.

(i) It is only in Jesus Christ that the world can become one. Egerton Young was the first missionary to the Red Indians. In Saskatchewan he went out and told them of the love of God. To the Indians it was like a new revelation. When the missionary had told his message, an old chief said: " When you spoke of the great Spirit just now, did I hear you say, ' Our Father '? " " Yes," said Egerton Young. " That is very new and sweet to

me," said the chief. " We never thought of the great Spirit as
Father. We heard him in the thunder; we saw him in the
lightning, the tempest and the blizzard, and we were afraid. So
when you tell us that the great Spirit is *our Father*, that is very
beautiful to us." The old man paused, and then he went on, as a
glimpse of glory suddenly shone on him. " Missionary, did you
say that the great Spirit is *your* Father? " " Yes," said the
missionary. " And," said the chief, " did you say that he is *the
Indians'* Father? " " I did," said the missionary. " Then," said
the old chief, like a man on whom a dawn of joy had burst,
" *you and I are brothers!* "

The only possible unity for men is in their common sonship
with God. In the world there is division between nation and
nation; in the nation there is division between class and class.
There can never be one nation; and there can never be one
class. The only thing which can cross the barriers and wipe out
the distinctions is the gospel of Jesus Christ telling men of the
universal fatherhood of God.

(ii) In the Authorized Version there is a mistranslation. It
has: " There shall be one *fold* and one shepherd." That mistranslation goes back to Jerome and the Vulgate. And on that
mistranslation the Roman Catholic Church has based the
teaching that, since there is only one fold, there can only be one
Church, the Roman Catholic Church, and that, outside it there
is no salvation. But the real translation beyond all possible
doubt as given in the Revised Standard Version, is: " There
shall be one *flock*, one shepherd," or, even better, " They shall
become one flock and there shall be one shepherd." The unity
comes from the fact, not that all the sheep are forced into one
fold, but they all hear, answer and obey one shepherd. It is not
an ecclesiastical unity; it is a unity of loyalty to Jesus Christ.
The fact that there is one flock does not mean that there can be
only one Church, one method of worship, one form of ecclesiastical administration. But it does mean that all the different
churches are united by a common loyalty to Jesus Christ.

(ii) But this saying of Jesus becomes very personal; for it is a
dream which every one of us can help Jesus to realize. Men

cannot hear without a preacher; the other sheep cannot be gathered in unless someone goes out to bring them in. Here is set before us the tremendous missionary task of the Church. And we must not think of that only in terms of what we used to call *foreign* missions. If we know someone here and now who is outside his love, we can find him for Christ. The dream of Christ depends on us; it is we who can help him make the world one flock with him as its shepherd.

LOVE'S CHOICE

John 10: 17, 18

> " The reason why my Father loves me is that I lay down my life that I may take it again. No one takes it from me, but I lay it down of my own free will. I have full authority to lay it down, and I have full authority to take it again. I have received this injunction from my Father."

FEW passages in the New Testament tell us so much about Jesus in so short a compass.

(i) It tells us that Jesus saw his whole life as an act of obedience to God. God had given him a task to do, and he was prepared to carry it out to the end, even if it meant death. He was in a unique relationship to God which we can describe only by saying that he was the Son of God. But that relationship did not give him the right to do what he liked; it depended on his doing always, cost what it may, what God liked. Sonship for him, and sonship for us, could never be based on anything except obedience.

(ii) It tells us that Jesus always saw the Cross and the glory together. He never doubted that he must die; and equally he never doubted that he would rise again. The reason was his confidence in God; he was sure that God would never abandon him. All life is based on the fact that anything worth getting is hard to get. There is always a price to be paid. Scholarship can be bought only at the price of study; skill in any craft or technique can be bought only at the price of practice; eminence in any sport can be bought only at the price of training and discipline. The world is full of people who have missed their destiny because they would not pay the price. No one can take the easy way and enter into glory or greatness; no one can take the hard way and fail to find these things.

(iii) It tells us in a way that we cannot possibly mistake that Jesus's death was entirely voluntary. Jesus stresses this again and again. In the garden he bade his would-be defender put up his sword. If he had wished, he could have called in the hosts of heaven to his defence (*Matthew* 26: 53). He made it quite clear that Pilate was not condemning him, but that he was accepting death (*John* 19: 10, 11). He was not the victim of circumstance. He was not like some animal, dragged unwillingly and without understanding to the sacrifice. Jesus laid down his life because he chose to do so.

It is told that in the First World War there was a young French soldier who was seriously wounded. His arm was so badly smashed that it had to be amputated. He was a magnificent specimen of young manhood, and the surgeon was grieved that he must go through life maimed. So he waited beside his bedside to tell him the bad news when he recovered consciousness. When the lad's eyes opened, the surgeon said to him: " I am sorry to tell you that you have lost your arm." " Sir," said the lad, " I did not lose it; I gave it —for France."

Jesus was not helplessly caught up in a mesh of circumstances from which he could not break free. Apart from any divine power he might have called in, it is quite clear that to the end he could have turned back and saved his life. He did not lose his life: he gave it. The Cross was not thrust upon him: he willingly accepted it—for us.

MADMAN OR SON OF GOD

John 10: 19–21

> There was again a division among the Jews because of these
> words. Many of them said: " He has an evil spirit, and he is mad.
> Why do you listen to him? " Others said: " These are not the
> words of a man possessed by an evil spirit. Can a man with an evil
> spirit open the eyes of the blind? "

THE people who listened to Jesus on this occasion were
confronted with a dilemma which is for ever confronting men.
Either Jesus was a megalomaniac madman, or he was the Son
of God. There is no escape from that choice. If a man speaks
about God and about himself in the way in which Jesus spoke,
either he is completely deluded, or else he is profoundly right.
The claims which Jesus made signify either insanity or divinity.
How can we assure ourselves that they were indeed justified and
not the world's greatest delusion?

(i) The words of Jesus are not the words of a madman. We
could cite witness after witness to prove that the teaching of
Jesus is the supreme sanity. Thinking men and women in every
generation have judged the teaching of Jesus the one hope of
sanity for a mad world. His is the one voice which speaks
God's sense in the midst of man's delusions.

(ii) The deeds of Jesus are not the deeds of a madman. He
healed the sick and fed the hungry and comforted the sorrowing. The madness of megalomania is essentially selfish. It seeks
for nothing but its own glory and prestige. But Jesus's life was
spent in doing things for others. As the Jews themselves said, a
man who was mad would not be able to open the eyes of the
blind.

(iii) The effect of Jesus is not the effect of a madman. The
undeniable fact is that millions upon millions of lives have been
changed by the power of Jesus Christ. The weak have become
strong, the selfish have become selfless, the defeated have
become victorious, the worried have become serene, the bad

have become good. It is not madness which produces such a change, but wisdom and sanity.

The choice remains—Jesus was either mad or divine. No honest person can review the evidence and come to any other conclusion than that Jesus brought into the world, not a deluded madness, but the perfect sanity of God.

THE CLAIM AND THE PROMISE

John 10: 22–28

It was the Festival of the Dedication in Jerusalem. It was wintry weather, and Jesus was walking in the Temple precincts in Solomon's Porch. So the Jews surrounded him. " How long," they said to him, " are you going to keep us hanging in suspense? If you really are God's Anointed One, tell us plainly." Jesus answered them: " I did tell you and you did not believe me. The works that I do in the name of my Father, these are evidence about me. But you do not believe because you are not among the number of my sheep. My sheep hear my voice, and I know them, and they follow me. And I give them eternal life, and they will never perish, and no one will snatch them from my hand."

JOHN begins by giving us both the date and the place of this discussion. The date was the Festival of the Dedication. This was the latest of the great Jewish festivals to be founded. It was sometimes called The Festival of Lights; and its Jewish name was *Hanukkah*. Its date is the 25th of the Jewish month called Chislew which corresponds with our December. This Festival therefore falls very near our Christmas time and is still universally observed by the Jews.

The origin of the Festival of the Dedication lies in one of the greatest times of ordeal and heroism in Jewish history. There was a king of Syria called Antiochus Epiphanes who reigned from 175 to 164 B.C. He was a lover of all things Greek. He decided that he would eliminate the Jewish religion once and for all, and introduce Greek ways and thoughts, Greek religion and gods into Palestine. At first he tried to do so by peaceful penetration of ideas. Some of the Jews welcomed the new ways, but most were stubbornly loyal to their ancestral faith.

It was in 170 B.C. that the deluge really came. In that year Antiochus attacked Jerusalem. It was said that 80,000 Jews perished, and as many were sold into slavery. 1,800 talents—a talent is equal to £240—were stolen from the Temple treasury. It became a capital offence to possess a copy of the law, or to circumcise a child; and mothers who did circumcise their children were crucified with their children hanging round their necks. The Temple courts were profaned; the Temple chambers were turned into brothels; and finally Antiochus took the dreadful step of turning the great altar of the burnt-offering into an altar to Olympian Zeus, and on it proceeded to offer swine's flesh to the pagan gods.

It was then that Judas Maccabaeus and his brother arose to fight their epic fight for freedom. In 164 B.C. the struggle was finally won; and in that year the Temple was cleansed and purified. The altar was rebuilt and the robes and the utensils were replaced, after three years of pollution. It was to commemorate that purification of the Temple that the Feast of the Dedication was instituted. Judas Maccabaeus enacted that " the days of the dedication of the altar should be kept in their season from year to year, by the space of eight days, from the five and twentieth day of the month of Chislew, with gladness and joy " (1 *Maccabees* 4: 59). For that reason the festival was sometimes called the Festival of the Dedication of the Altar, and sometimes the Memorial of the Purification of the Temple.

But as we have already seen, it had still another name. It was often called the Festival of Lights. There were great illuminations in the Temple; and there were also illuminations in every Jewish home. In the window of every Jewish house there were set lights. According to Shammai, eight lights were set in the window, and they were reduced each day by one until on the last day only one was left burning. According to Hillel, one light was kindled on the first day, and one was added each day until on the last day eight were burning. We can see these lights in the windows of every devout Jewish home to this day.

These lights had two significances. First, they were a reminder that at the first celebrating of the festival the light of freedom had come back to Israel. Second, they were traced back to a very old legend. It was told that when the Temple had been purified and the great sevenbranched candlestick re-lit, only one little cruse of unpolluted oil could be found. This cruse was still intact, and still sealed with the impress of the ring of the High Priest. By all normal measures, there was only oil enough in that cruse to light the lamps for one single day. But by a miracle it lasted for eight days, until new oil had been prepared according to the correct formula and had been consecrated for its sacred use. So for eight days the lights burned in the Temple and in the homes of the people in memory of the cruse which God had made to last for eight days instead of one.

It is not without significance that it must have been very close to this time of illumination that Jesus said: " I am the Light of the world." When all the lights were being kindled in memory of the freedom won to worship God in the true way, Jesus said: " I am the Light of the world; I alone can light men into the knowledge and the presence of God."

John also gives us the place of this discussion, Solomon's Porch. The first court in the Temple precincts was the Court of the Gentiles. Along two sides of it ran two magnificent colonnades called the Royal Porch and Solomon's Porch. They were rows of magnificent pillars, almost forty feet high and roofed over. People walked there to pray and meditate; and Rabbis strolled there as they talked to their students and expounded the doctrines of the faith. It was there that Jesus was walking, because, as John says with a pictorial touch, " it was wintry weather."

THE CLAIM AND THE PROMISE

John 10: 22–28 (*continued*)

As Jesus walked in Solomon's Porch the Jews came to him. " How long," they said to him, " are you going to keep us in suspense? Tell us plainly, are you or are you not God's promised Anointed One? " There is no doubt that behind that question were two attitudes of mind. There were those who genuinely wished to know. They were on an eager tip-toe of expectation. But there were others who beyond a doubt asked the question as a trap. They wished to inveigle Jesus into making a statement which could be twisted either into a charge of blasphemy with which their own courts could deal or a charge of insurrection with which the Roman governor would deal.

Jesus's answer was that he had already told them who he was. True, he had not done so in so many words; for, as John tells the story, Jesus's two great claims had been made in private. To the Samaritan woman he had revealed himself as the Messiah (*John* 4: 26) and to the man born blind he had claimed to be the Son of God (*John* 9: 37). But there are some claims which do not need to be made in words, especially to an audience well-qualified to perceive them. There were two things about Jesus which placed his claim beyond all doubt whether he stated it in words or not. First, there were his *deeds*. It was Isaiah's dream of the golden age: " Then the eyes of the blind shall be opened, and the ears of the deaf unstopped; then shall the lame man leap like a hart, and the tongue of the dumb sing for joy " (*Isaiah* 35: 5, 6). Every one of Jesus's miracles was a claim that the Messiah had come. Second, there were his *words*. Moses had forecast that God would raise up the Prophet who must be listened to (*Deuteronomy* 18: 15). The very accent of authority with which Jesus spoke, the way in which he regally abrogated the old law and put his own teaching in its place, was a claim that God was speaking in him. The words and deeds of Jesus were a continuous claim to be the Anointed One of God.

But the great majority of the Jews had not accepted that claim. As we have seen in Palestine the sheep knew their own shepherd's special call and answered it; these were not of Jesus's flock. In the fourth gospel there is behind it all a doctrine of predestination, things were happening all the time as God meant them to happen. John is really saying that these Jews were predestined not to follow Jesus. Somehow or other the whole New Testament keeps two opposite ideas in balance—— the fact that everything happens within the purpose of God and yet in such a way that man's free-will is responsible. These had made themselves such that they were predestined not to accept Jesus; and yet, as John sees it, that does not make them any the less to be condemned.

But though most did not accept Jesus, some did; and to them Jesus promised three things.

(i) He promised *eternal life.* He promised that if they accepted him as Master and Lord, if they became members of his flock, all the littleness of earthly life would be gone and they would know the splendour and the magnificence of the life of God.

(ii) He promised a *life that would know no end.* Death would not be the end but the beginning; they would know the glory of indestructible life.

(iii) He promised a *life that was secure.* Nothing could snatch them from his hand. This would not mean that they would be saved from sorrow, from suffering and from death; but that in the sorest moment and the darkest hour they would still be conscious of the everlasting arms underneath and about them. Even in a world crashing to disaster they would know the serenity of God.

THE TREMENDOUS TRUST AND THE TREMENDOUS CLAIM

John 10: 29, 30

> My Father, who gave them to me, is greater than all; and no one
> can snatch them from the hand of the Father. I and the Father are
> one.

THIS passage shows at one and the same time the tremendous trust and the tremendous claim of Jesus.

His trust was something which traced everything back to God. He has just been speaking about *his* sheep and *his* flock; he has just been saying that no one will ever snatch his own from *his* hand, that he is the shepherd who will keep the sheep for ever safe. At first sight, and if he had stopped there, it would have seemed that Jesus put his trust in his own keeping power. But now we see the other side of it. It is his Father who gave him his sheep; that both he and his sheep are in his Father's hand. Jesus was so sure of himself because he was so sure of God. His attitude to life was not self-confidence, But God-confidence. He was secure, not in his own power, but in God's. He was so certain of ultimate safety and ultimate victory, not because he arrogated all power to himself, but because he assigned all power to God.

Now we come to the supreme claim. " I and the Father are one," said Jesus. What did he mean? Is it absolute mystery, or can we understand at least a little of it? Are we driven to interpret it in terms of essence and hypostasis and all the rest of the metaphysical and philosophic notions about which the makers of the creeds fought and argued? Has one to be a theologian and a philosopher to grasp even a fragment of the meaning of this tremendous statement?

If we go to the Bible itself for the interpretation, we find that it is in fact so simple that the simplest mind can grasp it. Let us turn to the seventeeenth chapter of John's gospel, which tells of the prayer of Jesus for his followers before he went to his death:

" Holy Father, keep them in thy name, which thou hast given me, *that they may be one, even as we are one* " (*John* 17: 11). Jesus conceived of the unity of Christian with Christian as the same as his unity with God. In the same passage he goes on: " I do not pray for these only, but also for those who believe in me through their word, that they may all be one; even as thou, Father, art in me, and I in thee, that they also may be in us, so that the world may believe that thou hast sent me. The glory which thou hast given me I have given to them, that they may be one even as we are one " (*John* 17: 20–22). Jesus is saying with simplicity and a clarity none can mistake that the end of the Christian life is that Christians should be one as he and his Father are one.

What is the unity which should exist between Christian and Christian? Its secret is *love*. " A new commandment I give to you, That you love one another; even as I have loved you, that you also love one another " (*John* 13: 34). Christians are one because they love one another; even so, Jesus is one with God because of his love of God. But we can go further. What is the only test of love? Let us go again to the words of Jesus. " If you keep my commandments, you will abide in my love; just as I have kept my Father's commandments and abide in his love " (*John* 15: 10). " If man loves me, he will keep my word " (*John* 14: 23, 24). " If you love me, you will keep my commandments " (*John* 14: 15). " He who has my commandments and keeps them, he it is who loves me " (*John* 14: 21).

Here is the essence of the matter. The bond of unity is love; the proof of love is obedience. Christians are one with each other when they are bound by love, and obey the words of Christ. Jesus is one with God, because as no other ever did, he obeyed and loved him. His unity with God is a unity of perfect love, issuing in perfect obedience.

When Jesus said: " I and the Father are one," he was not moving in the world of philosophy and metaphysics and abstractions; he was moving in the world of *personal relationships*. No one can really understand what a phrase like " a unity of essence " means; but any one can understand what a unity of heart means. Jesus's unity with God came from the twin facts of perfect love and perfect obedience. He was one with God because he loved and obeyed him perfectly; and he came to this world to make us what he is.

INVITING THE ACID TEST

John 10: 31–39

> The Jews again lifted up stones to stone him. Jesus said to them: " I have showed you many lovely deeds, which came from my Father. For which of these deeds are you trying to stone me? " The Jews answered him: " It is not for any lovely deed that we propose to stone you; it is for insulting God, and because you, being a man, make yourself God." " Does it not stand written in your law," Jesus answered them, " ' I said you are gods' ? If he called those to whom the word came gods—and the scripture cannot be destroyed—are you going to say about me, whom the Father consecrated and despatched into the world: ' You insult God,' because I said: ' I am the Son of God '? If I do not do the works of my Father, do not believe me' But if I do, even if you do not believe me, believe the works, that you may know and recognize that the Father is in me, and I am in the Father." They again tried to lay violent hands on him, but he evaded their grasp.

To the Jews Jesus's statement that he and the Father were one was blasphemy. It was the invasion by a man of the place which belonged to God alone. The Jewish law laid down the penalty of stoning for blasphemy. " He who blasphemes the name of the Lord shall be put to death; all the congregation shall stone him " (*Leviticus* 24: 16). So they made their preparations to stone Jesus. The Greek really means that they went and fetched stones to fling at him. Jesus met their hostility with three arguments.

(i) He told them that he had spent all his days doing lovely things, healing the sick feeding the hungry, and comforting the sorrowing, deeds so full of help and power and beauty that they obviously came from God. For which of these deeds did they

wish to stone him? Their answer was that it was not for
anything he had done that they wished to stone him, but for the
claim he was making.

(ii) This claim was that he was the Son of God. To meet
their attack Jesus used two arguments. The first is a purely
Jewish argument which is difficult for us to understand. He
quoted *Psalm* 82: 6. That psalm is a warning to unjust judges to
cease from unjust ways and defend the poor and the innocent.
The appeal concludes: " I say, ' You are gods, sons of the Most
High, all of you. ' " The judge is commissioned by God to be
god to men. This idea comes out very clearly in certain of the
regulations in *Exodus*. *Exodus* 21: 1–6 tells how the Hebrew
servant may go free in the seventh year. As the Authorized
Version has it, verse 6 says " Then his master shall bring him
unto the *judges*." But in the Hebrew, the word which is translated *judges* is actually *elohim*, which means *gods*. The same
form of expression is used in *Exodus* 22: 9, 28. Even scripture
said of men who were specially commissioned to some task by
God that they were gods. So Jesus said: " If scripture can
speak like that about men, why should I not speak so about
myself? "

Jesus claimed two things for himself. (*a*) He was *consecrated*
by God to a special task. The word for *to consecrate* is
hagiazein, the verb from which comes the adjective *hagios*,
holy. This word always has the idea of rendering a person or a
place or a thing different from other persons and places and
things, because it is set aside for a special purpose or task. So,
for instance, the Sabbath is *holy* (*Exodus* 20: 11). The altar is
holy (*Leviticus* 16: 19). The priests are *holy* (2 *Chronicles* 26:
18). The prophet is *holy* (*Jeremiah* 1: 5). When Jesus said that
God had *consecrated* him, made him *holy*, he meant that he had
set him apart from other men, because he had given him a
special task to do. The very fact that Jesus used this word
shows how conscious he was of his special task. (*b*) He said that
God had *despatched* him into the world. The word used is the
one which would be used for sending a messenger or an
ambassador or an army. Jesus did not so much think of himself

as *coming* into the world, as being *sent* into the world His coming was an act of God; and he came to do the task which God had given him to do.

So Jesus said: " In the old days it was possible for scripture to speak of judges as gods, because they were commissioned by God to bring his truth and justice into the world. Now I have been set apart for a special task; I have been despatched into the world by God; how can you then object if I call myself the Son of God? I am only doing what scripture does." This is one of those biblical arguments the force of which it is difficult for us to feel; but which to a Jewish Rabbi would have been entirely convincing.

(iii) Jesus went on to invite the acid test. " I do not ask you," he said in effect, " to accept my words. But I do ask you to accept my deeds." A word is something about which a man can argue; but a deed is something beyond argument. Jesus is the perfect teacher in that he does not base his claims on what he says, but on what he is and does. His invitation to the Jews was to base their verdict on him, not on what he said, but on what he did; and that is a test which all his followers ought to be able and willing to meet. The tragedy is that so few can meet it, still less invite it.

PEACE BEFORE THE STORM

John 10: 40, 41

> And he went away again to the other side of Jordan, to the place where John first used to baptize; and he stayed there. And many came to him, and they kept saying: " John did no sign; but everything John said about this man is true." And then many believed in him.

FOR Jesus the time was running out; but he knew his hour. He would not recklessly court danger and throw his life away; nor would he in cowardice avoid danger to preserve his life. But he desired quietness before the final struggle. He always armed himself to meet men by first meeting God. That is why he retired to the other side of Jordan. He was not running away: he was preparing himself for the final contest.

The place to which Jesus went is most significant. He went to the place where John had been accustomed to baptize, the place where he himself had been baptized. It was there that the voice of God had come to him and assured him that he had taken the right decision and was on the right way. There is everything to be said for a man returning every now and then to the place where he had the supreme experience of his life. When Jacob was up against it, when things had gone wrong and badly wrong, he went back to Bethel (*Genesis* 35: 1–5). When he needed God, he went back to the place where he had first found him. Jesus, before the end, went back to the place where the beginning had happened. It would often do our souls a world of good to make a pilgrimage to the place where we first found God.

Even on the far side of Jordan the Jews came to Jesus, and they too thought of John. They remembered that he had spoken with the words of a prophet; but had done no mighty deeds. They saw that there was a difference between Jesus and John. To John's proclamation Jesus added God's power. John could diagnose the situation; Jesus brought the power to deal with the situation. These Jews had looked on John as a prophet; now they saw that what John had foretold of Jesus was true, and many of them believed.

It often happens that a man for whom a great future is painted, and who sets out with the hopes of men upon him, disappoints that future and belies these hopes. But Jesus was even greater than John had said he would be. Jesus is the one person who never disappoints those who set their hopes upon him. In him the dream always comes true.

ON THE ROAD TO GLORY

John 11: 1–5

There was a man Lazarus, who came from Bethany from the village where Mary and her sister Martha lived, and he was ill. It was Mary who had anointed the Lord with perfumed ointment, and who had wiped his feet with her hair, and it was her brother Lazarus who was ill. So the sisters sent a message to Jesus. " Lord," they said, " See! The one you love is ill." When Jesus heard the message, he said: " This illness is not going to prove fatal; rather it has happened for the sake of the glory of God, so that God's Son should be glorified by means of it." Jesus loved Martha and her sister and Lazarus.

IT is one of the most precious things in the world to have a house and a home into which one can go at any time and find rest and understanding and peace and love. That was doubly true for Jesus, for he had no home of his own; he had nowhere to lay his head (*Luke* 9: 58). In the home at Bethany he had just such a place. There were three people who loved him; and there he could find rest from the tension of life.

The greatest gift any human being can give another is understanding and peace. To have someone to whom we can go at any time knowing that they will not laugh at our dreams or misunderstand our confidences is a most wonderful thing. It is open to us all to make our own homes like that. It does not cost money, and does not need lavish hospitality. It costs only the understanding heart. Sir William Watson, in his poem *Wordsworth's Grave*, paid a great tribute to Wordsworth:

" What hadst thou that could make so large amends,
 For all thou hadst not and thy peers possessed?
Motion and fire, swift means to radiant ends?—
 Thou hadst for weary feet, the gift of rest."

No man can have a greater gift to offer his fellow men than rest for weary feet; and that is the gift which Jesus found in the house in Bethany, where Martha and Mary and Lazarus lived.

The name *Lazarus* means *God is my help*, and is the same
name as *Eleazar*. Lazarus fell ill, and the sisters sent to Jesus a
message that it was so. It is lovely to note that the sisters'
message included no request to Jesus to come to Bethany. They
knew that was unnecessary; they knew that the simple statement that they were in need would bring him to them. Augustine noted this, and said it was sufficient that Jesus should
know; for it is not possible that any man should at one and the
same time love a friend and desert him. C. F. Andrews tells of
two friends who served together in the First World War. One of
them was wounded and left lying helpless and in pain in
no-man's-land. The other, at peril of his life, crawled out to help
his friend; and, when he reached him, the wounded man looked
up and said simply: " I knew you would come." The simple fact of
human need brings Jesus to our side in the twinkling of an eye.

When Jesus came to Bethany he knew that whatever was
wrong with Lazarus he had power to deal with it. But he went
on to say that his sickness had happened for God's glory and
for his. Now this was true in a double sense—and Jesus knew
it. (i) The cure would undoubtedly enable men to see the glory
of God in action. (ii) But there was more to it than that. Again
and again in the Fourth Gospel Jesus talks of his glory in
connection with the Cross. John tells us in 7: 39 that the Spirit
had not yet come because Jesus was not yet *glorified*, that is to
say, because he had not yet died upon his Cross. When the
Greeks came to him, Jesus said: " The hour has come for the
Son of Man to be *glorified* " (*John* 12: 23). And it was of his
Cross that he spoke, for he went straight on to speak of the corn
of wheat which must fall into the ground and die. In *John* 12:
16 John says that the disciples remembered these things after
Jesus had been *glorified*, that is after he had died and risen
again. In the Fourth Gospel it is clear that Jesus regarded the
Cross both as his supreme glory and as the way to glory. So
when he said that the cure of Lazarus would glorify him, he was
showing that he knew perfectly well that to go to Bethany and
to cure Lazarus was to take a step which would end in the
Cross—as indeed it did.

With open eyes Jesus accepted the Cross to help his friend. He knew the cost of helping and was well prepared to pay it.

When some trial or affliction comes upon us, especially if it is the direct result of fidelity to Jesus Christ, it would make all the difference in the world if we saw that the cross we have to bear is our glory and the way to a greater glory still. For Jesus there was no other way to glory than through the Cross; and so it must ever be with those who follow him.

TIME ENOUGH BUT NOT TOO MUCH

John 11: 6–10

> Now, when Jesus had received the news that Lazarus was ill, he continued to stay where he was for two days. But after that he said to his disciples: " Let us go to Judaea again." His disciples said to him: " Rabbi, things had got to a stage when the Jews were trying to find a way to stone you, and do you propose to go back there? " Jesus answered: " Are there not twelve hours in the day? If a man walks in the day-time, he does not stumble because he has the light of this world. But if a man walks in the night-time, he does stumble because the light is not in him."

WE may find it strange that John shows us Jesus staying two whole days where he was when he received the news about Lazarus. Commentators have advanced different reasons to explain this delay. (i) It has been suggested that Jesus waited so that when he arrived Lazarus would be indisputably dead. (ii) It has therefore been suggested that Jesus waited because the delay would make the miracle he proposed to perform all the more impressive. The wonder of raising to life a man who had been dead for four days would be all the greater. (iii) The real reason why John tells the story in this way is that he always shows us Jesus taking action entirely on his own initiative and not on the persuasion of anyone else. In the story of the turning of the water into wine at Cana of Galilee (*John* 2: 1–11) John shows us Mary coming to Jesus and telling him of the problem.

Jesus's first answer to Mary is: " Don't bother about this. Let me handle it in my own way." He takes action, not be ause he is persuaded or compelled to do so, but entirely on hie own initiative. When John tells the story of Jesus's brothers trying to dare him into going to Jerusalem (*John* 7: 1–10), he shows us Jesus at first refusing to go to Jerusalem and then going in his own good time. It is always John's aim to show that Jesus did things, not because he was pressed to do them, but because he chose to do them in his own good time. That is what John is doing here. It is a warning to us. So often we would like Jesus to do things in our way; we must leave him to do them in his own way.

When Jesus finally announced that he was going to Judaea, his disciples were shocked and staggered. They remembered that the last time he was there the Jews had tried to find a way to kill him. To go to Judaea at that time seemed to them—as indeed humanly speaking it was—the surest way to commit suicide.

Then Jesus said something which contains a great and permanent truth. " Are there not," he asked, " twelve hours in the day? " There are three great truths implied in that question.

(i) A day cannot finish before it ends. There are twelve hours in the day, and they will be played out no matter what happens. The day's period is fixed, and nothing will shorten or lengthen it. In God's economy of time a man has his day, whether it be short or long.

(ii) If there are twelve hours in the day there is time enough for everything a man should do. There is no need for a rushed haste.

(iii) But, even if there are twelve hours in the day, there are *only* twelve hours. They cannot be extended; and therefore, time cannot be wasted. There is time enough, but not too much; the time we have must be used to the utmost.

The legend of Dr Faustus was turned into great drama and poetry by Christopher Marlowe. Faustus had struck a bargain with the devil. For twenty-four years the devil would be his servant and his every wish would be realized; but at the end of the years the devil would claim his soul. The twenty-four years have run their course, the last hour has come, and Faustus now sees what a terrible bargain he has struck.

> " Ah, Faustus,
>   Now hast thou but one bare hour to live,
>   And then thou must be damn'd perpetually;
>   Stand still, you ever-moving spheres of heaven,
>   That time may cease, and midnight never come.
>   Fair Nature's eye, rise, rise again and make
>   Perpetual day; or let this hour be but
>   A year, a month, a week, a natural day,
>   That Faustus may repent and save his soul!
>   *O lente, lente currite, noctis equi*!
>   The stars move still, time runs, the clock will strike,
>   The devil will come, and Faustus must be damn'd."

Nothing in the world could give Faustus more time. That is one of the great threatening facts in the life of man. There are twelve hours in the day—but there are *only* twelve hours in the day. There is no necessity for haste; but, equally, there is no room for waste. There is time enough in life, but there is never time to spare.

THE DAY AND THE NIGHT

John 11: 6–10 (*continued*)

JESUS goes on to develop what he has just said about time. He says that if a man walks in the light, he will not stumble; but if he tries to walk in the night, he will stumble.

John again and again says things which have two meanings, one which lies on the surface and is true, and another which lies below the surface and is truer yet. It is so here.

(i) There is a surface meaning which is perfectly true and which we must learn. The Jewish day, like the Roman day, was divided into twelve equal hours, from sunrise to sunset. That of course means that the length of an hour varied according to the length of the day and the season of the year. On the surface Jesus simply means that a man will not stumble when the sun is shining, but when the dark comes down he cannot see the way. There was no street lighting in those days, at least not in the country places. With the dark, the time for journeying was done.

Jesus is saying that a man must finish the day's work within the day, for the night comes when work is ended. If a man had one wish it might well be that he might come to the end of each day with its work completed. The unrest and the hurry of life are so often simply due to the fact that we are trying to catch up on work which should have been done before. A man should so spend his precious capital of time and not dissipate it on useless extravagances, however pleasant, that at the end of each day he is never in debt to time.

(ii) But below the surface meaning is another meaning. Who can hear the phrase *the light of the world* without thinking of Jesus? Again and again John uses the words the *dark* and the *night* to describe life without Christ, life dominated by evil. In his dramatic account of the last meal together, John describes how Judas went out to make the dreadful final arrangements for the betrayal. " So, after receiving the morsal, he immediately went out; and it was night " (*John* 13: 30). The night is the time when a man goes from Christ and when evil possesses him.

The gospel is based on the love of God; but whether we like it or not, there is a threat also at its heart. A man has only so much time to make his peace with God through Christ; and if he does not do so the judgment must follow. So Jesus says: " Finish your greatest work; finish the work of getting yourself right with God while you have the light of the world; for the time comes when for you, too, the dark must come down and then it will be too late."

No gospel is so sure that God loved the world as the Fourth Gospel is; but also no gospel is so sure that love may be refused. It has in it two notes—the glory of being *in time*; and the tragedy of being *too late*.

THE MAN WHO WOULD NOT QUIT

John 11: 11–16

> Jesus said these things, and then he went on to say: " Our friend
> Lazarus is sleeping; but I am going to waken him up." " Lord,"
> the disciples said to him, " if he is sleeping he will recover." But
> Jesus had spoken about his death. They thought that he was
> speaking about the sleep of natural sleep. So Jesus then said to
> them plainly: " Lazarus has died, and, for your sakes, I am glad
> that I was not there, because it is all designed in order that you
> may come to believe. But let us go to him." Thereupon Thomas,
> who was called Didymus, said: " Let us, too, go that we may die
> with him."

JOHN here uses his normal method of relating a conversation of
Jesus. In the Fourth Gospel, Jesus's conversations always
follow the same pattern. Jesus says something which sounds
quite simple. His saying is misunderstood, and he goes on to
explain more fully and unmistakably what he meant. So it is
with his conversation with Nicodemus about being born again
(*John* 3: 3–8); and his conversation with the woman at the well
about the water of life (*John* 4: 10–15).

Jesus here began by saying that Lazarus was sleeping. To the
disciples that sounded good news, for there is no better
medicine than sleep. But the word *sleep* has always had a
deeper and a more serious meaning. Jesus said of Jairus's
daughter that she was asleep (*Matthew* 9: 24); at the end of
Stephen's martyrdom we are told that he fell asleep (*Acts* 7: 60).
Paul speaks about those who sleep in Jesus (1 *Thessalonians* 4:
13); and of those witnesses of the Resurrection who are now
fallen asleep (1 *Corinthians* 15: 6). So Jesus had to tell them
plainly that Lazarus was dead; and then he went on to say that
for their sake this was a good thing, because it would produce
an event which would buttress them even more firmly in their
faith.

The final proof of Christianity is the sight of what Jesus
Christ can do. Words may fail to convince, but there is no

argument against God in action. It is the simple fact that the power of Jesus Christ has made the coward into a hero, the doubter into a man of certainty, the selfish man into the servant of all. Above all, it is the plain fact of history that again and again the power of Christ has made the bad man good.

That is what lays so tremendous a responsibility on the individual Christian. The design of God is that every one of us should be a living proof of his power. Our task is not so much to commend Christ in words—against which there is always an argument, for no one can ever write Q.E.D. after a Christian verbal proof—but to demonstrate in our lives what Christ has done for us. Sir John Reith once said: " I do not like crises; but I like the opportunities which they supply." The death of Lazarus brought a crisis to Jesus, and he was glad, because it gave him the opportunity to demonstrate in the most amazing way what God can do. For us every crisis should be a like opportunity.

At that moment the disciples might well have refused to follow Jesus; then one lonely voice spoke up. They were all feeling that to go to Jerusalem was to go to their deaths, and they were hanging back. Then came the voice of Thomas: " Let us, too, go that we may die with him."

All Jews in those days had two names—one a Hebrew name by which a man was known in his own circle, the other a Greek name by which he was known in a wider circle. *Thomas* is the *Hebrew* and *Didymus* the *Greek* for a *twin*. So *Peter* is the Greek and *Cephas* is the *Hebrew* for a rock; *Tabitha* is the *Hebrew*, and *Dorcas* the *Greek* for a *gazelle*. In later days the apocryphal Gospels wove their stories around Thomas, and they actually in the end came to say that he was the twin of Jesus himself.

At this moment Thomas displayed the highest kind of courage. In his heart, as R. H. Strachan said, " There was not expectant faith, but loyal despair." But upon one thing Thomas was determined—come what may, he would not quit.

Gilbert Frankau tells of an officer friend of his in the 1914–18 war, an artillery observation officer. His duty was to go up in a captive balloon and to indicate to the gunners whether their shells fell short of or over the target. It was one of the most dangerous assignments that could be given. Because the balloon was captive, there was no way to dodge; he was a sitting target for the guns and planes of the enemy. Gilbert Frankau said of his friend: " Every time he went up in that balloon he was sick with nerves, but he wouldn't quit."

That is the highest form of courage. It does not mean not being afraid. If we are not afraid it is the easiest thing in the world to do a thing. Real courage means being perfectly aware of the worst that can happen, being sickeningly afraid of it, and yet doing the *right* thing. That was what Thomas was like that day. No man need ever be ashamed of being afraid; but he may well be ashamed of allowing his fear to stop him doing what in his heart of hearts he knows he ought to do.

THE HOUSE OF MOURNING

John 11: 17–19

> So, when Jesus came, he found that Lazarus had already been in the tomb for four days. Bethany was near Jerusalem, less than two miles away. Many of the Jews had gone to Martha and Mary to comfort them about their brother.

IN order to visualize this scene we must first see what a Jewish house of mourning was like. Normally in Palestine, because of the climate, burial followed death as quickly as possible. There was a time when a funeral was an exceedingly costly thing. The finest spices and ointments were used to anoint the body; the body itself was clothed in the most magnificent robes; all kinds of valuables were buried in the tomb along with the body. By midway through the first century all this had become a ruinous expenditure. Naturally no one wished on such an occasion to be outdone by his neighbour, and the wrappings and robes with which the body was covered, and the treasures left in the tomb, became ever more expensive. The matter had become almost an

intolerable burden which no one liked to alter—until the advent
of a famous Rabbi called Gamaliel the Second. He gave orders
that he was to be buried in the simplest possible linen robe, and
so broke the extravagance of funeral customs. To this day at
Jewish funerals a cup is drunk to Rabbi Gamaliel who rescued
the Jews from their own ostentatious extravagance. From his
time on the body was wrapped in a simple linen dress which
was sometimes called by the very beautiful name of *the
travelling-dress*.

As many as possible attended a funeral. Everyone who could
was supposed, in courtesy and respect, to join the procession on
its way. One curious custom was that the woman walked first,
for it was held that since woman by her first sin brought death
into the world, she ought to lead the mourners to the tomb. At
the tomb memorial speeches were sometimes made. Everyone
was expected to express the deepest sympathy, and, on leaving
the tomb, the others stood in two long lines while the principal
mourners passed between them. But there was this very wise
rule—the mourners were not to be tormented by idle and
uninvited talk. They were to be left, at that moment, alone with
their sorrow.

In the house of mourning there were set customs. So long as
the body was in the house it was forbidden to eat meat or to
drink wine, to wear phylacteries or to engage in any kind of
study. No food was to be prepared in the house, and such food
as was eaten must not be eaten in the presence of the dead. As
soon as the body was carried out all furniture was reversed, and
the mourners sat on the ground or on low stools.

On the return from the tomb a meal was served, which had
been prepared by the friends of the family. It consisted of bread,
hard-boiled eggs and lentils; the round eggs and lentils symbolized life which was always rolling to death.

Deep mourning lasted for seven days, of which the first three
were days of weeping. During these seven days it was forbidden
to anoint oneself, to put on shoes, to engage in any kind of
study or business, and even to wash. The week of deep
mourning was followed by thirty days of lighter mourning.

So when Jesus found a crowd in the house at Bethany, he
found what anyone would expect to find in a Jewish house of
mourning. It was a sacred duty to come to express loving
sympathy with the sorrowing friends and relations of one who
had died. The *Talmud* says that whoever visits the sick shall
deliver his soul from Gehenna; and Maimonides, the great
medieval Jewish scholar, declared that to visit the sick takes
precedence of all other good works. Visits of sympathy to the
sick, and to the sorrowing, were an essential part of Jewish
religion. A certain Rabbi expounded the text in *Deuteronomy*
13: 4: " You shall walk after the Lord your God." He said that
text commands us to imitate the things which God is depicted
as doing in scripture. God clothed the naked (*Genesis* 3: 21);
God visited the sick (*Genesis* 18: 1). God comforted the
mourners (*Genesis* 25: 11); God buried the dead (*Deuteronomy*
34: 6). In all these things we must imitate the actions of God.

Respect for the dead and sympathy for the mourner were an
essential part of Jewish duty. As the mourners left the tomb,
they turned and said: " Depart in peace," and they never
mentioned the name of the one who had died without invoking
a blessing on it. There is something very lovely in the way in
which the Jews stressed the duty of showing sympathy to
the mourner.

It would be to a household crowded with sympathizers that
Jesus came that day.

THE RESURRECTION AND THE LIFE

John 11: 20–27

So when Martha heard that Jesus was coming, she went to meet
him, but Mary remained sitting in the house. So Martha said to
Jesus: " Lord, if you had been here, my brother would not have
died. And even as things are, I know that whatever you ask God,
God will give you." Jesus said to her: " Your brother will rise
again." Martha said to him: " I know that he will rise at the
resurrection on the last day." Jesus said to her: " I am the

Resurrection and the Life. He who believes in me will live even if
he has died; and everyone who lives and believes in me shall never
die. Do you believe this? " She said to him; " Yes, Lord. I am
convinced that you are God's Anointed One, the Son of God, the
One who is to come into the world."

IN this story, too, Martha is true to character. When Luke tells
us about Martha and Mary (*Luke* 10: 38–42), he shows us
Martha as the one who loved action, and Mary as the one
whose instinct was to sit still. It is so here. As soon as it was
announced that Jesus was coming near, Martha was up to meet
him, for she could not sit still, but Mary lingered behind.

When Martha met Jesus her heart spoke through her lips.
Here is one of the most human speeches in all the Bible, for
Martha spoke, half with a reproach that she could not keep
back, and half with a faith that nothing could shake. " If you
had been here," she said, " my brother would not have died."
Through the words we read her mind. Martha would have liked
to say: " When you got our message, why didn't you come at
once? And now you have left it too late." No sooner are the
words out than there follow the words of faith, faith which
defied the facts and defied experience: " Even yet," she said
with a kind of desperate hope, " even yet, I know that God will
give you whatever you ask."

Jesus said " Your brother will rise again." Martha answered:
" I know quite well that he will rise in the general resurrection
on the last day." Now that is a notable saying. One of the
strangest things in scripture is the fact that the saints of the
Old Testament had practically no belief in any real life after
death. In the early days, the Hebrews believed that the soul of
every man, good and bad alike, went to Sheol. Sheol is wrong-
ly translated *Hell*; for it was not a place of torture, it was the land
of the shades. All alike went there and they lived a vague,
shadowy, strengthless, joyless ghostly kind of life. This is the
belief of by far the greater part of the Old Testament. " In death
there is no remembrance of thee: in Sheol who can give thee
praise? " (*Psalm* 6: 5). " What profit is there in my death if I go
down to the pit? Will the dust praise thee? Will it tell of thy

faithfulness? " (*Psalm* 30: 9). The Psalmist speaks of " the slain that lie in the grave, like those whom thou dost remember no more; for they are cut off from thy hand " (*Psalm* 88: 5). " Is thy steadfast love declared in the grave," he asks, " or thy faithfulness in Abaddon? Are thy wonders known in the darkness, or thy saving help in the land of forgetfulness? " (*Psalm* 88: 10–12). " The dead do not praise the Lord, nor do any that go down into silence " (*Psalm* 115: 17). The preacher says grimly: " Whatever your hand finds to do, do it with your might; for there is no work or thought or knowledge or wisdom in Sheol, to which you are going " (*Ecclesiastes* 9: 10). It is Hezekiah's pessimistic belief that: " For Sheol cannot thank thee, death cannot praise thee; those who go down to the pit cannot hope for thy faithfulness " (*Isaiah* 38: 18). After death came the land of silence and of forgetfulness, where the shades of men were separated alike from men and from God. As J. E. McFadyen wrote: " There are few more wonderful things than this in the long history of religion, that for centuries men lived the noblest lives, doing their duties and bearing their sorrows, without hope of future reward."

Just very occasionally someone in the Old Testament made a venturesome leap of faith. The Psalmist cries: " My body also dwells secure. For thou dost not give me up to Sheol, or let thy godly one see the pit. Thou dost show me the path of life; in thy presence there is fullness of joy, in thy right hand are pleasures for evermore " (*Psalm* 16: 9–11). " I am continually with thee; thou dost hold my right hand. Thou dost guide me with thy counsel, and afterward thou wilt receive me to glory " (*Psalm* 73: 23, 24). The Psalmist was convinced that when a man entered into a real relationship with God, not even death could break it. But at that stage it was a desperate leap of faith rather than a settled conviction. Finally in the Old Testament there is the immortal hope we find in *Job*. In face of all his disasters Job cried out:

> " I know that there liveth a champion,
>   Who will one day stand over my dust;
>   Yea, another shall rise as my witness,

> And, as sponsor, shall I behold—God;
> Whom mine eyes shall behold, and no stranger's."

(*Job* 14: 7–12; translated by J. E. McFadyen).

Here in *Job* we have the real seed of the Jewish belief in immortality.

The Jewish history was a history of disasters, of captivity, slavery and defeat. Yet the Jewish people had the utterly unshakable conviction that they were God's own people. This earth had never shown it and never would; inevitably, therefore, they called in the new world to redress the inadequacies of the old. They came to see that if God's design was ever fully to be worked out, if his justice was ever completely to be fulfilled, if his love was ever finally to be satisfied, another world and another life were necessary. As Galloway (quoted by McFadyen) put it: " The enigmas of life become at least less baffling, when we come to rest in the thought that this is not the last act of the human drama." It was precisely that feeling that led the Hebrews to a conviction that there was a life to come.

It is true that in the days of Jesus the Sadducees still refused to believe in any life after death. But the Pharisees and the great majority of the Jews did. They said that in the moment of death the two worlds of time and of eternity met and kissed. They said that those who died beheld God, and they refused to call them the dead but called them the living. When Martha answered Jesus as she did she bore witness to the highest reach of her nation's faith.

THE RESURRECTION AND THE LIFE

John 11: 20–27 (*continued*)

WHEN Martha declared her belief in the orthodox Jewish belief in the life to come, Jesus suddenly said something which brought to that belief a new vividness and a new meaning. " I am the Resurrection and the Life," he said. " He who believes in me will live even if he has died; and everyone who lives and believes in me shall never die." What exactly did he mean? Not even a lifetime's thinking will reveal the full meaning of this; but we must try to grasp as much of it as we can.

One thing is clear—Jesus was not thinking in terms of physical life; for, speaking physically, it is not true that the man who believes in him will never die. The Christian experiences physical death as any other man does. We must look for a more than physical meaning.

(i) Jesus was thinking of the death of sin. He was saying: " Even if a man is dead in sin, even if, through his sins, he has lost all that makes life worth calling life, I can make him alive again." In point of historical fact that is abundantly true. A. M. Chirgwin quotes the example of Tokichi Ishii. Ishii had an almost unparalleled criminal record. He had murdered men, women and children in the most brutal way. Anyone who stood in his way was pitilessly eliminated. Now he was in prison awaiting death. While in prison he was visited by two Canadian women who tried to talk to him through the bars, but he only glowered at them like a caged and savage animal. In the end they abandoned the attempt; but they gave him a Bible, hoping that it might succeed where they had failed. He began to read it, and, having started, could not stop. He read on until he came to the story of the Crucifixion. He came to the words: " Father, forgive them, for they know not what they do," and these words broke him. " I stopped," he said. " I was stabbed to the heart, as if pierced by a five-inch nail. Shall I call it the love of Christ? Shall I call it his compassion? I do not know what to call it. I only know that I believed, and my hardness of heart was changed." Later, when the condemned man went to the scaffold, he was no longer the hardened, surly brute he once had been, but a smiling radiant man. The murderer had been born again; Christ had brought Tokichi Ishi to life.

It does not need to be so dramatic as that. A man can become so selfish that he is dead to the needs of others. A man can become so insensitive that he is dead to the feelings of others. A man can become so involved in the petty dishonesties and the petty disloyalties of life, that he is dead to honour. A man can become so hopeless that he is filled with an inertia, which is spiritual death. Jesus Christ can resurrect these men. The witness of history is that he has resurrected millions and millions of people like them and his touch has not lost its ancient power.

(ii) Jesus was also thinking of the life to come. He brought into life the certainty that death is not the end. The last words of Edward the Confessor were: " Weep not, I shall not die; and as I leave the land of the dying I trust to see the blessings of the Lord in the land of the living." We call this world *the land of the living*; but it would in fact be more correct to call it *the land of the dying*. Through Jesus Christ we know that we are journeying, not to the sunset, but to the sunrise; we know, as Mary Webb put it, that death is a gate on the sky-line. In the most real sense we are not on our way to death, but on our way to life.

How does this happen? It happens when we believe in Jesus Christ. What does that mean? To believe in Jesus means to accept everything that Jesus said as absolutely true, and to stake our lives upon that in perfect trust. When we do that we enter into two new relationships.

(i) We enter into a new relationship with God. When we believe that God is as Jesus told us that he is, then we become absolutely sure of his love; we become absolutely sure that he is above all a redeeming God. The fear of death vanishes, for death means going to the great lover of the souls of men.

(ii) We enter into a new relationship with life. When we accept Jesus's way, when we take his commands as our laws, and when we realize that he is there to help us to live as he has commanded, life becomes a new thing. It is clad with a new loveliness, a new winsomeness, a new strength. And when we accept Christ's way as our way, life becomes so lovely a thing that we cannot conceive of it ending incomplete.

When we believe in Jesus, when we accept what he says about God and about life and stake everything on it, in truth we are resurrected for we are freed from the fear which is characteristic of the godless life; we are freed from the frustration

which is characteristic of the sin-ridden life; we are freed from
the futility of the Christless life. Life is raised from sin's death
and becomes so rich that it cannot die but must find in death
only the transition to a higher life.

THE EMOTION OF JESUS

John 11: 28–33

> When Martha had said this, she went away and called Mary her
> sister. Without letting the rest of the people know, she said to her:
> " The Teacher has arrived and is calling for you." When she heard
> this, she rose quickly and began to go to him. Jesus had not yet
> come into the village, but he was still in the place where Martha
> met him. So when the Jews, who were in the house with Mary, and
> who were condoling with her, saw her rise quickly and go out,
> they followed her, for they thought that she was going back to the
> tomb to weep there. When Mary came to where Jesus was, when
> she saw him, she knelt at his feet. " Lord," she said, " if you had
> been here, my brother would not have died." When Jesus saw her
> weeping, and when he saw the Jews who had come with her
> weeping, he was deeply moved in spirit so that an involuntary
> groan burst from him, and he trembled with deep emotion.

MARTHA went back to the house to tell Mary that Jesus had
come. She wanted to give the news to her secretly, without
letting the visitors know, because she wanted Mary to have a
moment or two alone with Jesus, before the crowds engulfed
them and made privacy impossible. But when the visitors saw
Mary rise quickly and go out, they immediately assumed that
she had gone to visit the tomb of Lazarus. It was the custom,
especially for the women, for a week after the burial to go to the
tomb to weep on every possible occasion. Mary's greeting was
exactly the same as that of Martha. If only Jesus had come in
time, Lazarus would still be alive.

Jesus saw Mary and all the sympathizing crowd weeping.
We must remember that this would be no gentle shedding of
tears. It would be almost hysterical wailing and shrieking, for it

was the Jewish point of view that the more unrestrained the weeping, the more honour it paid to the dead.

Now we have a problem of translation. The word which the Authorized Version and the Revised Standard Version translate as *deeply moved* in spirit comes from the verb *embrimasthai*. It is used three other times in the New Testament. It is used in *Matthew* 9: 30 when Jesus *sternly charged* the blind men not to publish abroad the fact that he had given them their sight. It is used in *Mark* 1: 43 when Jesus *sternly charged* the leper not to publish the fact that he had healed him. It is used in *Mark* 14: 5 when the spectors *reproached* the woman who anointed Jesus's head with the costly ointment, because they thought that this deed of love was wastefully extravagant. In every one of these instances the word has a certain sternness, almost anger, in it. It means rather to rebuke, to give a stern order to. Some who wish to take it in that way and would translate: " Jesus was moved to anger in his spirit."

Why the anger? It is suggested that the display of tears by the Jewish visitors to Bethany was sheer hypocrisy, that this artificial grief raised Jesus's wrath. It is possible that this was true of the visitors, although there is no indication that their grief was synthetic. But it was certainly not true of Mary and it an hardly be right here to take *embrimasthai* to imply anger. Moffatt translates it: " Jesus *chafed* in spirit," but *chafed* is weak. The Revised Standard Version translates: " Jesus was deeply moved in spirit," but again that is colourless for this most unusual word. Rieu translates: " He gave way to such distress of spirit as made his body tremble." With this we are getting nearer the real meaning. In ordinary classical Greek the usual usage of *embrimasthai* is of a horse *snorting*. Here it must mean that such deep emotion seized Jesus that an involuntary groan was wrung from his heat.

Here is one of the most precious things in the gospel. So deeply did Jesus enter into men's sorrows that his heart was wrung with anguish

> " In ev'ry pang that rends the heart,
> The Man of Sorrows had a part."

But there is more. To any Greek reading this—and we must remember that it was written for Greeks—this would be a staggering and incredible picture. John had written his whole gospel on the theme that in Jesus we see the mind of God. To the Greek the primary characteristic of God was what he called *apatheia, which means total inability to feel any emotion whatsoever.*

How did the Greeks come to attribute such a characteristic to God? They argued like this. If we can feel sorrow or joy, gladness or grief, it means that someone can have an effect upon us. Now, if a person has an effect upon us, it means that for the moment that person has power over us. No one can have any power over God; and this must mean that God is essentially incapable of feeling any emotion whatsoever. The Greeks believed in an isolated, passionless and compassionless God.

What a different picture Jesus gave. He showed us a God whose heart is wrung with anguish for the anguish of his people. The greatest thing Jesus did was to bring us the news of a God who cares.

THE VOICE THAT WAKES THE DEAD

John 11: 34–44

Jesus said to them: " Where have you laid him? " " Lord," they said to him: " Come and see." Jesus wept. So the Jews said: " Look how he loved him! " Some of them said: " Could not this man who opened the eyes of the blind have so acted that Lazarus would not have died? " Again a groan was wrung from Jesus's inner being. He went to the tomb. It was a cave; and a stone had been laid upon it. Eesus said: " Take away the stone." Martha, the dead man's sister, said to him: " Lord, by this time the stench of death is on him, for he has been in the tomb for four days." Jesus said to her: " Did I not tell you that, if you believe, you will see the glory of God? " So they took the stone away. Jesus lifted up his eyes and said: " Father, I thank you that you have heard me. I knew that you always hear me. But I said this for the sake of the

crowd which is standing round, because I want them to believe
that you sent me." When he had said this, he cried with a loud
voice: " Lazarus, come out! " The man who had been dead came
out, bound hand and foot in grave-clothes, and with his face
encircled with a napkin. Jesus said to them: " Set him free from
his wrappings and let him go! "

WE come to the last scene. Once again we are shown the picture
of Jesus wrung with anguish as he shared the anguish of the
human heart. To the Greek reader that little sentence: " Jesus
wept," would be the most astonishing thing in an astonishing
story. That the Son of God could weep would be almost beyond
belief.

We must have in our minds a picture of the usual Palestinian
tomb. It was either a natural cave or hewn out of the rock. There
was an entrance in which the bier was first laid. Beyond that was a
chamber, usually about six feet long, nine feet wide and ten feet
high. There were usually eight shelves cut in the rock, three on
each side and two on the wall facing the entrance, and on these
shelves the bodies were laid. The bodies were enveloped in linen
but the hands and feet were swathed in bandage-like wrappings and
the head was wrapped separately. The tomb had no door, but
in front of the opening ran a groove in which was set a great
stone like a cartwheel that was rolled across the entrance to seal
the grave.

Jesus asked that the stone should be moved. Martha could
think of only one reason for opening the tomb—that Jesus wished
to look on the face of his dead friend for the last time. Martha
could see no consolation there. She pointed out that Lazarus had
been in the tomb for four days. The point is this. It was Jewish
belief that the spirit of the departed hovered around his tomb for
four days, seeking an entrance again into his body. But after four
days the spirit finally left for the face of the body was so decayed
that it could no longer be recognized.

Then Jesus spoke his word of command which even death was
powerless to oppose.

> " He speaks, and, listening to his voice,
> New life the dead receive."

And Lazarus came forth. It is weird to think of the bandaged figure staggering out from the tomb. Jesus told them to unloose the hampering grave-clothes and wrappings and let him go.

There are certain things to note.

(i) Jesus prayed. The power which flowed through him was not his; it was God's, " Miracles," said Godet, " are just so many answered prayers."

(ii) Jesus sought only the glory of God; he did not do this to glorify himself. When Elijah had his epic contest with the prophets of Baal, he prayed: " Answer me, O Lord, that this people may know that thou art God " (1 *Kings* 18: 37).

Everything Jesus did was due to the power of God and designed for the glory of God. How different men are! So much that we do is attempted in our own power and designed for our own prestige. It may be that there would be more wonders in our life, too, if we ceased to act by ourselves and for ourselves and set God in the central place.

THE RAISING OF LAZARUS

John 11: 1–44

WE have tried to expound the raising of Lazarus simply as the story stands written. But we can not evade the fact that of all the miracles of Jesus this presents the greatest problem. Let us honestly face the difficulties.

(i) In the other three gospels there are accounts of people being raised from the dead. There is the story of the raising of Jairus's daughter (*Matthew* 9: 18–26; *Mark* 5: 21–43; *Luke* 8: 40–56). There is the story of the raising of the widow's son at Nain (*Luke* 7: 11–16). In both cases the raising followed *immediately* after death. It would be quite possible to believe that in both these miracles the person raised was in a coma. We have seen how burial had to follow hard upon death in the climate of Palestine; and we know from the evidence of the graves that people were not infrequently buried alive, because of that haste. It could well be that these were miracles of diagnosis in which Jesus saved two young people from a dreadful death. But there is no parallel whatever for the raising of a man who had been dead for four days and whose body had begun to putrefy.

(ii) In the other three gospels there is no account, not even a mention, of the raising of Lazarus. If the other writers knew about this miracle, how could they possibly omit it? If it actually happened, how could they fail to know of it? It has been suggested that the answer is this. We know that Mark drew his information from Peter. The fact is that Peter does not appear in the Fourth Gospel at all in chapters 5 and chapters 7 to 12. Thomas is, in fact, the spokesman of the disciples. It has been suggested that Peter was not with Jesus at this time, and only came up later to the Passover Feast. On the face of it that does not seem likely, and, even if Peter was not there, surely the writers of the gospels must have heard from other sources of so amazing a miracle.

(iii) Perhaps the greatest difficulty is that John sees in this miracle the essential cause which moved the Jewish authorities to take definite steps to have Jesus eliminated (*John* 11: 47–54). In other words, the raising of Lazarus was the direct cause of the Cross. In the other three gospels the great moving cause of the crucifixion was the Cleansing of the Temple. It is difficult to understand why the other three gospel writers have nothing to say of it, if indeed it was the immediate cause of Jesus's crucifixion.

(iv) On the other hand, it might well be argued that the Triumphal Entry is inexplicable without this miracle to go before it. Why otherwise did Jesus receive that tremendous reception whn he arrived in Jerusalem? Yet the fact remains that, in the story as the other three gospels tell it, there is just no space into which this miracle can be fitted.

If, then, this is not a record of actual historical fact, how can we explain it?

(i) Renan suggested that the whole thing was a deliberate fraud arranged by Jesus and Martha and Mary and Lazarus.

That explanation has only to be stated to be dismissed as incredible; and, later, Renan himself departed from it.

(ii) It has been suggested that Lazarus was in a coma. It would be impossible to argue that from the story as it stands. The details of death are too vivid.

(iii) It has been suggested that the story is an allegory written round the saying of Jesus: " I am the Resurrection and the Life," a story composed to illustrate that saying and to give it a setting. That may be an oversimplified and overstated version of the truth.

(iv) It has been suggested that the story is to be connected with the Parable of Dives and Lazarus (*Luke* 16: 19–31). That story ends with the saying that even if someone was raised from the dead the Jews would still not believe. It is suggested that the story was produced to show that someone did rise from the dead and the Jews did not believe.

When we consider the difficulties of this story, we are in the end compelled to say that we do not know what happened, although undoubtedly something tremendous did happen. It is worth noting that to this day Bethany is known as Azariyeh, which is derived from the name Lazaruṣ. But we do know for certain the truth which it teaches.

Robert McAfee Brown, an American professor, tells of something which this story did. He was an American army chaplain on a troopship in which 1,500 marines were returning from Japan to America for discharge. Greatly to his surprise he was approached by a small group to do Bible study with them. He leapt at the opportunity. Near the end of the voyage, they were studying this chapter and afterwards a marine came to him. " Everything in that chapter," he said, " is pointing at me." He went on to say that he had been in hell for the last six months. He had gone straight into the marines from college. He had been sent out to Japan. He had been bored with life; and he had gone out and got into trouble—bad trouble. Nobody knew about it—except God. He felt guilty; he felt his life was ruined; he felt he could never face his family although they need never know; he felt he had killed himself and was a dead man.

" And," said this young marine, " after reading this chapter I have come alive again. I know that this resurrection Jesus was talking about is real here and now, for he has raised me from death to life." That lad's troubles were not finished; he had a hard road to go; but in his sin and his sense of guilt he had found Jesus as the resurrection and the life.

That is the end of the whole matter. It does not really matter whether or not Jesus literally raised a corpse to life in A.D. 30, but it matters intensely that Jesus is the Resurrection and the Life for every man who is dead in sin and dead to God today. There may be problems in this story; we may never know what exactly happened at Bethany so many years ago; but we do know for certain that Jesus is still the Resurrection and the Life. That is what this story tells us—and that is what really matters.

THE TRAGIC IRONY

John 11: 47–53

> The chief priests and Pharisees assembled the Sanhedrin: " What are we going to do? " they said, " because this man does many signs. If we leave him alone like this, all will believe in him, and the Romans will come and will take away our place and will destroy our nation." One of them, called Caiaphas, who was High Priest for that year, said to them: " You are witless creatures. You do not think it out that it is to our good that one man should die for the people, rather than that the whole nation should perish." It was not he who was responsible for what he said; but, since he was High Priest for that year, he was really prophesying that Jesus was going to die for the nation, and, not only for the nation, but that the scattered children of God should be gathered into one. So from that day they plotted to kill him.

THE Jewish authorities are very vividly sketched before us. The wonderful happening at Bethany had forced their hand; it was impossible to allow Jesus to continue unchecked, otherwise the people would follow him in ever larger numbers. So the Sanhedrin was called to deal with the situation.

In the Sanhedrin there were both Pharisees and Sadducees. The Pharisees were not a political party at all; their sole interest was in living according to every detail of the law; and they cared not who governed them so long as they were allowed to continue in meticulous obedience to the law. On the other hand, the Sadducees were intensely political. They were the wealthy and aristocratic party. They were also the collaborationist party. So long as they were allowed to retain their wealth, comfort and position of authority, they were well content to collaborate with Rome. All the priests were Sadducees. And it is clear that it was the priests who dominated this meeting of the Sanhedrin. That is to say, it was the Sadducees who did all the talking.

With a few masterly strokes John delineates their characteristics. First, they were notoriously discourteous. Josephus said of them (*The Wars of the Jews* 2: 8, 14) that: " The behaviour of the Sadducees to one another is rather rude, and their intercourse with their equals is rough, as with strangers." " You know nothing at all," said Caiaphas (verse 49). " You are witless, brainless creatures." Here we see the innate, domineering arrogance of the Sadducees in action; this was exactly in character. Their contemptuous arrogance is an implicit contrast to the accents of love of Jesus.

Second, the one thing at which the Sadducees always aimed was the retention of their political and social power and prestige. What they feared was that Jesus might gain a following and raise a disturbance against the government. Now, Rome was essentially tolerant, but, with such a vast empire to govern, it could never afford civil disorder, and always quelled it with a firm and merciless hand. If Jesus was the cause of civil disorder, Rome would descend in all her power, and, beyond a doubt the Sadducees would be dismissed from their positions of authority. It never even occurred to them to ask whether Jesus was right or wrong. Their only question was: " What effect will this have on our ease and comfort and authority? " They judged things, not in the light of principle but in the light of their own career. And it is still possible for a man to set his own career before the will of God.

Then comes the first tremendous example of dramatic irony. Sometimes in a play a character says something whose full significance he does not realize; that is dramatic irony. So the Sadducees insisted that Jesus must be eliminated or the Romans would come and take their authority away. In A.D. 70 that is exactly what happened. The Romans, weary of Jewish stubbornness, besieged Jerusalem, and left it a heap of ruins with a plough drawn across the Temple area. How different things might have been if the Jews had accepted Jesus! The very steps they took to save their nation destroyed it. This destruction happened in A.D. 70; John's gospel was written about A.D. 100; and all who read it would see the dramatic irony in the words of the Sadducees.

Then Caiaphas, the High Priest, made his two-edged statement. " If you had any sense," he said, " you would come to the conclusion that it is far better that one man should perish for the nation than that the whole nation should perish." It was the Jewish belief that when the High Priest asked God's counsel for the nation, God spoke through him. In the old story Moses chose Joshua to be his successor in the leadership of Israel. Joshua was to have a share in his honour and when he wished for God's counsel he was to go to Eleazar the High Priest: " And he shall stand before Eleazar the priest, who shall inquire for him ... at his word they shall go out, and at his word they shall come in " (*Numbers* 27: 18–21). The High Priest was to be the channel of God's word to the leader and to the nation. That is what Caiaphas was that day.

Here is another tremendous example of dramatic irony. Caiaphas meant that it was better that Jesus should die than that there should be trouble with the Romans. It was true that Jesus must die to save the nation. That was true—but not in the way that Caiaphas meant. It was true in a far greater and more wonderful way. God can speak through the most unlikely people; sometimes he sends his message through a man without the man being aware; he can use even the words of bad men.

Jesus was to die for the nation and also for all God's people throughout the world. The early Church made a very beautiful use of these words. Its first service order book was called the *Didache*, or *The Teaching of the Twelve Apostles*. It dates back to shortly after A.D. 100. When the bread was being broken, it was laid down that it should be said: " Even as this bread was scattered upon the mountains, and was brought into one, so let thy Church be brought together from the ends of the earth into the kingdom " (*Didache* 9: 4). The bread had been put together from the scattered elements of which it was composed; so some day the scattered elements of the Church must be united into one. That is something about which to think as we look on the broken bread of the Sacrament.

JESUS THE OUTLAW

John 11: 54–57

So Jesus walked no longer openly among the Jews, but he went away from them to a place near the wilderness, to a town called Ephraim, and he stayed there with his disciples.

Now the Passover Feast of the Jews was near; and many from the country areas went up to Jerusalem before the Passover Feast to purify themselves. So they were looking for Jesus; and, as they stood in the Temple precincts, they were talking with each other and saying: " What do you think? Surely it is impossible that he should come to the Feast? " Now the chief priests and Pharisees had given orders that if anyone knew where Jesus was, he should lodge information with them, that they might seize him.

JESUS did not unnecessarily court danger. He was willing to lay down his life, but not so foolishly reckless as to throw it away before his work was done. So he retired to a town called Ephraim, which was near Bethel in the mountainous country north of Jerusalem (cp. 2 *Chronicles* 13: 19).

By this time Jerusalem was beginning to fill up with people. Before the Jew could attend any feast he had to be ceremonially clean; and uncleanness could be contracted by touching a vast number of things and people. Many of the Jews, therefore, came up to the city early to make the necessary offerings and go through the necessary washings in order to ensure ceremonial cleanness. The law had it: " Every man is bound to purify himself before the Feast."

These purifications were carried out in the Temple. They took time, and in the time of waiting the Jews gathered in excited little groups. They knew what was going on. They knew about this mortal contest of wills between Jesus and the authorities; and people are always interested in the man who gallantly faces fearful odds. They wondered if he would appear at the feast; and concluded that he could not possible come. This Galilean carpenter could not take on the whole might of Jewish ecclesiastical and political officialdom.

But they had underrated Jesus. When the time arrived for him to come, nothing on earth would stop him coming. Martin Luther was a man who hurled defiance at cautious souls who sought to hold him back from being too venturesome. He took what seemed to him the right course " despite all cardinals, popes, kings and emperors, together with all devils and hell." When he was cited to appear at Worms to answer for his attack on the abuses of the Roman Catholic Church, he was well warned of the danger. His answer was: " I would go if there were as many devils in Worms as there are tiles on the housetops." When told that Duke George would capture him, he answered: " I would go if it rained Duke Georges." It was not that Luther was not afraid, for often he made his greatest statements when both voice and knees were shaking; but he had a courage which conquered fear. The Christian does not fear the consequences of doing the right thing; he fears rather the consequences of *not* doing it.

From the concluding verses of the chapter, it seems that by this time, Jesus had been classed as an outlaw. It may be that the authorities had offered a reward for information leading to his apprehension and that it was this that Judas sought and received. In spite of that Jesus came to Jerusalem, and not skulking in the back streets but openly and in such a way as to focus attention upon himself. Whatever else we may say of Jesus, we must bow in admiration before his death-defying courage. For these last days of his life he was the bravest outlaw of all time.

LOVE'S EXTRAVAGANCE

John 12: 1–8

> Now six days before the Passover Jesus went to Bethany, where Lazarus was whom he raised from the dead. So they made him a meal there, and Martha was serving while Lazarus was one of those who reclined at table with him. Now Mary took a pound of very precious genuine spikenard ointment, and anointed Jesus's feet, and wiped his feet with her hair; and the house was filled with the perfume of the ointment. But Judas Iscariot, one of his disciples, the one who was going to betray him, said: " Why was this ointment not sold for ten pounds, and the proceeds given to the poor? " He said this, not that he cared for the poor, but because he was a thief and had charge of the money-box, and pilfered from what was put into it. So Jesus said: " Let her observe it now against the day of my burial. The poor you have always with you, but me you have not always."

WE have seen on other occasions that many scholars believe that certain parts of John's gospel have become displaced. Some suspect a dislocation here. Moffatt, for instance, prints it in the order verses 19–29; verses 1–18 and verse 30; verses 31 to 42. We have retained the order of the Authorized Version (and the Revised Standard Version) for our studies, but if the reader will read the chapter in the rearranged order he will see the connection of events and thought more clearly.

It was coming very near the end for Jesus. To come to Jerusalem for the Passover was an act of the highest courage, for the authorities had made him in effect an outlaw (*John* 11): 57). So great were the crowds who came to the Passover that they could not all possibly obtain lodging within the city itself, and Bethany was one of the places outside the city boundaries which the law laid down as a place for the overflow of the pilgrims to stay.

When Jesus came to Bethany they made him a meal. It must have been in the house of Martha and Mary and Lazarus, for where else would Martha be serving but in her own house? It was then that Mary's heart ran over in love. She had a pound of very precious spikenard ointment. Both John and Mark describe it by the adjective *pistikos* (*Mark* 14: 3). Oddly enough, no one really knows what that word means. There are four possibilities. It may come from the adjective *pistos* which means *faithful* or *reliable*, and so may mean *genuine*. It may come from the verb *pinein* which means *to drink*, and so may mean *liquid*. It may be a kind of trade name, and may have to be translated simply *pistic nard*. It may come from a word meaning the *pistachio nut*, and be a special kind of essence extracted from it. In any event it was a specially valuable kind of perfume. With this perfume Mary anointed Jesus's feet. Judas ungraciously questioned her action as sheer waste. Jesus silenced him by saying that money could be given to the poor at any time, but a kindness done to him must be done now, for soon the chance would be gone for ever.

There is a whole series of little character sketches here.

(i) There is the character of Martha. She was serving at table. She loved Jesus; she was a practical woman; and the only way in which she could show her love was by the work of her hands. Martha always gave what she could. Many and many a great man has been what he was only because of someone's loving care for his creature comforts in his home. It is just as possible to serve Jesus in the kitchen as on the public platform or in a career lived in the eyes of men.

(ii) There is the character of Mary. Mary was the one who above all loved Jesus; and here in her action we see three things about love.

(*a*) We see love's extravagance. Mary took the most precious thing she possessed and spent it all on Jesus. Love is not love if it nicely calculates the cost. It gives its all and its only regret is that it has not still more to give. O. Henry, the master of the short story, has a moving story called *The Gift of the Magi*. A young American couple, Della and Jim, were very poor but very much in love. Each had one unique possession. Della's hair was her glory. When she let it down it almost served as a robe. Jim had a gold watch which had come to him from his father and was his pride. It was the day before Christmas, and Della had exactly one dollar eighty-seven cents to buy Jim a present. She went out and sold her hair for twenty dollars; and with the proceeds bought a platinum fob for Jim's precious watch. When Jim came home at night and saw Della's shorn head, he stopped as if stupefied. It was not that he did not like it or love her any less; for she was lovelier than ever. Slowly he handed her his gift; it was a set of expensive tortoise-shell combs with jewelled edges for her lovely hair—and he had sold his gold watch to buy them. Each had given the other all there was to give. Real love cannot think of any other way to give.

(*b*) We see love's humility. It was a sign of honour to anoint a person's head. " Thou anointest my head with oil," says the psalmist (*Psalm* 23: 5). But Mary would not look so high as the head of Jesus; she anointed his feet. The last thing Mary thought of was to confer an honour upon Jesus; she never dreamed she was good enough for that.

(*c*) We see love's unselfconsciousness. Mary wiped Jesus's feet with the hair of her head. In Palestine no respectable woman would ever appear in public with her hair unbound. On the day a girl was married her hair was bound up, and never again would she be seen in public with her long tresses flowing loose. That was the sign of an immoral woman. But Mary never even thought of that. When two people really love each other they live in a world of their own. They will wander slowly down a crowded street hand in hand heedless of what other people think. Many are self-conscious about showing their Christianity, concerned always about what others are thinking about them. Mary loved Jesus so much that it was nothing to her what others thought.

But there is something else about love here. John has the sentence: " The house was filled with the fragrance of the ointment." We have seen that so many of John's statements have two meanings, one which lies on the surface and one

which is underneath. Many fathers of the Church and many
scholars have seen a double meaning here. They have taken it to
mean that the whole Church was filled with the sweet memory
of Mary's action. A lovely deed becomes the possession of the
whole world and adds to the beauty of life in general, something
which time cannot ever take away.

LOVE'S EXTRAVAGANCE

John 12: 1–8 (*continued*)

(iii) THERE is the character of Judas. There are three things here
about him.

(*a*) We see Jesus's trust in Judas. As far back as *John* 6: 70,
71, John shows us Jesus well aware that there was a traitor
within the ranks. It may well be that he tried to touch Judas's
heart by making him the treasurer of the apostolic company. It
may well be that he tried to appeal to his sense of honour. It
may well be that he was saying in effect to him: " Judas, here's
something that you can do for me. Here is proof that I need you
and want you." That appeal failed with Judas, but the fact
remains that often the best way to reclaim someone who is on
the wrong path is to treat him not with suspicion but with trust;
not as if we expected the worst, but as if we expected the best.

(*b*) We see one of the laws of temptation. Jesus would not
have put Judas in charge of the money-box unless he had some
capabilities in that direction. Westcott in his commentary said:
" Temptation commonly comes through that for which we are
naturally fitted." If a man is fitted to handle money, his temptation may be to regard money as the most important thing in
the world. If a man is fitted to occupy a place of prominence,
his temptation may be to think first and foremost of reputation. If
a man has a particular gift, his temptation may be to become
conceited about that gift. Judas had a gift for handling money
and became so fond of it that he became first a thief and then a
traitor for its sake. The Authorized Version says that he

bare the bag. The verb is *bastazein*; *bastazein* does not mean to *bear*, or *carry*, or *lift*. But in colloquial English to *lift* a thing can also mean to *steal* it. We talk, for instance, of a *shop-lifter*. And Judas did not only carry the bag; he pilfered from it. Temptation struck him at the point of his special gift.

(*c*) We see how a man's view can be warped. Judas had just seen an action of surpassing loveliness; and he called it extravagant waste. He was an embittered man and he took an embittered view of things. A man's sight depends on what is inside him. He sees only what he is fit and able to see. If we like a person, he can do little wrong. If we dislike him, we may misinterpret his finest action. A warped mind brings a warped view of things; and, if we find ourselves becoming very critical of others and imputing unworthy motives to them, we should, for a moment, stop examining them and start examining ourselves.

Lastly, there is here one great truth about life. Some things we can do almost any time, but some things we will never do, unless we grasp the chance when it comes. We are seized with the desire to do something fine and generous and big-hearted. But we put it off—we will do it tomorrow; and the fine impulse goes, and the thing is never done. Life is an uncertain thing. We think to utter some word of thanks or praise or love but we put it off; and often the word is never spoken.

Here is one tragic instance of how a man realized too late the things he had never said and done. Thomas Carlyle loved Jane Welsh Carlyle, but he was a cross-grained, irritable creature and he never made life happy for her. Unexpectedly she died. J. A. Froude tells us of Carlyle's feelings when he lost her. " He was looking through her papers, her notebooks and journals; and old scenes came mercilessly back to him in the vistas of mournful memory. In his long sleepless nights, he recognized too late what she had felt and suffered under his childish irritabilities. His faults rose up in remorseless judgment, and as he had thought too little of them before, so now he exaggerated them to himself in his helpless repentance ... ' Oh!' he cried again and again, ' if I could see her but once more, were it but for five minutes, to let her know that I always loved her through all that. She never did know it, never.' " There is a time for doing and for saying things; and, when it is past, they may never be said and never be done.

It was Judas's ill-natured complaint that the money which that ointment could have raised should have been given to the poor. But as scripture said: " The poor will never cease out of the land; therefore I command thee saying, You shall open wide your hand to your brother, to the needy and to the poor, in the land " (*Deuteronomy* 15: 11). To help the poor was something that could be done any time. To show the heart's devotion to Jesus had to be done before the Cross on Calvary took him to its cruel arms. Let us remember to do things now, for the chance so often never comes again, and the failure to do them, especially the failure to express love brings bitter remorse.

A PLAN TO DESTROY THE EVIDENCE

John 12: 9–11

> The mob of the Jews knew that Jesus was there; and they came, not only because of Jesus, but to see Lazarus, whom he had raised from the dead. The chief priests plotted to kill Lazarus too, because many of the Jews were withdrawing from them because of him and were coming to believe in Jesus.

FOR the leaders of the Jews things were getting into an impossible position. This was specially the case for the Sadducees, to which party belonged all the priests, for them the position was doubly threatening.

First, it was threatening from the political point of view. The Sadducees were the wealthy aristocratic class and they worked in close collaboration with the Roman government. Their aim was to ensure their own wealth and ease and comfort. So long as they were allowed to retain the ruling places in the government they were quite prepared to collaborate. The Romans allowed their subject kingdoms a large amount of freedom.

Broadly speaking, under a Roman governor, they allowed them to govern themselves, but at the slightest outbreak of civil disorder Rome's hand came down heavily, and those who were responsible for good government and had failed to produce it were summarily dismissed. The Sadducees saw Jesus as the possible leader of a rebellion. He was stealing away the hearts of the people. The atmosphere was electric; and the Sadducees were determined to get rid of him in case there should be an uprising of the people and their own ease and comfort and authority be threatened.

Second, they regarded it as theologically intolerable. Unlike the Pharisees, the Sadducees did not believe in the resurrection of the dead; and, here they were confronted with Lazarus who had been raised from the grave. Unless they could do something about it, the foundations of their power, their influence and their teaching, were slipping from beneath their feet.

So they proposed to destroy the evidence by doing away with Lazarus. H. G. Wood tells of a remark of two old ladies in the days when Charles Darwin had made public the conception of evolution and when it was thought that that meant that man was sprung from and akin to the beasts. They were heard to say: " Let's hope it's not true, and, if it is, let's hush it up! " When a man has to support a position by destroying the evidence which threatens it, it means that he is using dishonest methods to support a lie—and knows it.

The Sadducees were prepared to suppress the truth to further their own self-interest. For many people self-interest is the most powerful motive in life. Many discoveries which might produce cheaper goods never see the light of day because the patents are bought up and rendered inoperative by those whose products they threaten. Self-interest dictates policy and action.

In order to maintain their own place and their own influence the priests and the Sadducees were prepared to destroy the evidence for the truth. A man has come to a sorry pass when he is afraid of the truth and sets his personal prestige and profit before it.

A KING'S WELCOME

John 12: 12–19

On the next day the great crowd that was coming to the Feast heard that Jesus was on his way to Jerusalem. They took the branches of palm trees and went out to meet him. They kept up a shout: " Hosanna! Blessed is he who comes in the name of the Lord, he who is the King of Israel! " Jesus found a young ass and sat on it, as it stands written: " Fear not, daughter of Zion. Look! Your King is coming sitting upon an ass's colt." At first the disciples did not realize the significance of these things; but when Jesus was glorified then they remembered that these things were written about him, and that they had done these things to him. The crowd who were with him testified that he had called Lazarus from the tomb, and had raised him from among the dead. It was because they had heard that he had performed this sign that the crowd went out to meet him. So the Pharisees said to each other: " You can see that all the steps you have taken have been completely ineffective. See! The whole world has gone off after him! "

PASSOVER, Pentecost and Tabernacles were the three compulsory festivals of the Jews. To the Passover in Jerusalem Jews came from the ends of the earth. Wherever a Jew might live it was his ambition to observe one such Passover. To this day, when Jews in foreign lands observe the Passover, they say: " This year here; next year in Jerusalem."

At such a time Jerusalem and the villages round about were crowded. On one occasion a census was taken of the lambs slain at the Passover Feast. The number was given as 256,000. There had to be a minimum of ten people per lamb; and if that estimate is correct it means that there must have been as many as 2,700,000 people at that Passover Feast. Even if that figure is exaggerated, it remains true that the numbers must have been immense.

News and rumour had gone out that Jesus the man who had raised Lazarus from the dead was on his way to Jerusalem.

There were two crowds, the crowd which was accompanying
Jesus from Bethany, and the crowd which surged out from
Jerusalem to see him; and they must have flowed together in a
surging mass like two tides of the sea. Jesus came riding on a
ass's colt. As the crowds met him they received him like a
conqueror. And the sight of this tumultuous welcome sent the
Jewish authorities into the depths of despair, for it seemed that
nothing they could do could stop the tide of the people who had
gone after Jesus. This is an incident so important that we must
try to understand just what was happening.

(i) Certain among the crowds were simply sightseeing. Here
was a man who, as rumour had it, had raised a man from the
dead; and many had simply gone out to gaze on a sensational
figure. It is always possible to attract people *for a time by*
sensationalism and shrewd publicity; but it never lasts. Those
who were that day regarding Jesus as a sensation were within a
week shouting for his death.

(ii) Many among these crowds were greeting Jesus as a
conqueror. That, in fact, is the predominant atmosphere of the
whole scene. They greeted him with the words: " Hosanna!
Blessed is he who is coming in the name of the Lord! " The
word *Hosanna* is the Hebrew for " Save now! " And the shout of
the people was almost precisely: " God save the King! "

The words with which the people greeted Jesus are illuminating. They are a quotation from *Psalm* 118: 25, 26. That
psalm had many connections, which were bound to be in the
minds of the people. It was the last psalm of the group
(113–118) known as the *Hallel*. The word *Hallel* means *Praise
God!* and these are all praising psalms. They were part of the
first memory work every Jewish boy had to do; they were sung
often at great acts of praise and thanksgiving in the Temple;
they were an integral part of the Passover ritual. Further, this
particular psalm was intimately connected with the ritual of the
Feast of Tabernacles. At that feast worshippers carried bundles
made up of palm, myrtle and willow branches called *lulabs*.
Daily they went with them to the Temple. On every day of the
feast they marched round the great altar of the burnt offer-

ing—once on each of the first six days, seven times on the seventh—and as they marched they triumphantly sang verses from this psalm and especially these very ones. In fact it may well be that this psalm was written for the first celebration of the Feast of Tabernacles when Nehemiah had rebuilt the shattered walls and city and the Jews came home from Babylon and could worship again (*Nehemiah* 8: 14–18). This was indeed the psalm of the great occasion—and the people knew it.

Further, this was characteristically the conqueror's psalm. To take but one instance, these very verses were sung and shouted by the Jerusalem crowd when they welcomed back Simon Maccabaeus after he had conquered Acra and wrested it from Syrian dominion more than a hundred years before. There is no doubt that when the people sang this psalm they were looking on Jesus as God's Anointed One, the Messiah, the Deliverer, the One who was to come. And there is no doubt that they were looking on him as the Conqueror. To them it must have been only a matter of time until the trumpets rang out and the call to arms sounded and the Jewish nation swept to its long delayed victory over Rome and the world. Jesus approached Jerusalem with the shout of the mob hailing a conqueror in his ears—and it must have hurt him, for they were looking in him for that very thing which he refused to be.

A KING'S WELCOME

John 12: 12–19 (*continued*)

(iii) IN such a situation it was obviously impossible for Jesus to speak to the crowd. His voice could not have reached that vast assembly of people. So he did something that all could see; he came riding upon an ass's colt. Now that was two things. First, it was a deliberate claim to be the Messiah. It was a dramatic enactment of the words of Zechariah the prophet (*Zechariah* 9: 9). John does not quote accurately because obviously he is quoting from memory. Zechariah had said: " Rejoice greatly, O daughter of Zion; shout aloud, O daughter of Jerusalem, Lo your king comes to you; triumphant and victorious is he, humble and riding on an ass, on a colt the foal of an ass." There is no doubt at all that Jesus's claim was a messianic claim.

But, second, it was a claim to be a particular kind of Messiah. We must not misunderstand this picture. With us the ass is lowly and despised; but in the East it was a noble animal. Jair, the Judge, had thirty sons who rode on asses' colts (*Judges* 10: 4). Ahithopel rode upon an ass (2 *Samuel* 17: 23). Mephibosheth, the royal prince, the son of Saul, came to David riding upon an ass (2 *Samuel* 19: 26). The point is that a king came riding upon a horse when he was bent on *war*; he came riding upon an ass when he was coming in *peace*. This action of Jesus is a sign that he was not the warrior figure men dreamed of, but the Prince of Peace. No one saw it that way at that time, not even the disciples, who should have known so much better. The minds of all were filled with a kind of mob hysteria. Here was the one who was to come. But they looked for the Messiah of their own dreams and their own wishful thinking; they did not look for the Messiah whom God had sent. Jesus drew a dramatic picture of what he claimed to be, but none understood the claim.

(iv) In the background there were the Jewish authorities. They felt frustrated and helpless; nothing they could do seemed able to stop the attraction of this Jesus. " The whole world," they said, " is gone of after him! " In this saying of the authorities there is a magnificent example of that irony in which John is so skilled. No writer in the New Testament can say so much with such amazing reticence. It was because God so loved *the world* that Jesus came into the world; and here, all unwittingly, his enemies are saying that the world has gone after him. In the very next section John is going to tell of the coming of the Greeks to Jesus. The first representatives of that wider world, the first seekers from outside, are about to come. The Jewish authorities were speaking truer than they knew.

We cannot leave this passage without noticing the simplest thing of all. Seldom in the world's history has there been such a display of magnificently deliberate courage as the Triumphal Entry. We must remember that Jesus was an outlaw and that the authorities were determined to kill him. All prudence would have warned him to turn back and make for Galilee or the desert places. If he was to enter Jerusalem at all, all caution would have demanded that he enter secretly and go into hiding; but he came in such a way as to focus every eye upon himself. It was an act of the most superlative courage, for it was the defiance of all that man could do; and it was an act of the most superlative love, for it was love's last appeal before the end.

THE SEEKING GREEKS

John 12: 20–22

> There were some Greeks among those whose practice it was to come up to the feast. Now these came to Philip, who came from Bethsaida in Galilee, and made a request to him. " Sir," they said, " we wish to see Jesus." Philip went and told Andrew, and Andrew and Philip went and told Jesus.

NONE of the other gospels tells of this incident, but it is very fitting to find it in the Fourth. The Fourth Gospel was the one written to present the truth of Christianity in a way that the Greeks could appreciate and understand; and it is natural that in it the first Greeks to come to Jesus should find a place.

It need not seem strange to find Greeks in Jerusalem at the Passover time. They need not even have been proselytes. The Greek was an inveterate wanderer, driven by wanderlust and by the desire to find out new things. " You Athenians," said one of the ancients, " will never rest yourselves, nor will you ever let anyone else rest." " You Greeks," said another, " are like children, always young in your souls." More than five hundred years before this Herodotus had travelled the world, as he said himself, to find things out. Far up the Nile to this day there stands a great Egyptian statue on which a Greek tourist, even as modern tourists do, had scratched his name. The Greek voyaged for trade and for commerce of course; but he was the first man to wander for the sake of wandering in the ancient world. There is no need to be surprised to find a detachment of sightseeing Greeks even in Jerusalem.

But the Greek was more than that. He was characteristically a seeker after truth. It was no unusual thing to find a Greek who had passed through philosophy after philosophy, and religion after religion, and gone from teacher to teacher in the search for truth. The Greek was the man with the seeking mind.

How had these Greeks come to hear of Jesus and to be interested in him? J. H. Bernard throws out a most interesting suggestion. It was in the last week of his ministry that Jesus cleansed the Temple and swept the money-changers and the sellers of doves from the Temple court. Now these traders had their stance in the Court of the Gentiles, that great court which was the first of the Temple courts and where Gentiles were allowed to come but no further. If these Greeks were in Jerusalem at all they would be certain to visit the Temple and to stand in the Court of the Gentiles. Perhaps they had actually witnessed that tremendous scene when Jesus had driven the traders from the Temple court; and perhaps they wished to know more of a man who could do things like that.

However that may be, this is one of the great moments of the story, for here is the first faint hint of a gospel which is to go out to all the world.

The Greeks came with their request to Philip. Why Philip? No one can say for certain, but Philip is a Greek name and perhaps they thought that a man with a Greek name would treat them sympathetically. But Philip did not know what to do, and he went to Andrew. Andrew was in no doubt and he led them to Jesus.

Andrew had discovered that no one could ever be a nuisance to Jesus. He knew that Jesus would never turn any seeking soul away.

THE AMAZING PARADOX

John 12: 23–26

> Jesus answered them: " The hour has come that the Son of Man should be glorified. This is the truth I tell you—unless a grain of wheat falls into the ground and dies, it remains all by itself alone; but, if it dies, it bears much fruit. He who loves his life is losing it; and he who hates his life in this world will keep it to life eternal. If anyone will serve me, let him follow me; and where I am, there will my servants also be."

HARDLY any passage in the New Testament would come with such a shock to those who heard it for the first time as this. It begins with a saying which everyone would expect; and it finishes with a series of sayings which were the last things anyone would expect.

" The hour has come," began Jesus. " when the Son of Man should be glorified." It was clear that things had been building up to a crisis and that crisis had now come. But Jesus's idea of what that crisis involved was quite different from anyone else's. When he talked about the *Son of Man*, he did not mean what other people meant. To understand the shocking nature of this short paragraph we must grasp something of what the Jews understood by Son of Man. That term took its origin in *Daniel* 7: 13. In that passage the Authorized Version mistranslates. It has it that one like unto *the Son of Man* came to the Ancient of Days, and received a kingdom, a glory and a dominion that were to be universal and for ever. The correct translation is not *the Son of Man*, but *a son of man* as the Revised Standard Version has it.

The point of the passage is this. In *Daniel* 7: 1–8 the writer has been describing the world powers which have held sway, the Assyrians, the Babylonians, the Medes and the Persians. They were so cruel, so savage, so sadistic that they could be described only under the imagery of wild beasts—the lion with the eagle's wings, the bear with the three ribs between its teeth, the leopard with the four wings and the four heads, and the terrible beast with iron teeth and ten horns. These were the symbols of the powers which had hitherto held sway. But it was the dream of the seer that into the world there was going to come a new power, and that power was to be gentle and humane and gracious, so that it could be depicted under the symbol, not of a savage beast, but of a man. This passage means that the day of savagery would pass and the day of humanity was coming.

That was the dream of the Jews, the golden age, when life would be sweet and they would be masters of the world. But how was that age to come? It became clearer and clearer to them that their nation was so small and their power so weak, that the golden age could never come by human means and human power; it must come by the direct intervention of God. He would send his champion to bring it in. So they thought back to the picture in the book of *Daniel,* and what more natural than that they should call the champion the *Son of Man*? The phrase which had once been merely a symbol came to describe a person. Between the Old and the New Testament there arose a whole series of books about the golden age and how it was to come. Amidst their troubles and their sufferings, in their subjections and their slaveries, the Jews never forgot and never gave up their dream. One of these books was specially influential—the *Book of Enoch* and it repeatedly speaks about *that Son of Man.* In *Enoch* The Son of Man is a tremendous figure who, as it were, is being held in leash by God. But the day will come when God will release him and he will come with a divine power against which no man and no kingdom will be able to stand, and smash the way to world empire for the Jews.

To the Jews the Son of Man stood for the undefeatable world conqueror sent by God. So Jesus says: " The hour has come when the Son of Man must be glorified." When he said that, the listeners would catch their breath. They would believe that the trumpet call of eternity had sounded, that the might of heaven was on the march, and that the campaign of victory was on the move. But Jesus did not mean by *glorified* what they understood. They meant that the subjected kingdoms of the earth would grovel before the conqueror's feet; by *glorified* he meant *crucified*. When the Son of Man was mentioned they thought of the conquest of the armies of God; he meant the conquest of the Cross.

The first sentence which Jesus spoke would excite the hearts of those who heard it; then began a succession of sayings which must have left them staggered and bewildered by their sheer incredibility, for they spoke, not in terms of conquest, but in terms of sacrifice and death. We will never understand Jesus nor the attitude of the Jews to him, until we understand how he turned their ideas upside down, replacing a dream of conquest with a vision of a Cross. No wonder they did not understand him; the tragedy is that they refused to try.

THE AMAZING PARADOX

John 12: 23–26 (*continued*)

WHAT was this amazing paradox which Jesus was teaching? He was saying three things, which are all variations of one central truth and all at the heart of the Christian faith and life.

(i) He was saying that only by death comes life. The grain of wheat was ineffective and unfruitful so long as it was preserved, as it were, in safety and security. It was when it was thrown into the cold ground, and buried there as if in a tomb, that it bore fruit. It was by the death of the martyrs that the Church grew. In the famous phrase: " The blood of the martyrs was the seed of the Church."

It is always because men have been prepared to die that the great things have lived. But it becomes more personal than that. It is sometimes only when a man buries his personal aims and ambitions that he begins to be of real use to God. Cosmo Lang became Archbishop of Canterbury. At one time he had had great worldly ambitions. A godly friend's influence led him to abandon these and enter the Church of England. When he was studying for the ministry at Cuddesdon, one day as he was praying in the chapel he heard unmistakably a voice saying to him: " You are wanted! " It was when he had buried his personal ambitions that he became useful to God.

By death comes life. By the loyalty which was true to death there have been preserved and born the most precious things which humanity possesses. By the death of personal desire and personal ambition a man becomes a servant of God.

(i) He was saying that only by spending life do we retain it. The man who loves his life is moved by two aims, by selfishness and by the desire for security. Not once or twice but many times Jesus insisted that the man who hoarded his life must in the end lose it, and the man sho spent his life must in the end gain it. There was a famous evangelist called Christmas Evans who was always on the move preaching for Christ. His friends besought him to take things easier but his answer always was: " It is better to burn out than to rust out." When Joan of Arc knew that her enemies were strong and her time was short, she prayed to God: " I shall only last a year, use me as you can." Again and again Jesus laid down this law (*Mark* 8: 35; *Matthew* 16: 25; *Luke* 9: 24; *Matthew* 10: 39; *Luke* 17: 33).

We have only to think of what this world would have lost if there had not been men prepared to forget their personal safety, security, selfish gain and selfish advancement. The world owes everything to people who recklessly spent their strength and gave themselves to God and to others. No doubt we will exist longer if we take things easily, if we avoid all strain, if we sit at the fire and husband life, if we look after ourselves as a hypochondriac looks after his health. No doubt we will *exist* longer—but we will never *live*.

(iii) He was saying that only by service comes greatness. The people whom the world remembers with love are the people who serve others. A certain Mrs Berwick had been very active in Salvation Army work in Liverpool. She retired to London. There came the war and the air raids. People get queer ideas and the idea got about that somehow Mrs Berwick's poor house and her shelter were specially safe. She was old now; her

Liverpool days of social service were long behind her; but she felt she must do something about it. So she got together a simple first-aid box and she put a notice on her window: " If you need help, knock here." That is the Christian attitude to our fellow men.

Once a schoolboy was asked what parts of speech *my* and *mine* are. He answered—more truly than he knew—that they were *aggressive* pronouns. It is all too true that in the modern world the idea of service is in danger of getting lost. So many people are in business only for what they can get out of it. They may well become rich, but one thing is certain—they will never be loved, and love is the true wealth of life.

Jesus came to the Jews with a new view of life. They looked on glory as conquest, the acquisition of power, the right to rule. He looked on it as a cross. He taught men that only by death comes life; that only by spending life do we retain it; that only by service comes greatness. And the extraordinary thing is that when we come to think of it, Christ's paradox is nothing other than the truth of common sense.

FROM TENSION TO CERTAINTY

John 12: 27–34

" Now, my soul is troubled. And what shall I say? ' Father, rescue me from this hour.' But it was for this reason that I came to this hour. Father, glorify your name." A voice came from heaven: " I have both glorified it and I will glorify it again." So the crowd who were standing by, and who heard it, said that there had been thunder. Others said: " An angel spoke to him." Jesus answered: " It was not for my sake that this voice came, but for yours. Now is the judgment of this world. Now will the ruler of this world be cast out. And I, if I be lifted up from the earth, will draw all men to myself." He said this in indication of what death he was going to die by. The crowd answered him: " We have heard from the law that God's Anointed One remains for ever. And do you say: ' The Son of Man must be lifted up '? Who is this Son of Man? "

IN this passage John shows us both Jesus's tension and his triumph, and shows us what turned the tension into the triumph.

(i) John does not tell us of the agony in Gethsemane. It is here that he shows us Jesus fighting his battle with his human longing to avoid the Cross. No one wishes to die at thirty-three; and no one wishes to die upon a cross. There would have been no virtue in Jesus's obedience to God, if it had come easily and without cost. Real courage does not mean not being afraid. It means to be terribly afraid, and yet to do the thing that ought to be done. That was the courage of Jesus. As Bengel put it: " Here there met the horror of death and the ardour of obedience." God's will meant the Cross and Jesus had to nerve himself to accept it.

(ii) But the end of the story is not tension; it is triumph and certainty. Jesus was certain that if he went on, something would happen which would break the power of evil once and for all. If he was obedient to the Cross, he was sure that a death-blow would be struck to the ruler of this world, Satan. It was to be one last struggle which would break for ever the power of evil. Further, he was certain that if he went to the Cross, the sight of his upraised and crucified figure would in the end draw all men to him. Jesus, too, wanted conquest; he, too, wanted to subdue men; but he knew that the only way to conquer and to subdue the hearts of men for ever was to show himself to them on the Cross. He began with the tension; he ended with the triumph.

(iii) What came between the tension and the triumph and changed the one into the other? It was the voice of God. Behind this coming of the voice of God lies something great and deep.

There was a time when the Jews really and fully believed that God spoke direct to men. It was directly that God spoke to the child Samuel (*1 Samuel* 3: 1–14). It was directly that God spoke to Elijah, when he had fled from the avenging Jezebel (*1 Kings* 19: 1–18). It was directly that Eliphaz the Temanite had claimed to hear the voice of God (*Job* 4: 16). But by the time of Jesus they had ceased to believe that God spoke directly. The great days were past; God was far too far away now; the voice that had spoken to the prophets was silent. Nowadays they believed in what they called the *Bath qol*, a Hebrew phrase which means *the daughter voice* or *the daughter of a voice*. When the *Bath qol* spoke it quoted scripture most often. It was not really the direct voice of God; it was what we might call the echo of his voice, a distant, faint whisper instead of a direct, vital communication.

But it was not the echo of his voice that Jesus heard; it was the very voice of God Himself. Here is a great truth. With Jesus there comes to men not some distant whisper of the voice of God, not some faint echo from the heavenly places, but the unmistakeable accents of God's direct voice.

It is to be noted that the voice of God came to Jesus at all the great moments of his life. It came at his baptism when he first set out upon the work God had given him to do (*Mark* 1: 11). It came on the Mount of Transfiguration when he finally decided to take the way which led to Jerusalem and the Cross (*Mark* 9: 7). And now it came to him when his human flesh and blood had to be strengthened by divine aid for the ordeal of the Cross.

What God did for Jesus, he does for every man. When he sends us out upon a road, he does not send us without directions and without guidance. When he gives us a task, he does not leave us to do it in the lonely weakness of our own strength. God is not silent, and ever and again, when the strain of life is too much for us, and the effort of his way is beyond our human resources, if we listen we will hear him speak, and we will go on with his strength surging through our frame. Our trouble is not that God does not speak, but that we do not listen.

FROM TENSION TO CERTAINTY

John 12: 27–34 (*continued*)

JESUS claimed that, when he was lifted up, he would draw all men to him. Some take this to refer to the Ascension and think it means that when Jesus was exalted in his risen power, he would draw all men to him. But that is far from the truth. Jesus was referring to his Cross—and the people knew it. And once again—inevitably—they were moved to incredulous astonishment. How could anyone possibly connect the Son of Man and a cross? Was not the Son of Man the invincible leader at the head of the irresistible armies of heaven? Was not his kingdom to last for ever? " His dominion is an everlasting dominion, which shall not pass away, and his kingdom one that shall not be destroyed " (*Daniel* 7: 14). Was it not said of the prince of the golden age: " David my servant shall be their prince for ever "? (*Ezekiel* 37: 25). Had Isaiah not said of the ruler of the new world: " Of the increase of his government and of peace there shall be no end "? (*Isaiah* 9: 7). Did the Psalmists not sing of this endless kingdom? " I will establish your descendants for ever, and build your thrones for all generations " (*Psalm* 89: 4). The Jews connected the Son of Man with an everlasting kingdom, and here was he, who claimed to be the Son of Man, talking about being lifted up upon a cross. Who was this Son of Man, whose kingdom was to end before it had begun?

The lesson of history is that Jesus was right. It was on the magnet of the Cross that he pinned his hopes; and he was right because love will live long after might is dead.

As Kipling had it:

> " Far-called our navies melt away;
>   On dune and headland sinks the fire;
>   Lo, all our pomp of yesterday
>   Is one with Nineveh and Tyre! "

Nineveh and Tyre are only names now, but Christ lives on.

One of the great sonnets of the English language is *Ozymandias* by Shelley:

> " I met a traveller from an antique land
>   Who said: ' Two vast and trunkless legs of stone
>   Stand in the desert. Near them, on the sand
>   Half sunk, a shatter'd visage lies, whose frown
>   And wrinkled lip and sneer of cold command

Tell that sculptor well those passions read
Which yet survive, stamp'd on these lifeless things,
The hand that mock'd them and the heart that fed:
And on the pedestal these words appear:
' My name is Ozymandias, king of kings:
Look on my works, ye Mighty, and despair! '
Nothing beside remains. Round the decay
Of that colossal wreck, boundless and bare,
The lone and level sands stretch far away."

Ozymandias was king of kings, yet all that he has left is a shattered statue in the desert, and a name that a chance sonnet keeps alive.

H. E. Fosdick quotes a poem in one of his books:

" I saw the conquerors riding by
    With cruel lips and faces wan:
Musing on kingdoms sacked and burned
    There rode the Mongol Genghis Khan;

And Alexander, like a god,
    Who sought to weld the world in one:
And Caesar with his laurel wreath;
    And like a thing from Hell the Hun;

And, leading like a star, the van,
    Heedless of upstretched arm and groan,
Inscrutable Napoleon went,
    Dreaming of Empire, and alone. . . .

Then all they perished from the earth,
    As fleeting shadows from a glass,
And, conquering down the centuries,
    Came Christ the swordless on an ass."

The empires founded on force have vanished, leaving only a memory which with the years becomes ever fainter. But the empire of Christ, founded upon a Cross, each year extends its sway.

In Shaw's play, when Joan of Arc knows that she has been betrayed to the stake by the leaders of her own people, she turns to them and says: " I will go out now to the common people,

and let the love in their eyes comfort me for the hate in yours.
You will all be glad to see me burnt; but if I go through the fire
I shall go through it to their hearts for ever and ever." That is
a parable of what happened to Jesus. His death upon the Cross
made him go through men's hearts for ever and for ever. The
conquering Messiah of the Jews is a figure about whom
scholars write their books; but the Prince of Love on the Cross
is a king who has his throne for ever in the hearts of men. The
only secure foundation for a kingdom is sacrificial love.

SONS OF THE LIGHT

John 12: 35, 36

> Jesus said to them: " For a little while yet the light is among you.
> Walk while you have the light that the darkness may not overtake
> you. He who walks in the darkness does not know where he is
> going. While you have the light, believe in the light, that you may
> become the sons of the light."

THERE is in this passage the implicit promise and the implicit
threat which are never very far from the heart of the Christian
faith.

(i) There is the promise of light. The man who walks with
Jesus is delivered from the shadows. There are certain shadows
which cast their shade sooner or later on every light. There is
the shadow of fear. Sometimes we are afraid to look forward.
Sometimes, especially when we see what they can do to others,
we are afraid of the chances and the changes of life. There are
the shadows of doubts and uncertainties. Sometimes the way
ahead is far from being clear and we feel like people groping
among the shadows with nothing firm to cling to. There are the
shadows of sorrow. Sooner or later the sun sets at midday and
the lights go out. But the man who walks with Jesus is delivered
from fear; he is liberated from doubt; he has a joy that no man
takes from him.

(ii) There is the implicit threat. The decision to trust life and all things to Jesus, the decision to take him as Master and Guide and Saviour, must be made in time. In life all things must be done in time, or they will not be done at all. There is work which we can do only when we have the physical strength to do it. There is study which can be carried out only when our minds are keen enough and our memories retentive enough to cope with it. There are things which have to be said and done or the time for saying and doing them is gone for ever. It is so with Jesus. At the actual moment Jesus said this, he was appealing to the Jews to believe in him before the Cross came and he was taken from them. But this is an eternal truth. It is a statistical fact that there is a steep rise in the number of conversions up to the age of seventeen and an equally steep fall afterwards. The more a man lets himself become fixed in his ways the harder it is to jerk himself out of them. In Christ the supreme blessedness is offered to men; in one sense it is never too late to grasp it; but nonetheless it remains true that it must be grasped in time.

BLIND UNBELIEF

John 12: 37–41

> When Jesus had said these things, he went away and hid himself from them. Although he had done such great signs in their presence they did not believe in him. It happened thus that the word which Isaiah the prophet spoke should be fulfilled: " Lord, who has believed what he heard from us? And to whom has the arm of the Lord been revealed? " It was for this reason that they could not believe, because Isaiah said again: " He has blinded their eyes, he has hardened their heart, so that they may not see with their eyes and understand with their heart. and turn, and I will heal them." Isaiah said these things because he saw his glory and spoke about him.

THIS is a passage which is bound to trouble many minds. John quotes two passages from *Isaiah*. The first is from *Isaiah* 53: 1, 2. In it the prophet asks if there is anyone who has believed what he has been saying, and if there is anyone who recognizes the power of God when it is revealed to him. But it is the second passage which troubles the mind. The original is in *Isaiah* 6: 9, 10. It runs: " And God said, Go and tell this people, Hear ye indeed, but understand not; and see ye indeed, but perceive not. Make the heart of this people fat, and make their ears heavy, and shut their eyes; lest they see with their eyes, and hear with their ears, and understand with their heart, and turn, and be healed." That is a passage which runs all through the New Testament. It is quoted or echoed in *Matthew* 13: 14, 15; *Mark* 4: 12; *Luke* 8: 10; *Romans* 11: 8; 2 *Corinthians* 3: 14; *Acts* 28: 27. The terrible and the troubling thing is that it seems to say that man's unbelief is due to God's action; that God has ordained that certain people must not and will not believe. Now in whatever way we explain this passage, we cannot believe that the God whom Jesus told us about would make it impossible for his children to believe.

There are two things to be said.

(i) We must try to think ourselves back into Isaiah's heart and mind. He had proclaimed the word of God and put everything he had into his message. And men had refused to listen. In the end he was forced to say: " For all the good I have done I might as well never have spoken. Instead of making men better my message seems to have made them worse. They might as well never have heard it, for they are simply confirmed in their lethargy and their disobedience and their unbelief. You would think that God had meant them not to believe." Isaiah's words spring from a broken heart. They are the words of a man bewildered by the fact that his message seemed to make men worse instead of better. To read them with cold literalness is completely to misunderstand.

(ii) But there is something else. It was a basic belief of the Jews that God is behind *everything*. They believed that *nothing* could happen outside the purpose of God. If that is so they were bound to believe that when men would not accept God's message their unbelief was still within God's purpose. To put that into modern terms and into our way of thought—we would not say that unbelief is God's purpose, but we *would* say that

God in his controlling wisdom and power can use *even* men's unbelief for his purposes. That is how Paul saw it. He saw God using the unbelief of the Jews for the conversion of the Gentiles.

We must understand this passage to mean, not that God predestined certain people to unbelief, but that even man's unbelief can be used to further God's eternal purposes. These Jews did not believe in Jesus; that was not God's fault but theirs; but even that has somehow its place in God's scheme. " Ill that he blesses is our good." God is so great that there is nothing in this world, not even sin, which is outside his power.

THE COWARD'S FAITH

John 12: 42, 43

> Nevertheless many of the rulers believed in him, but they did not publicly confess their faith for they did not wish to be excommunicated; for they loved the glory of men rather than the glory of God.

JESUS did not speak entirely to deaf ears; there were those even of the Jewish authorities, who in their heart of hearts believed. But they were afraid to confess their faith, because they did not wish to run the risk of being excommunicated from the synagogue. These people were seeking to carry out the impossible; they were trying to be secret disciples. Secret discipleship is a contradiction in terms for, " either the secrecy kills the discipleship, or the discipleship kills the secrecy."

They feared that by becoming confessed followers of Jesus they would lose so much. It is strange how often men have got their values mixed up. Again and again they have failed to support some great cause because it interfered with some lesser interest. When Joan of Arc realized that she stood forsaken and alone, she said: " Yes: I am alone on earth: I have always been alone. My father told my brothers to drown me if I would not stay to mind his sheep while France was bleeding to death; France might perish if only our lambs were safe." That French farmer preferred the safety of his sheep to the safety of his country. These Jewish rulers were a little like that. They knew that Jesus was right; they knew that their fellow-rulers were out to destroy him and all that he was seeking to do for God; but they were not prepared to take the risk of openly declaring for him. It would have meant an end of their place, their profit, and their prestige. They would have been ostracised from society and banished from orthodox religion. It was too high a price to pay. So they lived a lie because they were not big enough to stand up for the truth.

In one vivid phrase John diagnoses their position. They preferred to stand well with men rather than with God. No doubt they thought themselves wise and prudent; but their wisdom did not extend to remembering that while the opinion of men might matter for the few years in which they lived upon this earth, the judgment of God mattered for all eternity. It is true wisdom and prudence to prefer the good opinion of God to the good opinion of men; it is always better to be right for eternity than to be right for time.

THE INESCAPABLE JUDGMENT

John 12: 44–50

Jesus cried and said: " He who believes in me does not believe in me, but in him who sent me. And he who looks upon me, looks upon him who sent me. It was as light that I came into the world, that every one who believes in me should not remain in darkness. And, if anyone hears my words and does not keep them, it is not I who judge him. I did not come to judge the world but to save the world. He who completely disregards me as of no account, and who does not receive my words, has one who judges him. The word which I spoke, that will judge him on the last day. That is so because it was not out of my own self that I spoke. But the Father who sent me, it was he who gave me the commandment which laid down what I should speak and what I should say. And I know that his commandment is eternal life. The things that I speak, I speak as the Father spoke to me."

THESE, according to John, are Jesus's last words of public teaching. Hereafter he will teach his disciples and hereafter he will stand before Pilate, but these are the last words he will address to people at large.

Jesus makes the claim which is the basis of his whole life, that in him men are confronted with God. To listen to him is to listen to God; to see him is to see God. In him God meets man, and man meets God. That confrontation has two results and both have in them the core of judgment.

(i) Once again Jesus returns to a thought that is never far away in the Fourth Gospel. He did not come into the world to condemn; he came to save. It was not the wrath of God which sent Jesus to men; it was his love. Yet the coming of Jesus inevitably involves judgment. Why should that be? Because by his attitude to Jesus a man shows what he is and therefore judges himself. If he finds in Jesus an infinite magnetism and attraction, even if he never succeeds in making his life what he knows he ought to make it, he has felt the tug of God upon his heart; and therefore he is safe. If on the other hand he sees in Jesus nothing lovely and his heart remains completely untouched in his presence, it means that he is impervious to God; and he has therefore judged himself. Always in the Fourth Gospel there is this essential paradox; Jesus came in love, yet his coming is a judgment. As we have said before, we can in perfect, unmixed love offer a person some great experience, and find that he sees nothing in it; the experience offered in love has become a judgment. Jesus is God's touchstone. By a man's attitude to him he himself stands revealed.

(ii) Jesus said that at the last day the words which these people had heard would be their judges. That is one of the great truths of life. A man cannot be blamed for not knowing. But if he knows the right and does the wrong his condemnation is all the more serious. Therefore every wise thing that we have heard, and every opportunity we have had to know the truth, will in the end be a witness against us.

An old eighteenth century divine wrote a kind of catechism of the Christian faith for ordinary people. At the end there was a question which asked what would happen to a person if he disregarded the Christian message. The answer was that condemnation would follow, " and so much the more because thou hast read this book."

All that we have known and did not do will be a witness against us at the last.

THE ROYALTY OF SERVICE

John 13: 1–17

Before the Festival of the Passover, Jesus, in the knowledge that his hour had come to leave this world and to go to the Father, although he had always loved his own people in the world, decided to show them what his love was like in a way which went to the ultimate limit. The meal was in progress; and the devil had already put it into his heart that Judas Iscariot, the son of Simon, should betray him. Well knowing that the Father had given all things into his hands, and that he had come forth from God, and that he was going back to God, Jesus rose from the meal and laid aside his outer robe, and took a towel and put it round himself. Then he poured water into a ewer and began to wash the feet of his disciples and to wipe them with the towel which he had put round himself. He came to Simon Peter. Peter said to him: " Lord, are you going to wash my feet? " Jesus answered him: " You do not know now what I am doing, but you will understand afterwards." Peter said to him: " You will never wash my feet." Jesus answered him: " If I do not wash you, you have no part with me." Simon Peter said to him: " Lord, if that is so, do not wash my feet only, but my hands and my head too." Jesus said to him: " He who has been bathed has need only to have his feet washed. After that is done, he is altogether clean. And you are clean —but not all of you." He knew the one who was engineering his betrayal. That is why he said: " You are not all clean." So when he had washed their feet, and when he had taken his outer robe again, and when he had taken his place at table, he said to them: " Do you understand what I have done to you? You call me ' Teacher,' and you call me ' Lord.' And you are quite right to do so, for so I am. If then I, the Teacher and Lord, have washed your

feet, so you ought to wash each other's feet, for I have given you
an example, that, as I have done to you, you too should do to each
other. This is the truth I tell you—the servant is not greater than
his master, nor he who is sent greater than he who sent him. If you
know these things you are blessed if you do them."

WE shall have to look at this passage in far more aspects than
one, but first of all we must take it as a whole.

Few incidents in the gospel story so reveal the character of
Jesus and so perfectly show his love. When we think of what
Jesus might have been and of what he might have done the
supreme wonder of what he was and did comes home to us.

(i) Jesus knew all things had been given into his hands. He
knew that his hour of humiliation was near, but he knew that
his hour of glory was also near. Such a consciousness might
well have filled him with pride; and yet, with the knowledge of
the power and the glory that were his, he washed his disciples'
feet. At that moment when he might have had supreme pride, he
had supreme humility. Love is always like that. When, for
example, someone falls ill, the person who loves him will
perform the most menial services and delight to do them,
because love is like that. Sometimes men feel that they are too
distinguished to do the humble things, too important to do some
menial task. Jesus was not so. He knew that he was Lord of all,
and yet he washed his disciples' feet.

(ii) Jesus knew that he had come from God and that he was
going to God. He might well have had a certain contempt for
men and for the things of this world. He might well have
thought that he was finished with the world now, for he was on
the way to God. It was just at that time when God was nearest
to him that Jesus went to the depths and the limits of his service
of men. To wash the feet of the guests at a feast was the office of
a slave. The disciples of the Rabbis were supposed to render
their masters personal service, but a service like this would
never have been dreamed of. The wonderful thing about Jesus
was that his nearness to God, so far from separating him from
men, brought him nearer than ever to them.

It is always true that there is no one closer to men than the man who is close to God. T. R. Glover said of certain clever intellectuals: " They thought they were being religious when they were merely being fastidious." There is a legend of St Francis of Assisi. In his early days he was very wealthy; nothing but the best was good enough for him; he was an aristocrat of the aristocrats. But he was ill at ease and there was no peace in his soul. One day he was riding alone outside the city when he saw a leper, a mass of sores, a horrible sight. Ordinarily the fastidious Francis would have recoiled in horror from this hideous wreck of humanity. But something moved within him; he dismounted from his horse and flung his arms around the leper; and as he embraced him the leper turned into the figure of Jesus. The nearer we are to suffering humanity, the nearer we are to God.

(iii) Jesus knew this also. He was well aware that he was about to be betrayed. Such knowledge might so easily have turned him to bitterness and hatred; but it made his heart run out in greater love than ever. The astounding thing was that the more men hurt him, the more Jesus loved them. It is so easy and so natural to resent wrong and to grow bitter under insult and injury; but Jesus met the greatest injury and the supreme disloyalty, with the greatest humility and the supreme love.

THE ROYALTY OF SERVICE

John 13: 1–17 (*continued*)

THERE is more in the background of this passage than even John tells us. If we turn to Luke's account of the last meal together, we find the tragic sentence: " A dispute also arose among them, which of them was to be regarded as greatest " (*Luke* 22: 24). Even within sight of the Cross, the disciples were still arguing about matters of precedence and prestige.

It may well be that this very argument produced the situation which made Jesus act as he did. The roads of Palestine were unsurfaced and uncleaned. In dry weather they were inches

deep in dust and in wet they were liquid mud. The shoes
ordinary people wore were sandals, which were simply soles
held on to the foot by a few straps. They gave little protection
against the dust or the mud of the roads. For that reason there
were always great waterpots at the door of a house; and a
servant was there with a ewer and a towel to wash the soiled
feet of the guests as they came in. Jesus's little company of
friends had no servants. The duties which servants would carry
out in wealthier circles they must have shared among each
other. It may well be that on the night of this last meal together
they had got themselves into such a state of competitive pride
that not one of them would accept the duty of seeing that the
water and the towels were there to wash the feet of the company
as they came in; and Jesus mended their omission in the most
vivid and dramatic way.

He himself did what none of them was prepared to do. Then
he said: " You see what I have done. You call me your master
and your Lord; and you are quite right; for so I am; and yet I
am prepared to do this for you. Surely you don't think that a
pupil deserves more honour than a teacher, or a servant than a
master. Surely if I do this, you ought to be prepared to do it. I
am giving you an example of how you ought to behave towards
each other."

This ought to make us think. So often, even in churches,
trouble arises because someone does not get his place. So often
even ecclesiastical dignitaries are offended because they did
not receive the precedence to which their office entitled them.
Here is the lesson that there is only one kind of greatness,
the greatness of service. The world is full of people who are
standing on their dignity when they ought to be kneeling at the
feet of their brethren. In every sphere of life desire for prominence and unwillingness to take a subordinate place wreck the
scheme of things. A player is one day omitted from the team
and refuses to play any more. An aspiring politician is passed
over for some office to which he thought he had a right and
refuses to accept any subordinate office. A member of a choir is
not given a solo and will not sing any more. In any society it

may happen that someone is given a quite unintentional slight and either explodes in anger or broods in sulkiness for days afterwards. When we are tempted to think of our dignity, our prestige, our rights, let us see again the picture of the Son of God, girt with a towel, kneeling at his disciples' feet.

That man is truly great who has this regal humility, which makes him both servant and king among men. In *The Beloved Captain* by Donald Hankey, there is a passage which describes how the beloved captain cared for his men after a route march. " We all knew instinctively that he was our superior—a man of finer fibre than ourselves, a ' toff ' in his own right. I suppose that was why he could be so humble without loss of dignity. For he was humble, too, if that is the right word, and I think it is. No trouble of ours was too small for him to attend to. When we started route marches, for instance, and our feet were blistered and sore, as they often were at first, you would have thought that they were his own feet from the trouble he took. Of course after the march there was always an inspection of feet. That is the routine. But with him it was no mere routine. He came into our room, and, if any one had a sore foot, he would kneel down on the floor and look at it as carefully as if he had been a doctor. Then he would prescribe, and the remedies were ready at hand, being borne by a sergeant. If a blister had to be lanced, he would very likely lance it himself there and then, so as to make sure it was done with a clean needle and that no dirt was allowed to get in. There was no affectation about this, no striving after effect. It was simply that he felt that our feet were pretty important, and that he knew that we were pretty careless. So he thought it best at the start to see to the matter himself. Nevertheless, there was in our eyes something almost religious about this care for our feet. It seemed to have a touch of Christ about it, and we loved and honoured him the more." The strange thing is that it is the man who stoops like that—like Christ—whom men in the end honour as a king, and the memory of whom they will not willingly let die.

THE ESSENTIAL WASHING

John 13: 1–17 (*continued*)

WE have already seen that in John we have always to be looking for two meanings, the meaning which lies on the surface and the meaning which is beneath the surface. In this story there is undoubtedly a second meaning. On the surface it is a dramatic and unforgettable lesson in humility. But there is more to it than that.

There is one very difficult passage. At first Peter refuses to allow Jesus to wash his feet. Jesus tells him that unless he accepts this washing, he will have no part with him. Peter then begs that not only his feet, but his hands and his head should also be washed. But Jesus tells him that it is enough that his feet should be washed. The difficult sentence and the one with an inner meaning, is: " He who has been bathed has need only to have his feet washed."

Beyond doubt there is a reference to Christian baptism here. " Unless you are washed you can have no part in me " is a way of saying: " Unless you pass through the gate of baptism, you have no part in the Church."

The point is this. It was the custom that before people went to a feast they bathed themselves. When they came to the house of their host, they did not need to be bathed again; all they needed was to have their feet washed. The washing of the feet was the ceremony which preceded entry into the house where they were to be guests. It was what we might call *the washing of entry into the house.* So Jesus says to Peter: " It is not the bathing of your body that you require. That you can do for yourself. What you need is the washing which marks entry into the household of the faith." This explains another thing. Peter at first is going to refuse to allow Jesus to wash his feet. Jesus says that if he does, he will have no part in him. It is as if Jesus said: " Peter, are you going to be proud to let me do this for you? If you are, you will lose everything."

In the early Church, and still today, the way in is the way of baptism; baptism is what we might call the washing of entry. This is not to say that a man cannot be saved unless he is baptized. But it does mean that if he is able to be baptized and is too proud to enter by that gate, his pride shuts him out from the family of the faith.

Things are different now. In the early days it was grown men and women who came to be baptized because they were coming direct from heathenism into the faith. Now in many of our churches we bring our children too. But in this passage Jesus was drawing a picture of the washing which is the entry to the Church and telling men that they must not be too proud to submit to it.

THE SHAME OF DISLOYALTY AND THE GLORY OF FIDELITY

John 13: 18–20

" It is not about you all that I am speaking. I know the kind of men whom I have chosen. It is all happening that the Scripture should be fulfilled: ' He who eats my bread has lifted up his heel against me.' I am telling you this now, before it happens, so that, when it does happen, you may believe that I am who I claim to be. This is the truth I tell you—he who receives whomsoever I will send, receives me; and he who receives me, receives him who sent me."

THERE are three things stressed in this passage.

(i) The sheer cruelty of Judas's disloyalty is vividly pictured in a way which would be specially poignant to an eastern mind. Jesus used a quotation from *Psalm* 41: 9. In full the quotation runs: " Even my bosom friend in whom I trusted, who ate of my bread, has lifted his heel against me." In the east to eat bread with anyone was a sign of friendship and an act of loyalty. 2 *Samuel* 9: 7, 13 tell how David granted it to Mephibosheth to eat bread at his table, when he might well have eliminated him

as a descendant of Saul. 1 *Kings* 18: 19 tells how the prophets
of Baal ate bread at the table of Jezebel. For one who had eaten
bread at someone's table to turn against the person, to whom by
that very act he had pledged his friendship, was a bitter thing.
This disloyalty of friends is for the Psalmist the sorest of all
hurts. " It is not an enemy who taunts me—then I could bear
it—it is not an adversary who deals insolently with me—then I
could hide from him. But it is you, my equal, my companion,
my familiar friend. We used to hold sweet converse together;
within God's house we walked in fellowship " (*Psalm* 55:
12–14).

There is all the poignant sorrow in the world when a friend is
guilty of such heart-breaking disloyalty. The very phrase that is
used is full of cruelty. " He lifted up his heel against me."
Literally the Hebrew is, " He made great the heel," and it is a
phrase which describes " brutal violence." In this passage there
is no hint of anger, only of sorrow; Jesus, with a last appeal, is
revealing the wound upon his heart to Judas.

(ii) This passage also stresses the fact that all this tragedy is
somehow within the purpose of God, and that it is fully and
unquestionably accepted by Jesus. It was as Scripture said it
would be. There was never any doubt that the redeeming of the
world would cost the broken heart of God. Jesus knew what
was happening. He knew the cost and he was ready to pay it.
He did not want the disciples to think that he was caught up in
a blind web of circumstances from which he could not escape.
He was not going to be killed; he was choosing to die. At the
moment they did not, and could not, see that, but he wanted to
be sure that a day would come when they would look back and
remember and understand.

(iii) If this passage stresses the bitterness of disloyalty, it also
stresses the glory of fidelity. Some day these same disciples
would take the message of Jesus out to the world. When they
did, they would be nothing less than the representatives of God
himself. An ambassador does not go out as a private individual,
armed with only his own personal qualities and qualifications.
He goes out with all the honour and glory of his country upon

him. To listen to him is to listen to his country; to honour him is to honour the country he represents; to welcome him is to welcome the ruler who sent him out. The great honour and the great responsibility of being a pledged Christian is that we stand in the world for Jesus Christ. We speak for him; we act for him. The honour of the Eternal is in our hands.

LOVE'S LAST APPEAL

John 13: 21–30

When Jesus had said these things, he was troubled in spirit. Solemnly he declared: " This is the truth I tell you, one of you will betray me." The disciples began to look at each other, because they were at a loss to know about whom he was speaking. One of his disciples, the disciple whom Jesus loved, was reclining with his head on Jesus's breast. So Simon Peter made a sign to him and said to him: " Ask who it is that he is speaking about." The disciple who was reclining with his head on Jesus's breast said to him: " Lord who is it? " Jesus said: " It is he for whom I will dip the morsel in the dish and give it to him." So he took the morsel and dipped it in the dish and gave it to Judas Iscariot, the son of Simon. And after that man had received the morsel, Satan entered into him. So Jesus said to him: " Hurry on what you are going to do." None of those who were reclining at table understood why he said this to him. Some of them thought that, since Judas had the money-box, Jesus was saying to him: " Buy the things we need for the feast "; or that he was telling him to give something to the poor. So that man took the morsel and went out at once—and it was night.

WHEN we visualize this scene certain most dramatic things emerge.

The treachery of Judas is seen at its worst. He must have been the perfect actor and the perfect hypocrite. One thing is clear—if the other disciples had known what Judas was about, he would never have left that room alive. All the time Judas must have been putting on an act of love and loyalty which deceived everyone except Jesus. He was not only a bare-faced villain; he was a suave hypocrite. There is warning here. By our outward actions we may deceive men; but there is no hiding things from the eye of Christ.

There is more. When we understand aright what was happening, we can see that there was appeal after appeal to Judas. First, there were the seating arrangements at the meal. The Jews did not sit at table; they reclined. The table was a low solid block, with couches round it. It was shaped like a U and the place of the host was in the centre. They reclined on their left side, resting on the left elbow, thus leaving the right hand free to deal with the food. Sitting in such a way, a man's head was literally in the breast of the person reclining on his left. Jesus would be sitting in the place of the host, at the centre of the single side of the low table. The disciple whom Jesus loved must have been sitting on his *right*, for as he lent on his elbow at the table, his head was in Jesus's breast.

The disciple whom Jesus loved is never named. Some have thought that he was Lazarus, for Jesus loved Lazarus (*John* 11: 36). Some have thought that he was the rich young ruler, for Jesus loved him (*Mark* 10: 21); and it has been imagined that in the end he did decide to stake everything on Jesus. Some have thought that he was some otherwise unknown young disciple who was specially near and dear to Jesus. Some have thought that he was not a flesh and blood person at all, but only an ideal picture of what the perfect disciple ought to be. But the general opinion has always been that the beloved disciple was none other than John himself; and we may well believe that.

But it is the place of Judas that is of special interest. It is quite clear that Jesus could speak to him privately without the others overhearing. If that be so, there is only one place Judas could have been occupying. He must have been on Jesus's *left*, so that, just as John's head was in Jesus's breast, Jesus's head was in Judas's. The revealing thing is that *the place on the left of the host was the place of highest honour, kept for the most intimate friend*. When that meal began, Jesus must have said to Judas: " Judas, come and sit beside me tonight; I want specially to talk to you." The very inviting of Judas to that seat was an appeal.

But there is more. For the host to offer the guest a special tit-bit, a special morsel from the dish, was again a sign of special friendship. When Boaz wished to show how much he honoured Ruth, he invited her to come and dip her morsel in the wine (*Ruth* 2: 14). T. E. Lawrence told how when he sat with the Arabs in their tents, sometimes the Arab chief would tear a choice piece of fat mutton from the whole sheep before them and hand it to him (often a most embarrassing favour to a western palate, for it had to be eaten!) When Jesus handed the morsel to Judas, again it was a mark of special affection. And we note that even when Jesus did this the disciples did not gather the import of his words. That surely shows that Jesus was so much in the habit of doing this that it seemed nothing unusual. Judas had always been picked out for special affection.

There is tragedy here. Again and again Jesus appealed to that dark heart, and again and again Judas remained unmoved. God save *us* from being completely impervious to the appeal of love.

LOVE'S LAST APPEAL

John 13: 21–30 (*continued*)

So this tragic drama played itself out to the end. Again and again Jesus showed his affection to Judas. Again and again Jesus tried to save him from what he was planning to do.

Then quite suddenly the crucial moment came, the moment when the love of Jesus admitted defeat. " Judas," he said, " hurry on what you propose to do." There was no point in further delay. Why carry on this useless appeal in the mounting tension? If it was to be done, it were better done quickly.

Still the disciples did not see. They thought Judas was being despatched to make the arrangements for the feast. It was always the custom at the Passover that those who had shared with those who had not. It was the time of all times when people gave to the poor. To this day it is the custom in many churches to take a special offering at Communion services for those in need. So the disciples thought that Jesus was sending Judas out to give the usual present to the poor, that they too might be enabled to celebrate the Passover.

When Judas received the morsel, the devil entered into him. It is a terrible thing that what was meant to be love's appeal became hate's dynamic. That is what the devil can do. He can take the loveliest things and twist them until they become the agents of hell. He can take love and turn it into lust; he can take holiness and turn it into pride; he can take discipline and turn it into sadistic cruelty; he can take affection and turn it into spineless complacence. We must be on the watch so that in our lives the devil never warps the lovely things until he can use them for his own purposes.

Judas went out—and it was night. John has a way of using words in the most pregnant way. It was night for the day was late; but there was another night there. It is always night when a man goes from Christ to follow his own purposes. It is always night when a man listens to the call of evil rather than the summons of good. It is always night when hate puts out the light of love. It is always night when a man turns his back on Jesus.

If we submit ourselves to Christ we walk in the light; if we turn our backs on him we go into the dark. The way of light and the way of dark are set before us. God give us wisdom to choose aright—for in the dark a man always goes lost.

THE FOURFOLD GLORY

John 13: 31, 32

> When Judas had gone out, Jesus said: " Now the Son of Man has been glorified, and God has been glorified in him; and now God will glorify himself in him; and he will glorify him immediately."

THIS passage tells of the fourfold glory.

(i) The glory of Jesus has come; and that glory is the Cross. The tension is gone; any doubts that remained have been finally removed. Judas has gone out, and the Cross is a certainty. Here we are face to face with something which is of the very warp and woof of life. The greatest glory in life is the glory which comes from sacrifice. In any warfare the supreme glory belongs, not to those who survive but to those who lay down their lives. As Laurence Binyon wrote:

> " They shall grow not old, as we that are left grow old:
>   Age shall not weary them, nor the years condemn.
>   At the going down of the sun and in the morning
>   We will remember them."

In medicine it is not the physicians who made a fortune who are remembered; it is those who gave their lives that healing might come to men. It is the simple lesson of history that those who have made the great sacrifices have entered into the great glory.

(ii) In Jesus God has been glorified. It was the obedience of Jesus which brought glory to God. There is only one way for a man to show that he loves and admires and trusts a leader; and that is by obeying him, if need be to the bitter end. The only way in which a child can honour a parent is by obeying him. Jesus gave the supreme honour and the supreme glory to God, because he gave to God the supreme obedience, even to a Cross.

(iii) In Jesus God glorifies himself. It is a strange thought that the supreme glory of God lies in the Incarnation and the Cross. There is no glory like that of being loved. Had God remained aloof and majestic, serene and unmoved, untouched by any sorrow and unhurt by any pain, men might have feared him and men might have admired him; but they would never have loved him. The law of sacrifice is not only a law of earth; it is a law of heaven and earth. It is in the Incarnation and the Cross that God's supreme glory is displayed.

(iv) God will glorify Jesus. Here is the other side of the matter. At that moment the Cross was the glory of Jesus; but there was more to follow—the Resurrection; the Ascension; the full and final triumph of Christ, which is what the New Testament means when it talks of his Second Coming. In the Cross Jesus found his own glory; but the day came, and the day will come, when that glory will be demonstrated to all the world and all the universe. The vindication of Christ must follow his humiliation; the enthronement of Christ must follow his crucifixion; the crown of thorns must change into the crown of glory It is the campaign of the Cross, but the King will yet enter into a triumph which all the world can see.

THE FAREWELL COMMAND

John 13: 33–35

" Little children, I am still going to be with you for a little while. You will search for me; and, as I said to the Jews, so now I say to you too: ' You cannot go where I am going.' I give you a new commandment, that you love one another; that you too love one another, as I have loved you; it is by this that all will know that you are my disciples—if you have love amongst each other."

JESUS was laying down his farewell commandment to his disciples. The time was short; if they were ever to hear his voice they must hear it now. He was going on a journey on which none might accompany him; he was taking a road that he had to walk alone; and before he went, he gave them the commandment that they must love one another as he had loved them. What does this mean for us, and for our relationships with our fellow-men? How did Jesus love his disciples?

(i) He loved his disciples *selflessly*. Even in the noblest human love there remains some element of self. We so often think—maybe unconsciously—of what we are to get. We think of the happiness we will receive, or of the loneliness we will suffer if love fails or is denied. So often we are thinking: What will this love do for me? So often at the back of things it is *our* happiness that we are seeking. But Jesus never thought of himself. His one desire was to give himself and all he had for those he loved.

(ii) Jesus loved his disciples *sacrificially*. There was no limit to what his love would give or to where it would go. No demand that could be made upon it was too much. If love meant the Cross, Jesus was prepared to go there. Sometimes we make the mistake of thinking that love is meant to give us happiness. So in the end it does, but love may well bring pain and demand a cross.

(iii) Jesus loved his disciples *understandingly*. He knew his disciples through and through. We never really know people until we have lived with them. When we are meeting them only occasionally, we see them at their best. It is when we live with them that we find out their moods and their irritabilities and their weaknesses. Jesus had lived with his disciples day in and day out for many months and knew all that was to be known about them—and he still loved them. Sometimes we say that love is blind. That is not so, for the love that is blind can end in nothing but bleak and utter disillusionment. Real love is open-eyed. It loves, not what it imagines a man to be, but what he is. The heart of Jesus is big enough to love us as we are.

(iv) Jesus loved his disciples *forgivingly*. Their leader was to deny him. They were all to forsake him in his hour of need. They never, in the days of his flesh, really understood him. They were blind and insensitive, slow to learn, and lacking in understanding. In the end they were craven cowards. But Jesus held nothing against them; there was no failure which he could not forgive. The love which has not learned to forgive cannot do anything else but shrivel and die. We are poor creatures, and there is a kind of fate in things which makes us hurt most of all those who love us best. For that very reason all enduring love must be built on forgiveness, for without forgiveness it is bound to die.

THE FALTERING LOYALTY

John 13: 36–38

> Simon Peter said to him: " Lord, where are you going? " " Where
> I am going," Jesus answered, " you cannot now follow; but after-
> wards you will follow." Peter said to him: " Lord, why can I
> not follow you now? I will lay down my life for you." Jesus
> answered: " Will you lay down your life for me? This is the truth
> I tell you—the cock will not crow until you will deny me three
> times."

WHAT was the difference between Peter and Judas? Judas
betrayed Jesus, and Peter, in his hour of need, denied him even
with oaths and curses; and yet, while the name of Judas has
become one of blackest shame, there is something infinitely
lovable about Peter. The difference is this. Judas's betrayal of
Jesus was deliberate; it was carried out in cold blood; it must
have been the result of careful thought and planning; and in the
end it callously refused the most poignant appeal. But there was
never anything less deliberate than Peter's denial of Jesus. He
never meant to do it; he was swept away by a moment of
weakness. For the moment, his will was too weak, but his heart
was always right.

There is always a difference between the sin which is coldly
and deliberately calculated, and the sin which involuntarily
conquers a man in a moment of weakness or of passion; always
a difference between the sin which knows what it is doing, and
the sin that comes when a man is so weakened or so inflamed
that he scarcely knows what he is doing. God save us from
deliberately hurting himself or those who love us!

There is something very lovely in the relationship between
Jesus and Peter.

(i) Jesus knew Peter in all his weakness. He knew his
impulsiveness; he knew his instability; he knew how he had a
habit of speaking with his heart before he had thought with his
head. He knew well the strength of his loyalty and the weakness
of his resolution. Jesus knew Peter as he was.

(ii) Jesus knew Peter in all his love. He knew that whatever Peter did he loved him. If we would only understand that often when people hurt us, fail us, wound us, or disappoint us, it is not the real person who is acting. The real person is not the one who wounds us or fails us, but the one who loves us. The basic thing is not his failure, but his love. Jesus knew that about Peter. It would save us many a heartbreak and many a tragic breach if we remembered the basic love and forgave the moment's failure.

(iii) Jesus knew, not only what Peter was, but also what he could become. He knew that at the moment Peter could not follow him; but he was sure that the day would come when he, too, would take the same red road to martyrdom. It is the greatness of Jesus that he sees the hero even in the coward; he sees not only what we are, but also what he can make us. He has the love to see what we can be and the power to make us attain it.

THE PROMISE OF GLORY

John 14: 1–3

> " Do not let your heart be distressed. Believe in God and believe in me. There are many abiding-places in my Father's house. If it were not so, would I have told you that I am going to prepare a place for you? And, if I go and prepare a place for you, I am coming again, and I will welcome you to myself, that where I am, there you too may be."

IN a very short time life for the disciples was going to fall in. Their world was going to collapse in chaos around them. At such a time there was only one thing to do—stubbornly to hold on to trust in God. As the Psalmist had had it: " I believe that I shall see the goodness of the Lord in the land of the living " (*Psalm* 27: 13). " But my eyes are toward thee, O Lord God; in thee I seek refuge " (*Psalm* 141: 8). There comes a time when we have to believe where we cannot prove and to accept where we cannot understand. If, in the darkest hour, we believe that somehow there is a purpose in life and that that purpose is love, even the unbearable becomes bearable and even in the darkness there is a glimmer of light.

Jesus adds something to that. He says not only: " Believe in God." He says also:" Believe in me." If the Psalmist could believe in the ultimate goodness of God, how much can we. For Jesus is the proof that God is willing to give us everything he has to give. As Paul put it: " He who did not spare his own Son, but gave him up for us all, will he not also give us all things with him? " (*Romans* 8: 32). If we believe that in Jesus we see the picture of God, then, in face of that amazing love, it becomes, not easy, but at least possible, to accept even what we cannot understand, and in the storms of life to retain a faith that is serene.

Jesus went on to say: " There are many abiding places in my Father's house." By his Father's house he meant heaven. But what did he mean when he said there were many abiding places in heaven? The word used for *abiding places* is the word *monai* and there are three suggestions.

(i) The Jews held that in heaven there were different grades of blessedness which would be given to men according to their goodness and their fidelity on earth. In the *Book of the Secrets of Enoch* it is said:" In the world to come there are many mansions prepared for men; good for good; evil for evil." That picture likens heaven to a vast palace in which there are many rooms, with each assigned a room such as his life has merited.

(ii) In the Greek writer Pausanias the word *monai* means *stages upon the way*. If that is how to take it here, it means that there are many stages on the way to heaven and even in heaven there is progress and development and advance. At least some of the great early Christian thinkers had that belief. Origen was one. He said that when a man died, his soul went to some place called Paradise, which is still upon earth. There he received teaching and training and, when he was worthy and fit, his soul ascended into the air. It then passed through various *monai*, stages, which the Greeks called *spheres* and which the Christians called *heavens*, until finally it reached the heavenly kingdom. In so doing the soul followed Jesus who, as the writer to the Hebrews said, " passed through the heavens " (*Hebrews* 4: 14). Irenaeus speaks of a certain interpretation of the sentence which tells how the seed that is sown produces sometimes a hundredfold, sometimes sixtyfold and sometimes thirtyfold (*Matthew* 13: 8). There was a different yield and therefore a different reward. Some men will be counted worthy to pass all their eternity in the very presence of God; others will rise to Paradise; and others will become citizens of " the city." Clement of Alexandria believed that there were degrees of glory, rewards and stages in proportion to a man's achievement in holiness in this life.

There is something very attractive here. There is a sense in which the soul shrinks from what we might call a static heaven. There is something attractive in the idea of a development which goes on even in the heavenly places. Speaking in purely human and inadequate terms, we sometimes feel that we would be dazzled with too much splendour, if we were immediately ushered into the very presence of God. We feel that even in heaven we would need to be purified and helped until we could face the greater glory.

(iii) But it may well be that the meaning is very simple and very lovely. " There are many abiding-places in my Father's house " may simply mean that in heaven there is room for all. An earthly house becomes overcrowded; an earthly inn must sometimes turn away the weary traveller because its accommodation is exhausted. It is not so with our Father's house, for heaven is as wide as the heart of God and there is room for all. Jesus is saying to his friends: " Don't be afraid. Men may shut their doors upon you. But in heaven you will never be shut out."

THE PROMISE OF GLORY

John 14: 1–3 (*continued*)

THERE are certain other great truths within this passage.

(i) It tells us of the honesty of Jesus. " If it were not so," asked Jesus, " would I have told you that I am going to prepare a place for you? " No one could ever claim that he had been inveigled into Christianity by specious promises or under false pretences. Jesus told men bluntly that the Christian must bid farewell to comfort (*Luke* 9: 57, 58). He told them of the persecution, the hatred, the penalties they would have to bear (*Matthew* 10: 16–22). He told them of the cross which they must carry (*Matthew* 16: 24), even although he told them also of the glory of the ending of the Christian way. He frankly and honestly told men what they might expect both of glory and of pain if they followed him. He was not a leader who tried to bribe men with promises of an easy way; he tried to challenge them into greatness.

(ii) It tells us of the function of Jesus. He said, " I am going to prepare a place for you." One of the great thoughts of the New Testament is that Jesus goes on in front for us to follow. He opens up a way so that we may follow in his steps. One of the great words which is used to describe Jesus is the word *prodromos* (*Hebrews* 6: 20). The Authorized Version and the Revised Standard translate it *forerunner*. There are two uses of this word which light up the picture within it. In the Roman army the *prodromoi* were the reconnaissance troops. They went ahead of the main body of the army to blaze the trail and to ensure that it was safe for the rest of the troops to follow. The harbour of Alexandria was very difficult to approach. When the great corn ships came into it a little pilot boat was sent out to guide them along the channel into safe waters. That pilot boat was called the *prodromos*. It went first to make it safe for others to follow. That is what Jesus did. He blazed the way to heaven and to God that we might follow in his steps.

(iii) It tells us of the ultimate triumph of Jesus. He said: " I am coming again." The Second Coming of Jesus is a doctrine which has to a large extent dropped out of Christian thinking and preaching. The curious thing about it is that Christians seem either entirely to disregard it or to think of nothing else. It is true that we cannot tell when it will happen or what will happen, but one thing is certain—history is going somewhere. Without a climax it would be necessarily incomplete. History must have a consummation, and that consummation will be the triumph of Jesus Christ; and he promises that in the day of his triumph he will welcome his friends.

(iv) Jesus said: " Where I am, there you will also be." Here is a great truth put in the simplest way; for the Christian, heaven is where Jesus is. We do not need to speculate on what heaven will be like. It is enough to know that we will be for ever with him. When we love someone with our whole heart, we are really alive only when we are with that person. It is so with Christ. In this world our contact with him is shadowy, for we can see only through a glass darkly, and spasmodic, for we are poor creatures and cannot live always on the heights. But the best definition is to say that heaven is that state where we will always be with Jesus.

THE WAY, THE TRUTH AND THE LIFE

John 14: 4–6

> " And you know the way to where I go." Thomas said to him: " Lord, we do not know where you are going. How do we know the way? " Jesus said to him: " I am the Way, the Truth and the Life. No one comes to the Father except through me."

AGAIN and again Jesus had told his disciples where he was going, but somehow they had never understood. " Yet a little while I am with you," he said, " and then I go to him that sent me " (*John* 7: 33). He had told them that he was going to the Father who had sent him, and with whom he was one, but they still did not understand what was going on. Even less did they understand the way by which Jesus was going, for that way was the Cross. At this moment the disciples were bewildered men. There was one among them who could never say that he understood what he did not understand, and that was Thomas. He was far too honest and far too much in earnest to be satisfied with any vague pious expressions. Thomas had to be sure. So he expressed his doubts and his failure to understand,

and the wonderful thing is that it was the question of a doubting man which provoked one of the greatest things Jesus ever said. No one need be ashamed of his doubts; for it is amazingly and blessedly true that he who seeks will in the end find.

Jesus said to Thomas: " I am the Way, the Truth and the Life." That is a great saying to us, but it would be still greater to a Jew who heard it for the first time. In it Jesus took three of the great basic conceptions of Jewish religion, and made the tremendous claim that in him all three found their full realization.

The Jews talked much about the *way* in which men must walk and the *ways* of God. God said to Moses: " You shall not turn aside to the right hand or to the left. You shall walk in all the *ways* which the Lord your God has commanded you " (*Deuteronomy* 5: 32, 33). Moses said to the people: " I know that after my death you will surely act corruptly, and turn aside from the *way* which I have commanded you " (*Deuteronomy* 31: 29). Isaiah had said: " Your ears shall hear a word behind you saying, This is the *way*, walk in it " (*Isaiah* 30: 21). In the brave new world there would be a highway called *the Way of Holiness*, and in it the wayfaring man, even though a simple soul, would not go lost (*Isaiah* 35: 8). It was the Psalmist's prayer: " Teach me thy *way*, O Lord " (*Psalm* 27: 11). The Jews knew much about the way of God in which a man must walk. And Jesus said: " I am the Way."

What did he mean? Suppose we are in a strange town and ask for directions. Suppose the person asked says: " Take the first to the right, and the second to the left. Cross the square, go past the church, take the third on the right and the road you want is the fourth on the left." The chances are that we will be lost before we get half-way. But suppose the person we ask says: " Come. I'll take you there." In that case the person to us *is* the way, and we cannot miss it. That is what Jesus does for us. He does not only give advice and directions. He takes us by the hand and leads us; he strengthens us and guides us personally every day. He does not tell us about the way; he is the Way.

Jesus said: " I am the Truth." The Psalmist said: " Teach me

Thy way, O Lord, that I may walk in thy *truth* " (*Psalm* 86: 11). " For thy steadfast love is before my eyes," he said, " and I walk in faithfulness to thee " (*Psalm* 26: 3). " I have chosen the way of *truth*," he said (*Psalm* 119: 30). Many men have told us the truth, but no man ever embodied it. There is one all-important thing about moral truth. A man's character does not really affect his teaching of geometry or astronomy or Latin verbs. But if a man proposes to teach moral truth, his character makes all the difference in the world. An adulterer who teaches the necessity of purity, a grasping person who teaches the value of generosity, a domineering person who teaches the beauty of humility, an irascible creature who teaches the beauty of serenity, an embittered person who teaches the beauty of love, is bound to be ineffective. Moral truth cannot be conveyed solely in words; it must be conveyed in example. And that is precisely where the greatest human teacher must fall down. No teacher has ever embodied the truth he taught—except Jesus. Many a man could say: " I have taught you the truth." Only Jesus could say: " I am the Truth." The tremendous thing about Jesus is not simply that the *statement* of moral perfection finds its peak in him; it is that the *fact* of moral perfection finds its realization in him.

Jesus said: " I am the Life." The writer of the Proverbs said: " The commandment is a lamp, and the teaching a light; and the reproofs of discipline are the way of *life* " (*Proverbs* 6: 23). " He who heeds instructions is on the path to life " (*Proverbs* 10: 17). " Thou dost show me the path of *life*," said the Psalmist (*Psalm* 16: 11). In the last analysis what man is always seeking for is life. His search is not for knowledge for its own sake: but what will make life worth living. A novelist makes one of his characters who has fallen in love say: " I never knew what life was until I saw it in your eyes." Love had brought life. That is what Jesus does. Life with Jesus is life indeed.

And there is one way of putting all this. " No one," said Jesus, " comes to the Father except through me." He alone is the way to God. In him alone we see what God is like; and he alone can lead men into God's presence without fear and without shame.

THE VISION OF GOD

John 14: 7–11

" If you had known me, you would have known my Father too. From now on you are beginning to know him, and you have seen him." Philip said to him: " Lord, show us the Father, and that is enough for us." Jesus said to him: " Have I been with you for so long, and you did not know me, Philip? He who has seen me has seen the Father. How can you say: ' Show us the Father '? Do you not believe that I am in the Father and that the Father is in me? I am not the source of the words that I speak to you. It is the Father who dwells in me who is doing his own work. Believe me that I am in the Father and that the Father is in me. If you cannot believe it because I say it, believe it because of the very works I do."

IT may well be that to the ancient world this was the most staggering thing Jesus ever said. To the Greeks God was characteristically *The Invisible*, the Jews would count it as an article of faith that no man had seen God at any time. To people who thought like that Jesus said: " If you had known me, you would have known my Father too." Then Philip asked what he must have believed to be the impossible. Maybe he was thinking back to that tremendous day when God revealed his glory to Moses (*Exodus* 33: 12–32). But even in that great day. God had said to Moses: " You shall see my back: but my face shall not be seen." In the time of Jesus men were oppressed and fascinated by what is called the transcendence of God and by thought of the difference and the distance between God and man. They would never have dared to think that they could see God. Then Jesus says with utter simplicity: " He who has seen me has seen the Father."

To see Jesus is to see what God is like. A recent writer said that Luke in his gospel " domesticated God." He meant that

Luke shows us God in Jesus taking a share in the most intimate
and homely things. When we see Jesus we can say: " This is
God living our life." That being so, we can say the most
precious things about God.

(i) God entered into an ordinary home and into an ordinary
family. As Francis Thompson wrote so beautifully in *Ex Ore
Infantum*:

> " Little Jesus, wast thou shy
> Once, and just so small as I?
> And what did it feel to be
> Out of Heaven and just like me? "

Anyone in the ancient world would have thought that if God
did come into this world, he would come as a king into some
royal palace with all the might and majesty which the world
calls greatness. As George Macdonald wrote:

> " They all were looking for a king
> To slay their foes and lift them high;
> Thou cam'st, a little baby thing,
> That made a woman cry.

As the child's verse says:

> " There was a knight of Bethlehem
> Whose wealth was tears and sorrows;
> His men at arms were little lambs,
> His trumpeters were sparrows."

In Jesus, God once and for all sanctified human birth, sanctified
the humble home of ordinary folk and sanctified all childhood.

(ii) God was not ashamed to do a man's work. It was as a
working man that he entered into the world; Jesus was the
carpenter of Nazareth. We can never sufficiently realize the
wonder of the fact that God understands our day's work. He
knows the difficulty of making ends meet; he knows the
difficulty of the ill-mannered customer and the client who will
not pay his bills. He knew all the difficulty of living in an
ordinary home and in a big family, and he knew every problem
which besets us in the work of every day. According to the Old

Testament work is a curse; according to the old story, the curse on man for the sin of Eden was: " In the sweat of your face you shall eat bread " (*Genesis* 3: 19). But according to the New Testament, common work is tinged with glory for it has been touched by the hand of God.

(iii) God knows what it is to be tempted. The life of Jesus shows us, not the serenity, but the struggle of God. Anyone might conceive of a God who lived in a serenity and peace which were beyond the tensions of this world; but Jesus shows us a God who goes through the struggle that we must undergo. God is not like a commander who leads from behind the lines; he too knows the firing-line of life.

(iv) In Jesus we see God loving. The moment love enters into life pain enters in. If we could be absolutely detached, if we could so arrange life that nothing and nobody mattered to us, then there would be no such thing as sorrow and pain and anxiety. But in Jesus we see God caring intensely, yearning over men, feeling poignantly for them and with them, loving them until he bore the wounds of love upon his heart.

(v) In Jesus we see God upon a Cross. There is nothing so incredible as this in all the world. It is easy to imagine a god who condemns men; it is still easier to imagine a God who, if men oppose him, wipes them out. No one would ever have dreamed of a God who chose the Cross to obtain our salvation.

" He who has seen me has seen the Father." Jesus is the revelation of God and that revelation leaves the mind of man staggered and amazed.

THE VISION OF GOD

John 14: 7–11 (*continued*)

JESUS goes on to say something else. One thing no Jew would ever lose was the grip of sheer loneliness of God. The Jews were unswerving monotheists. The danger of the Christian faith is that we may set up Jesus as a kind of secondary God. But Jesus himself insists that the things he said and the things he did did not come from his own initiative or his own power or his own knowledge but from God. His words were God's voice speaking to men; His deeds were God's power flowing through him to men. He was the channel by which God came to men.

Let us take two simple and imperfect analogies, from the relationship between student and teacher. Dr Lewis Muirhead said of that great Christian and expositor, A. B. Bruce, that men " came to see in the man the glory of God." Every teacher has the responsibility of transmitting something of the glory of his subject to those who listen to him; and he who teaches about Jesus Christ can, if he is saint enough, transmit the vision and the presence of God to his students. That is what A. B. Bruce did, and in an infinitely greater way that is what Jesus did. He transmitted the glory and the love of God to men.

Here is the other analogy. A great teacher stamps his students with something of himself. W. M. Macgregor was a student of A. B. Bruce. A. J. Gossip tells in his memoir of W. M. Macgregor that, " when it was rumoured that Macgregor thought of deserting the pulpit for a chair, men, in astonishment, asked, Why? He replied, with modesty, that he had learned some things from Bruce that he would fain pass on." Principal John Cairns wrote to his teacher Sir William Hamilton: " I do not know what life, or lives, may lie before me. But I know this, that, to the end of the last of them, I shall bear your mark upon me." Sometimes if a divinity student has been trained by a great preacher whom he loves, we will see in the student something of the teacher and hear something of his voice. Jesus did something like that only immeasurably more so. He brought God's accent, God's message, God's mind, God's heart to men.

We *must* every now and then remember, that all is of God. It was not a self-chosen expedition to the world which Jesus made. He did not do it to soften a hard heart in God. He came because God sent him, because God so loved the world. At the back of Jesus, and in him, there is God.

Jesus went on to make a claim and to offer a test, based on two things; his *words* and his *works*.

(i) He claimed to be tested by what *he said*. It is as if Jesus said: " When you listen to me, can you not realize at once that what I am saying is God's own truth? " The words of any genius are always self-evidencing. When we read great poetry we cannot for the most part say why it is great and grips our heart. We may analyse the vowel sounds and so on, but in the end there is something which defies analysis, but nevertheless easily and immediately recognizable. It is so with the words of Jesus. When we hear them we cannot help saying: " If only the world would live on these principles, how different it would be! If only *I* would live on these principles, how different I would be! "

(ii) He claimed to be tested by his *deeds*. He said to Philip: " If you cannot believe in me because of what I say, surely you will allow what I can do to convince you." That was the same answer as Jesus sent back to John when he sent his messengers to ask whether Jesus was the Messiah, or if they must look for another. " Go back," he said, " and tell John what is happening—and that will convince him " (*Matthew* 11: 1–6). Jesus's proof is that no one else ever succeeded in making bad men good.

Jesus said in effect to Philip: " Listen to me! Look at me! And believe! " Still the way to Christian belief is not to argue about Jesus but to listen to him and to look at him. If we do that, the sheer personal impact will compel us to believe.

THE TREMENDOUS PROMISES

John 14: 12–14

" This is the truth I tell you—he that believes on me will do the works that I do, and he will do greater works than these, because I go to my Father. And I will do whatever you shall ask in my name, that the Father may be glorified in the Son. If you ask me anything in my name, I will do it."

THERE could scarcely be any greater promises than the two contained in this passage. But they are of such a nature that we must try to understand what they mean. Unless we do, the experience of life is bound to disappoint us.

(i) First of all Jesus said that one day his disciples would do what he did, and even greater works. What did he mean?

(*a*) It is quite certain that in the early days the early Church possessed the power of working cures. Paul enumerates among the gifts which different people had that of healing (1 *Corinthians* 12: 9, 28, 30). James urged that when any Christian was sick, the elders should pray over him and anoint him with oil (*James* 5: 14). But it is clear that that is by no means all that Jesus meant; for though it could be said that the early Church did the things which Jesus did, it certainly could not be said that it did greater things than he did.

(*b*) As time has gone on man has more and more learned to conquer disease. The physician and the surgeon nowadays have powers which to the ancient world would have seemed miraculous and even godlike. The surgeon with his new techniques, the physician with his new treatments and his miracle drugs, can now effect the most amazing cures. There is a long way to go yet, but one by one the citadels of pain and disease have been stormed. The salient thing about all this is that it was the power and the influence of Jesus Christ which brought it about. Why should men strive to save the weak and the sick and the dying, those whose bodies are broken and whose minds are darkened? Why is it that men of skill and science have felt moved, and even compelled, to spend their time and their strength, to ruin their health and sometimes to sacrifice their lives, to find cures for disease and relief from pain? The answer is that, whether they knew it or not, Jesus was saying to them through his Spirit: " These people must be helped and healed. You must do it. It is your responsibility and your privilege to do all you can for them." It is the Spirit of Jesus who has been behind the conquest of disease; and, as a result, men can do things nowadays which in the time of Jesus no one would ever have imagined possible.

(*c*) But we are still not at the meaning of this. Think of what Jesus in the days of his flesh had *actually done*. He had never preached outside Palestine. Within his lifetime Europe had never heard the gospel. He had never personally met moral degradation of a city like Rome. Even his opponents in Palestine were religious men; the Pharisees and the scribes had given their lives to religion as they saw it and there was never any doubt that they revered and practised purity of life. It was not in his lifetime that Christianity went out to a world where the marriage bond was set at nought, where adultery was not even a conventional sin, and where vice flourished like a tropical forest.

It was into that world the early Christians went; and it was that world which they won for Christ. When it came to a matter of numbers and extent and changing power, the triumphs of the message of the Cross were even greater than the triumphs of Jesus in the days of his flesh. It is of moral re-creation and spiritual victory that Jesus is speaking. He says that this will happen because he is going to his Father. What does he mean by that? He means this. In the days of his flesh he was limited to Palestine; when he had died and risen again, he was liberated from these limitations and his Spirit could work mightily anywhere.

(ii) In his second promise Jesus says that any prayer offered in his name will be granted. It is here of all places that we must understand. Note carefully what Jesus said—*not* that all our prayers would be granted, but that our prayers *made in his name* would be granted. The test of any prayer is: Can I make it in the name of Jesus? No man, for instance, could pray for personal revenge, for personal ambition, for some unworthy and unchristian object *in the name of Jesus*. When we pray, we must always ask: Can we honestly make this prayer *in the name of Jesus*? The prayer which can stand the test of that consideration, and which, in the end says, Thy will be done, is always answered. But the prayer based on self cannot expect to be granted.

THE PROMISED HELPER

John 14: 15–17

> " If you love me, keep my commandments; and I will ask the
> Father and he will give you another helper to be with you for ever,
> I mean the Spirit of Truth. The world cannot receive him, because
> it does not see him or know him. But you know him because he
> remains among you and will be within you."

To John there is only one test of love and that is obedience. It
was by his obedience that Jesus showed his love of God; and it
is by our obedience that we must show our love of Jesus. C. K.
Barrett says: " John never allowed love to devolve into a
sentiment or emotion. Its expression is always moral and is
revealed in obedience." We know all too well how there are
those who protest their love in words but who, at the same time,
bring pain and heartbreak to those whom they claim to love.
There are children and young people who say that they love
their parents, and who yet cause them grief and anxiety. There
are husbands who say they love their wives and wives who say
they love their husbands, and who yet, by their inconsiderate-
ness and their irritability and their thoughtless unkindness bring
pain the one to the other. To Jesus real love is not an easy thing.
It is shown only in true obedience.

But Jesus does not leave us to struggle with the Christian life
alone. He would send us another *Helper*. The Greek word is the
word *paraklētos* which is really untranslatable. The Authorized
Version renders it *Comforter*, which, although hallowed by time
and usage, is not a good translation. Moffatt translates it
Helper. It is only when we examine this word *paraklētos* in
detail that we catch something of the riches of the doctrine of
the Holy Spirit. It really means *someone who is called in*; but it
is the reason *why* the person is called in which gives the word its
distinctive associations. The Greeks used the word in a wide
variety of ways. A *paraklētos* might be a person *called in* to
give witness in a law court in someone's favour; he might be an

advocate *called in* to plead the cause of someone under a charge which would issue in serious penalty; he might be an expert *called in* to give advice in some difficult situation; he might be a person *called in* when, for example, a company of soldiers were depressed and dispirited to put new courage into their minds and hearts. Always a *paraklētos* is *someone called in to help* in time of trouble or need. *Comforter* was once a perfectly good translation. It actually goes back to Wicliffe, the first person to use it. But in his day it meant much more than it means now. The word comes from the Latin *fortis* which means *brave*; and a comforter was someone who enabled some dispirited creature to be brave. Nowadays *comfort* has to do almost solely with sorrow; and a comforter is someone who sympathizes with us when we are sad. Beyond a doubt the Holy Spirit does that, but to limit his work to that function is sadly to belittle him. We often talk of being able *to cope* with things. That is precisely the work of the Holy Spirit. He takes away our inadequacies and enables us to cope with life. The Holy Spirit substitutes victorious for defeated living.

So what Jesus is saying is: " I am setting you a hard task, and I am sending you out on a very difficult engagement. But I am going to send you someone, the *paraklētos*, who will guide you as to what to do and enable you to do it."

Jesus went on to say that the world cannot recognize the Spirit. By the world is meant that section of men who live as if there was no God. The point of Jesus's saying is: we can see only what we are fitted to see. An astronomer will see far more in the sky than an ordinary man. A botanist will see far more in a hedgerow than someone who knows no botany. Someone who knows about art will see far more in a picture than someone who is quite ignorant of art. Someone who understands a little about music will get far more out of a symphony than someone who understands nothing. Always what we see and experience depends on what we bring to the sight and the experience. A person who has eliminated God never listens for him; and we cannot receive the Holy Spirit unless we wait in expectation and in prayer for him to come to us.

The Holy Spirit gate-crashes no man's heart; He waits to be received. So when we think of the wonderful things which the Holy Spirit can do, surely we will set apart some time amidst the bustle and the rush of life to wait in silence for his coming.

THE WAY TO FELLOWSHIP AND TO REVELATION

John 14: 18–24

" I will not leave you forlorn. I am coming to you. In a little while the world will no longer see me; but you will see me because I will be alive and you too will be alive. In that day you will know that I am in the Father, and that you are in me, even as I am in you. It is he who grasps my commandments and keeps them who loves me. He who loves me will be loved by my Father, and I will love him and reveal myself to him." Judas, not Iscariot, said to him: " Why has it happened that you are going to reveal yourself to us, and not to the world? " Jesus answered: " If any man loves me, he will keep my word; and the Father will love him, and we will come to him, and we will make our abode with him. He who does not love me does not keep my words. And the word which you hear is not mine, but it belongs to the Father who sent me."

By this time a sense of foreboding must have enveloped the disciples. Even they must now have seen that there was tragedy ahead. But Jesus says: " I will not leave you forlorn." The word he uses is *orphanos*. It means *without a father*, but it was also used of disciples and students bereft of the presence and the teaching of a beloved master. Plato says that, when Socrates died, his disciples " thought that they would have to spend the rest of their lives forlorn as children bereft of a father, and they did not know what to do about it." But Jesus told his disciples that would not be the case with them. " I am coming back," he said.

He is talking of his Resurrection and his risen presence. They will see him because *he* will be alive; and because *they* will be alive. What he means is that they will be spiritually alive. At the

moment they are bewildered and numbed with the sense of
impending tragedy; but the day will come when their eyes will
be opened, their minds will understand and their hearts will be
kindled—and then they will really see him. That in fact is
precisely what happened when Jesus rose from the dead. His
rising changed despair to hope and it was then they realized
beyond a doubt that he was the Son of God.

In this passage John is playing on certain ideas which are
never far from his mind.

(i) First and foremost there is love. For John love is the basis
of everything. God loves Jesus; Jesus loves God; God loves
men; Jesus loves men; men love God through Jesus; men love
each other; heaven and earth, man and God, man and man are
all bound together by the bond of love.

(ii) Once again John stresses the necessity of obedience, the
only proof of love. It was to those who loved him that Jesus
appeared when he rose from the dead, not to the scribes and the
Pharisees and the hostile Jews.

(iii) This obedient, trusting love leads to two things. First, it
leads to ultimate safety. On the day of Christ's triumph those
who have been his obedient lovers will be safe in a crashing
world. Second, it leads to a fuller and fuller revelation. The
revelation of God is a costly thing. There is always a moral
basis for it; it is to the man who keeps his commandments that
Christ reveals himself. No evil man can ever receive the
revelation of God. He can be used by God, but he can have no
fellowship with him. It is only to the man who is looking for
him that God reveals himself; and it is only to the man who, in
spite of failure, is reaching up that God reaches down. Fellowship with God and the revelation of God are dependent on love;
and love is dependent on obedience. The more we obey God,
the more we understand him; and the man who walks in his
way inevitably walks with him.

THE BEQUESTS OF CHRIST

John 14: 25–31

> " I have spoken these things to you while to you while I am still with you. The Helper, the Holy Spirit, whom the Father will send in my name, will teach you all things, and will remind you of all that I have said. I am leaving you peace: I am giving you my peace. I do not give it to you as the world gives peace. Let not your heart be distressed or fear-stricken. You have heard that I said to you: ' I am going away and I am coming to you.' If you loved me, you would be glad that I am going to my Father, because the Father is greater than I. And now I have told you about it before it happens, so that whenever it does happen, you will believe. I shall not say much more to you, because the prince of this world is coming. He has no hold over me. His coming will only make the world know that I love the Father, and that I do as the Father has commanded me. Rise, let us be going."

THIS is a passage close-packed with truth. In it Jesus speaks of five things.

(i) He speaks of his *ally*, the Holy Spirit, and says two basic things about him.

(*a*) The Holy Spirit will teach us all things. To the end of the day the Christian must be a learner, for to the end of the day the Holy Spirit will be leading him deeper and deeper into the truth of God. There is never any excuse in the Christian faith for the shut mind. The Christian who feels that he has nothing more to learn is the Christian who has not even begun to understand what the doctrine of the Holy Spirit means.

(*b*) The Holy Spirit will remind us of what Jesus has said. This means two things. 1. In matters of belief, the Holy Spirit is constantly bringing back to us the things Jesus said. We have an obligation to think, but all our conclusions must be tested against the words of Jesus. It is not so much the truth that we have to discover; he told us the truth. What we have to discover is the meaning of that truth. The Holy Spirit saves us from arrogance and error of thought. 2. The Holy Spirit will keep us right in matters of conduct. Nearly all of us have this sort of experience in life. We are tempted to do something wrong and are on the very brink of doing it, when back into our mind comes a saying of Jesus, the verse of a psalm, the picture of Jesus, words of someone we love and admire, teaching we received when very young. In the moment of danger these things flash unbidden into our minds. That is the work of the Holy Spirit.

(ii) He speaks of his *gift*, and his gift is *peace*. In the Bible the word for *peace*, *shalōm*, never means simply the absence of trouble. It means everything which makes for our highest good. The peace which the world offers us is the peace of escape, the peace which comes from the avoidance of trouble and from refusing to face things. The peace which Jesus offers us is the peace of conquest. No experience of life can ever take it from us and no sorrow, no danger, no suffering can ever make it less. It is independent of outward circumstances.

(iii) He speaks of his *destination*. He is going back to his Father; and he says that if his disciples really loved him, they would be glad that it was so. He was being released from the limitations of this world; he was being restored to his glory. If we really grasped the truth of the Christian faith, we would always be glad when those whom we love go to be with God. That is not to say that we would not feel the sting of sorrow and the sharpness of loss; but even in our sorrow and our loneliness, we would be glad that after the troubles and the trials of earth those whom we loved have gone to something better. We would never grudge them their rest but would remember that they had entered, not into death, but into blessedness.

(iv) He speaks of his *struggle*. The Cross was the final battle of Jesus with the powers of evil. But he was not afraid of it, for he knew that evil had no ultimate power over him. He went to his death in the certainty, not of defeat, but of conquest.

(v) He speaks of his *vindication*. At the moment men saw in the Cross only his humiliation and his shame; but the time would come when they would see in it his obedience to God and his love to men. The very things which were the keynotes of Jesus's life found their highest expression in the Cross.

THE VINE AND THE BRANCHES

John 15: 1–10

" I am the real vine and my Father is the vine-dresser. He destroys every branch in me which does not bear fruit; and he cleanses every branch which does bear fruit, so that it may bear more fruit. You are already clean through the word which I have spoken to you. Abide in me even as I abide in you. As the branch cannot bear fruit in its own strength, unless it abides in the vine, so neither can you, unless you abide in me. I am the vine; you are the branches. The man who abides in me, and in whom I abide, bears much fruit, because without me you can do nothing. If anyone does not abide in me he will be cast out like a withered branch. And they gather such branches and throw them into the fire and they are burned. If you abide in me, and my words abide in you, ask what you will, and it will be given to you. It is by the fact that you bear such fruit, and that you show yourselves to be my disciples, that my Father is glorified. As the Father has loved me, so I have loved you. Abide in my love. As I have kept my Father's commandments, so I abide in his love."

JESUS, as so often, is working in this passage with pictures and ideas which were part of the religious heritage of the Jewish nation. Over and over again in the Old Testament, Israel is pictured as the vine or the vineyard of God. " The vineyard of the Lord is the house of Israel " (*Isaiah* 5: 1–7). " Yet I planted you a choice vine " is God's message to Israel through Jeremiah (*Jeremiah* 2: 21). *Ezekiel* 15 likens Israel to the vine, as does *Ezekiel* 19: 10. " Israel is a luxuriant vine," said Hosea (*Hosea* 10: 1). " Thou didst bring a vine out of Egypt," sang the Psalmist, thinking of God's deliverance of his people from bondage (*Psalm* 80: 8). The vine had actually become the symbol of the nation of Israel. It was the emblem on the coins of the Maccabees. One of the glories of the Temple was the great golden vine upon the front of the Holy Place. Many a great man had counted it an honour to give gold to mould a new bunch of grapes or even a new grape on to that vine. The

vine was part and parcel of Jewish imagery, and the very
symbol of Israel.

Jesus calls himself the *true* vine. The point of that word
alēthinos, true, real, genuine, is this. It is a curious fact that the
symbol of the vine is never used in the Old Testament apart
from the idea of *degeneration*. The point of Isaiah's picture is
that the vineyard has run wild. Jeremiah complains that the
nation has turned into " degenerate and become a wild vine." It
is as if Jesus said: " You think that because you belong to the
nation of Israel you are a branch of the true vine of God. But
the nation it is; a degenerate vine, as all your prophets saw. It is
I who am the true vine. The fact that you are a Jew will not save
you. The only thing that can save you is to have an intimate
living fellowship with *me*, for I am the vine of God and you
must be branches joined to me." Jesus was laying it down that
not Jewish blood but faith in him was the way to God's
salvation. No external qualification can set a man right with
God; only the friendship of Jesus Christ can do that.

THE VINE AND THE BRANCHES

John 15: 1–10 (*continued*)

WHEN Jesus drew his picture of the vine he knew what he was
talking about. The vine was grown all over Palestine as it still is.
It is a plant which needs a great deal of attention if the best fruit
is to be got out of it. It is grown commonly on terraces. The
ground has to be perfectly clean. It is sometimes trained on
trellisses; it is sometimes allowed to creep over the ground
upheld by low forked sticks; it sometimes even grows round the
doors of the cottages; but wherever it grows careful preparation
of the soil is essential. It grows luxuriantly and drastic pruning is necessary. So luxuriant is it that the slips are set in
the ground at least twelve feet apart, for it will creep over the
ground at speed. A young vine is not allowed to fruit for the
first three years and each year is cut drastically back to develop

and conserve its life and energy. When mature, it is pruned in December and January. It bears two kinds of branches, one that bears fruit and one that does not; and the branches that do not bear fruit are drastically pruned back, so that they will drain away none of the plant's strength. The vine can not produce the crop of which it is capable without drastic pruning—and Jesus knew that.

Further, the wood of the vine has the curious characteristic that it is good for nothing. It is too soft for any purpose. At certain times of the year, it was laid down by the law, the people must bring offerings of wood to the Temple for the altar fires. But the wood of the vine must not be brought. The only thing that could be done with the wood pruned out of a vine was to make a bonfire of it and destroy it. This adds to the picture Jesus draws.

He says that his followers are like that. Some of them are lovely fruit-bearing branches of himself; others are useless because they bear no fruit. Who was Jesus thinking of when he spoke of the fruitless branches? There are two answers. First, he was thinking of the Jews. They were branches of God's vine. Was not that the picture that prophet after prophet had drawn? But they refused to listen to him; they refused to accept him; therefore they were withered and useless branches. Second, he was thinking of something more general. He was thinking of Christians whose Christianity consisted of profession without practice, words without deeds; he was thinking of Christians who were useless branches, all leaves and no fruit. And he was thinking of Christians who became apostates, who heard the message and accepted it and then fell away, becoming traitors to the Master they had once pledged themselves to serve.

So then there are three ways in which we can be useless branches. We can refuse to listen to Jesus Christ at all. We can listen to him, and then render him a lip service unsupported by any deeds. We can accept him as Master, and then, in face of the difficulties of the way or the desire to do as we like, abandon him. One thing we must remember. It is a first principle of the New Testament that *uselessness invites disaster*. The fruitless branch is on the way to destruction.

THE VINE AND THE BRANCHES

John 15: 1–10 (*continued*)

IN this passage there is much about abiding in Christ. What is meant by that? It is true that there is a mystical sense in which the Christian is in Christ and Christ is in the Christian. But there are many—maybe they are in the majority—who never have this mystical experience. If we are like that, we must not blame ourselves. There is a much simpler way of looking at this and of experiencing it, a way open to anyone.

Let us take a human analogy. All analogies are imperfect but we must work with the ideas which we possess. Suppose a person is weak. He has fallen to temptation; he has made a mess of things; he is on the way down to degeneracy of mind and heart and mental fibre. Now suppose that he has a friend of a strong and lovely and loving nature, who rescues him from his degraded situation. There is only one way in which he can retain his reformation and keep himself on the right way. *He must keep contact with his friend.* If he loses that contact; all the chances are that his weakness will overcome him; the old temptations will rear their heads again; and he will fall. His salvation lies in continual contact with the strength of his friend.

Many a time a down-and-out has been taken to live with someone fine. So long as he continued in that fine home and that fine presence he was safe. But when he kicked over the traces and went off on his own, he fell. We must keep contact with the fine thing in order to defeat the evil thing. Robertson of Brighton was one of the great preachers. There was a tradesman who had a little shop; in the back room he kept a photograph of Robertson, for he was his hero and his inspiration. Whenever he was tempted to carry out a bit of sharp practice, he would rush into the back room and look at the photograph and the temptation was defeated. When Kingsley was asked the secret of his life, referring to F. D. Maurice he

said: " I had a friend." The contact with loveliness made him
lovely.

Abiding in Christ means something like that. The secret of
the life of Jesus was his contact with God; again and again he
withdrew into a solitary place to meet him. We must keep
contact with Jesus. We cannot do that unless we deliberately
take steps to do it. To take but one example—to pray in the
morning, if it be for only a few moments, is to have an
antiseptic for the whole day; for we cannot come out of the
presence of Christ to touch the evil things. For some few of us,
abiding in Christ will be a mystical experience which is beyond
words to express. For most of us, it will mean a constant
contact with him. It will mean arranging life, arranging prayer,
arranging silence in such a way that there is never a day when
we give ourselves a chance to forget him.

Finally, we must note that here there are two things laid
down about the good disciple. First, he enriches his own life; his
contact makes him a fruitful branch. Second, he brings glory to
God; the sight of his life turns men's thoughts to the God who
made him like that. God is glorified, when we bear much fruit
and show ourselves to be disciples of Jesus. The greatest glory
of the Christian life is that by our life and conduct we can bring
glory to God.

THE LIFE OF JESUS'S CHOSEN PEOPLE

John 15: 11–17

" I have spoken these things to you that my joy might be in you,
and that your joy might be complete. This is my commandment,
that you love one another, as I have loved you. No one has greater
love than this, that a man should lay down his life for his friend.
You are my friends, if you do what I command you. I no longer
call you slaves, because the slave does not know what his master
is doing. I have called you friends because I have made known to
you everything that I heard from my Father. You have not chosen
me, but I have chosen you, and I have appointed you to go out

and to bear fruit, of such a kind that it will remain. I have done so,
so that the Father will give you whatever you ask him in my
name. These are my orders to you, that you love one another."

THE central words of this passage are those in which Jesus says
that his disciples have not chosen him, but he has chosen them.
It was not we who chose God, but God who, in his grace,
approached us with a call and an offer made out of his love.

Out of this passage we can compile a list of things for which
we are chosen and to which we are called.

(i) We are chosen for *joy*. However hard the Christian way
is, it is, both in the travelling and in the goal, the way of joy.
There is always a joy in doing the right thing. The Christian
is the man of joy, the laughing cavalier of Christ. A gloomy
Christian is a contradiction in terms, and nothing in all religious
history has done Christianity more harm than its connection
with black clothes and long faces. It is true that the Christian
is a sinner, but he is a *redeemed* sinner; and therein lies his joy.
How can any man fail to be happy when he walks the ways of
life with Jesus?

(ii) We are chosen for *love*. We are sent out into the world to
love one another. Sometimes we live as if we were sent into the
world to compete with one another, or to dispute with one
another, or even to quarrel with one another. But the Christian
is to live in such a way that he shows what is meant by loving
his fellow men. It is here that Jesus makes another of his great
claims. If we ask him: What right have you to demand that we
love one another? His answer is: " No man can show greater
love than to lay down his life for his friends—and I did that."
Many a man tells men to love each other, when his whole life is
a demonstration that that is the last thing he does himself. Jesus
gave men a commandment which he had himself first fulfilled.

(iii) Jesus called us to be *his friends*. He tells his men that he
does not call them slaves any more; he calls them friends. Now
that is a saying which would be even greater to those who heard
it for the first time than it is to us. *Doulos*, the slave, the servant ✓
of God was no title of shame; it was a title of the highest
honour. Moses was the *doulos* of God (*Deuteronomy* 34: 5); so

was Joshua (*Joshua* 24: 29); so was David (*Psalm* 89: 20). It is
a title which Paul counted it an honour to use (*Titus* 1: 1); and
so did James (*James* 1: 1). The greatest men in the past had
been proud to be called the *douloi*, the slaves of God.
And Jesus says: "I have something greater for you yet, you are
no longer *slaves*; you are *friends*." Christ offers an intimacy
with God which not even the greatest men knew before he came
into the world.

The idea of being the friend of God has also a background.
Abraham was the *friend* of God (*Isaiah* 41: 8). In *Wisdom* 7: 27
Wisdom is said to make men the friends of God. But this phrase
is lit up by a custom which obtained both at the courts of the
Roman Emperors and of the eastern kings. At these courts
there was a very select group of men called *the friends of the
king*, or *the friends of the Emperor*. At all times they had access
to the king: they had even the right to come to his bedchamber
at the beginning of the day. He talked to them before he talked
to his generals, his rulers, and his statesmen. The friends of the
king were those who had the closest and the most intimate
connection with him.

Jesus called us to be his friends and the friends of God. That
is a tremendous offer. It means that no longer do we need to
gaze longingly at God from afar off; we are not like slaves who
have no right whatever to enter into the presence of the master;
we are not like a crowd whose only glimpse of the king is in the
passing on some state occasion. Jesus gave us this intimacy
with God, so that he is no longer a distant stranger, but our
close friend.

THE LIFE OF JESUS'S CHOSEN PEOPLE

John 15: 11–17 (*continued*)

(iv) Jesus did not only choose us for a series of tremendous
privileges. He called us to be his *partners*. The slave could never
be a partner. He was defined in Greek law as *a living tool*. His

master never opened his mind to him; the slave simply had to do what he was told without reason and without explanation. But Jesus said: " You are not my slaves; you are my partners. I have told you everything; I have told you what I am trying to do, and why I am trying to do it. I have told you everything which God told me." Jesus has given us the honour of making us partners in his task. He has shared his mind with us, and opened his heart to us. The tremendous choice laid before us is that we can accept or refuse partnership with Christ in the work of leading the world to God.

(v) Jesus chose to be *ambassadors*. " I have chosen you," he said, " *to send you out*." He did not choose us to live a life retired from the world, but to represent him in the world. When a knight came to the court of King Arthur, he did not come to spend the rest of his days in knightly feasting and in knightly fellowship there. He came to the king saying: " Send me out on some great task which I can do for chivalry and for you." Jesus chose us, first to come in to him, and then to go out to the world. And that must be the daily pattern and rhythm of our lives.

(vi) Jesus chose us to be *advertisements*. He chose us to go out *to bear fruit*, and to bear fruit which will stand the test of time. The way to spread Christianity is to be Christian. The way to bring others into the Christian faith is to show them the fruit of the Christian life. Jesus sends us out, not to argue men into Christianity, still less to threaten them into it, but to attract them into it; so to live that its fruits may be so wonderful that others will desire them for themselves.

(vii) Jesus chose us to be *privileged members of the family of God*. He chose us so that whatever we ask in his name the Father will give to us. Here again we are face to face with one of those great sayings about prayer which we must understand aright. If we come to it thoughtlessly, it sounds as if the Christian will receive everything for which he prays. We have already thought about this, but we may well think about it again. The New Testament lays down certain definite laws about prayer.

(*a*) Prayer must be *the prayer of faith* (*James* 5: 15). When it is a formality, merely the routine and conventional repetition of a form of words, it cannot be answered. When prayer is hopeless it cannot be effective. There is little use in a man praying to be changed, if he does not believe it possible that he can be changed. To pray with power a man must have an invincible belief in the all-sufficient love of God.

(*b*) Prayer must be *in the name of Christ*. We cannot pray for things of which we know that Jesus would disapprove. We cannot pray that we should be given possession of some forbidden person or some forbidden thing; we cannot pray that some personal ambition should be realized, if that ambition means that someone else must be hurt to fulfil it. We cannot pray in the name of him who is love for vengeance on our enemies. Whenever we try to turn prayer into something to enable us to realize our own ambitions and to satisfy our own desires, it must be ineffective, for it is not real prayer at all.

(*c*) Prayer must say: " *Thy will be done.*" When we pray we must first realize that we never know better than God. The essence of prayer is not that we say to God: " Thy will be changed," but that we say to him: " Thy will be done." So often real prayer must be, not that God would send us the things we wish, but that he would make us able to accept the things he wills.

(*d*) Prayer must never be *selfish*. Almost in the passing Jesus said a very illuminating thing. He said that, *if two people agreed* in asking anything in his name, it would be granted (*Matthew* 18: 19). We are not to take that with a crude literalism, because it would simply mean that if you can mobilize enough people to pray for anything you will get it. What it does mean is this—no man when he prays should think entirely of his own needs. To take the simplest example, the holiday-maker might be praying for sunshine while the farmer is praying for rain. When we pray, we must ask, not only: " Is this for my good? " but: " Is this for the good of all men? " The greatest temptation of all in prayer is to pray as if nobody but ourselves mattered.

Jesus chose us to be privileged members of the family of

God. We can and must take everything to God in prayer; but when we have done so we must accept the answer which God in his perfect wisdom and perfect love sends to us. And the more we love God, the easier it will be to do that.

THE WORLD'S HATRED

John 15: 18–21

" If the world hates you, you know that it hated me before it hated you. If you were of the world, the world would love its own; but the world hates you, because you are not of the world, but I have picked you out of the world. Remember the word which I spoke to you—the servant is not greater than his master. If they persecuted me, they will persecute you. If they kept my word, they will keep yours. But they will do these things to you because of my name, because they do not know him who sent me."

IT is always John's way to see things in terms of black and white. To him there are two great entities—the Church and the world. And there is no contact and no fellowship between them. To John it is,

" Stand thou on that side, for on this am I."

As he saw it, a man is either of the world or of Christ, and there is no stage between.

Further, we must remember that by this time the Church was living under the constant threat of persecution. Christians were indeed persecuted because of the name of Christ. Christianity was illegal. A magistrate needed only to ask whether or not a man was a Christian, and, if he was, no matter what he had done or had not done, he was liable to punishment by death. John was speaking of a situation which existed in the most clear-cut and agonizing way.

One thing is certain—no Christian who was involved in persecution could say that he had not been warned. On this matter Jesus was quite explicit. He had told his people before-hand what they might expect. " They will deliver you up to councils; and you will be beaten in synagogues and you will stand before governors and kings for my sake, to bear testimony before them.... And brother will deliver up brother to death, and the father his child, and children will rise against parents and have them put to death; and you will be hated by all for my name's sake " (*Mark* 13: 9–13; cp. *Matthew* 10: 17–22; 23–29; *Luke* 12: 2–9; 51–53).

When John wrote, this hatred had long since begun. Tacitus spoke of the people " hated for their crimes, whom the mob call Christians." Suetonius had spoken of " a race of men who belong to a new and evil superstition." Why was this hatred so virulent?

The Roman government hated the Christians because it regarded them as disloyal citizens. The position of the government was quite simple and understandable. The Empire was vast; it stretched from the Euphrates to Britain, from Germany to North Africa. It included all kinds of peoples and all kinds of countries within it. Some unifying force had to be found to weld this varied mass into one; and it was found in Caesar worship.

Now Caesar worship was not imposed on the world; it actually arose from the people themselves. Away back in the old days there had been the goddess Roma —the spirit of Rome. It is easy to see how men could think of that spirit of Rome symbolized in the Emperor. He stood for Rome; he embodied Rome; the spirit of Rome found its home in him. It is a great mistake to think that the subject peoples resented Roman government; for the most part they were profoundly grateful for it. Rome brought justice, and freed them from capricious kings. Rome brought peace and prosperity. The land was cleared of brigands and the sea of pirates. The *pax Romana*, the Roman peace, stretched over all the world.

It was in Asia Minor that men began to think of Caesar, the Emperor, as the god who embodied Rome, and they did so in sheer gratitude for the blessings Rome had brought. At first the Emperors discouraged and deprecated this worship; they insisted that they were men and must not be worshipped as gods. But they saw that they could not stop this movement. At first they confined it to the excitable Asiatics of Asia Minor, but soon it spread everywhere. Then the government saw that they could use it. Here was the unifying principle which was needed. So there came the day when once a year every inhabitant of the Empire had to burn his pinch of incense to the godhead of Caesar. By so doing, he showed that he was a loyal citizen of Rome. When he had done this, he received a certificate to say that he done it.

Here was the practice and the custom which made all men feel that they were part of Rome, and which guaranteed their loyalty to her. Now Rome was the essence of toleration. After he had burned his pinch of incense and said, " Caesar is Lord," a man could go away and worship any god he liked, so long as the worship did not affect public decency and public order. But that is precisely what the Christians would not do. They would call no man " Lord " except Jesus Christ. They refused to conform, and therefore the Roman government regarded them as dangerous and disloyal.

The government persecuted the Christians because they insisted they had no king but Christ. Persecution came to the Christians because they put Christ first. Persecution always comes to the man who does that.

THE WORLD'S HATRED

John 15: 18–21 (*continued*)

IT was not only that the government persecuted the Christians; the mob hated them. Why? It was because the mob believed certain slanderous things about the Christians. There is no doubt that the Jews were at least to some extent responsible for these slanders. It so happened that they had the ear of the government. To take but two examples, Nero's favourite actor Aliturus, and his harlot empress Poppaea, were both adherents of the Jewish faith. The Jews whispered their slanders to the government, slanders which they must have well known to be untrue, and four slanderous reports were spread about the Christians.

(i) They were said to be insurrectionaries. We have already seen the reason for that. It was futile for the Christians to point out that in fact they were the best citizens in the country. The fact remained they would not burn their pinch of incense and say, " Caesar is Lord," and so they were branded as dangerous and disloyal men.

(ii) They were said to be cannibals. This charge came from the words of the sacrament. " This is my body which is for you." " This cup is the new covenant in my blood." On the basis of these words, it was not difficult to disseminate amongst ignorant people, prepared to believe the worst, the story that the Christians' private meal was based on cannibalism. The charge stuck, and it is little wonder that the mob looked on the Christians with loathing.

(iii) They were said to practise the most flagrant immorality. The weekly meal of the Christians was called the *Agapē*, the Love Feast. When the Christians met each other in the early days they greeted each other with the kiss of peace. It was not difficult to spread abroad the report that the Love Feast was an orgy of sexual indulgence, of which the kiss of peace was the symbol and the sign.

(iv) They were said to be incendiaries. They looked to the Second Coming of Christ. To it they had attached all the Old Testament pictures of the Day of the Lord, which foretold of the flaming disintegration and destruction of the world. " The elements will be dissolved with fire, and the earth and the works that are upon it will be burned up " (2 *Peter* 3: 10). In the reign of Nero came the disastrous fire which devastated Rome and it was easy to connect it with people who preached of the consuming fire which would destroy the world.

(v) There was actually another charge brought and for this fifth charge there were understandable grounds. It was that the Christians " tampered with family relationships," divided families, split up homes and broke up marriages. In a way that was true. Christianity did bring not peace but a sword

(*Matthew* 10: 34). Often a wife became a Christian and a husband did not. Often children became Christians and parents did not. Then the home was split in two and the family divided.

These were the charges which were spread about the Christians with the help of the Jews. It is little wonder that the name of Christian was hated.

THE WORLD'S HATRED

John 15: 18–21 (*continued*)

SUCH were the causes of hatred in the early days. but it is still true that the world will hate the Christian. As we have already said, by the *world* John meant *human society organizing itself without God*. There is bound to be a cleavage between the man who regards God as the only reality in life and the man who regards God as totally irrelevant for life. In any event the world has certain characteristics, which are always part of the human situation.

(i) The world suspects people who are different. That comes out in the simplest ways. One of the commonest things in the world nowadays is an umbrella; but when Jonas Hanway tried to introduce the umbrella into England and walked down the street beneath one he was pelted with stones and dirt. In the early days of the Boys' Brigade, the boys who marched down the street in uniform often received similar treatment. Anyone who is different, who wears different clothes, who has different ideas, is automatically suspect. He may be regarded as an eccentric or a madman or a danger; but life is likely to be made uncomfortable for him.

(ii) The world acutely dislikes people whose lives are a condemnation of it. It is in fact dangerous to be good. The classic instance is the fate which befell Aristides in Athens. He was called Aristides the Just; and yet he was banished. When one of the citizens was asked why he had voted for his banishment, he answered: " Because I am tired of hearing him always called the Just." That was why men killed Socrates; they called him the human gadfly. He was always compelling men to think and to examine themselves, and men hated that and killed him. It is dangerous to practise a higher standard than the standard of the world. Nowadays a man can be persecuted even for working too hard or too long.

(ii) To put it at its widest—the world always suspects nonconformity. It likes a pattern; it likes to be able to label a person and to put him in a pigeon-hole. Anyone who does not conform to the pattern will certainly meet trouble. It is even said that if a hen with different markings is put among hens that are all alike, the others will peck her to death.

The basic demand on the Christian is the demand that he should have the courage to be different. To be different will be dangerous, but no man can be a Christian unless he accepts that risk, for there must be a difference between the man of the world and the man of Christ.

KNOWLEDGE AND RESPONSIBILITY

John 15: 22–25

" If I had not come and spoken to them, they would not be guilty of sin. As it is, they have no excuse for their sins. He who hates me hates the Father too. If I had not done deeds among them, which no one else had ever done, they would not be guilty of sin. As it is, they have seen and they have heard both me and my Father. But it has all happened that the word which stands written in their law might be fulfilled—' They have hated me without a cause.' "

HERE Jesus has returned to a thought which in the Fourth Gospel is never far from his mind, the conviction that knowledge and privilege bring with them responsibility. Until Jesus came men never had the opportunity really to know God; they had never fully heard his voice, and they had never seen perfectly demonstrated the kind of life he wished them to live. They could scarcely be blamed for being such as they were.

There are things which are allowable in a child which are not allowable in an adult, because the child does not know any better. There are things which are allowable in someone whose upbringing has been bad which are not allowable in someone who has been brought up in all the benefits of a Christian home. No one expects the same kind of conduct from a savage as from a civilized man. The more knowledge a man has and the more privileges he enjoys, the greater the responsibility laid upon him.

Jesus did two things. First, he exposed sin. He told men of the things which grieved God and of the way in which God wished them to walk. He set the true way before men. Second, he provided the remedy for sin; and he did that in a double sense. He opened the way to forgiveness for past sin, and he provided the power which would enable a man to overcome sin and do the right. These were the privileges and the knowledge which he brought to men. Suppose a man to be ill; suppose he consults a doctor, and the doctor diagnoses what is wrong and prescribes a cure. If that man disregards the diagnosis and refuses to use the cure, he has no one to blame but himself if he dies, or comes to a condition which makes life wretched for himself. That is what the Jews had done. As John saw it, they had only done what it was foretold they would do. Twice the Psalmist had said: " They hated me without a cause " (*Psalm* 35: 19; 69:4).

It is still possible for us to do the same. Not many are actively hostile to Christ, but many live their lives as if Christ had never come and simply disregard him. But no man can know life in this world or in the world to come if he disregards the Lord of all good life.

WITNESS DIVINE AND HUMAN

John 15: 26, 27

" When the Helper comes, the Helper whom I will send to you from my Father, I mean the Spirit of Truth who comes forth from

the Father, he will be a witness about me. And you will be witness
about me because you have been with me from the beginning."

HERE John uses two ideas which lie very close to his heart and
are constantly entwined in his thought.

The first is the witness of the Holy Spirit. What does he
mean by this? We shall have occasion to think of this again
very soon, but for the moment think of it this way. When the
story of Jesus is told us and his picture is set before us, what
makes us feel that this is none other than the picture of the Son
of God? That reaction of the human mind, that answer of the
human heart is the work of the Holy Spirit. It is the Holy Spirit
within us who moves us to respond to Jesus Christ.

The second is the witness which men must bear to Christ.
" You," said Jesus to his disciples, " will be witnesses about
me." There are three elements in Christian witness.

(i) Christian witness comes from long fellowship and intimacy with Christ. The disciples are his witnesses because they
have been with him from the beginning. A witness is a man who
says of something: " This is true, *and I know it*." There can be
no witness without personal experience. We can witness for
Christ only when we have been with him.

(ii) Christian witness comes from inner conviction. The
accent of personal inner conviction is one of the most unmis-
takable in the world. A man hardly starts to speak before we
know whether or not he really believes what he is saying. There
can be no effective Christian witness without this inner conviction which comes from personal intimacy with Christ.

(iii) Christian witness issues in outward testimony. A witness
is not only someone who knows that something is true; he is
someone who is prepared to say that he knows that it is true. A
Christian witness is a man who not only knows Christ but
wants others to know him too.

It is our privilege and our task to be witnesses for Christ in
the world; and we cannot be witnesses without the personal
intimacy, the inner conviction and the outward testimony to
our faith.

WARNING AND CHALLENGE

John 16: 1–4

> " I have spoken these things to you in case you should be caused
> to stumble in the way. They will excommunicate you from the
> synagogue. Yes, a time is coming when anyone who kills you will
> think that he is rendering a service to God; and they will do these
> things because they did not recognize the Father or me. But I have
> spoken these things to you, so that when their time comes, you
> will remember that I spoke them to you."

BY the time John was writing it was inevitable that some
Christians should fall away, for persecution had struck the
Church. *Revelation* condemns those who are unbelieving and
fearful (*Revelation* 21: 8). When Pliny, the governor of
Bithynia, was examining people to see whether or not they were
Christians, he wrote to his emperor Trajan to say that some
admitted " that they had been Christians, but they had ceased
to be so many years ago, some as much as twenty years ago."
Even amidst the heroism of the early Church, there were those
whose faith was not great enough to resist persecution and
whose endurance was not strong enough to stay the course.

Jesus foresaw this and gave warning beforehand. He did not
want anyone to be able to say that he had not known what
to expect when he became a Christian. When Tyndale was
persecuted and his enemies were out for his life because he
sought to give the Bible to the people in the English language,
he said calmly: " I never expected anything else." Jesus offered
men glory, but he offered them a cross as well.

Jesus spoke of two ways in which his followers would be
persecuted.

They would be excommunicated from the synagogue. This
for a Jew would be a very hard fate. The synagogue, the House
of God, had a very special place in Jewish life. Some of the
Rabbis went the length of saying that prayer was not effective
unless it was offered in the synagogue. But there was more to it

than that. It may be that a great scholar or a great theologian
does not need human company; he may be able to live alone
and solitary, keeping company with the great thoughts and
adventures of his mind. But the disciples were simple folk; they
needed fellowship. They needed the synagogue and its worship.
It would be hard for them to be ostracized, with all doors shut
against them. Men have sometimes to learn, as Joan of Arc
said, that: " It is better to be alone with God." Sometimes
loneliness among men is the price of fellowship with God.

Jesus also said that men would think they were rendering a
service to God when they killed his followers. The word Jesus
uses for service is *latreia*, which is the normal word for the
service that a priest rendered at the altar in the Temple of God
and is the standard word for religious service. One of the
tragedies of religion has been that men have so often thought
that they were serving God by persecuting those whom they
believed to be heretics. No man ever more truly thought that he
was serving God than Paul did, when he was trying to eliminate
the name of Jesus and to wipe out the Church (*Acts* 26: 9–11).
The torturers and judges of the Spanish Inquisition have left
a name which is loathed; yet they were quite sure that they
were serving God by torturing heretics into accepting what
they considered to be the true faith. As they saw it, they were
saving men from hell. " O Liberty," said Madame Roland, " what
crimes are committed in thy name! " And that is also true of
religion.

It happens, as Jesus said, because they do not recognize God.
The tragedy of the Church is that men have so often laboured
to propagate *their* idea of religion; they have so often believed
that *they* have a monopoly of God's truth and grace. The staggering fact is that it still happens; that is the barrier to union
and unity between the Churches. There will always be persecution—not necessarily killing and torture, but exclusion from the
house of God—so lonr as men believe that there is only one
way to him.

Jesus knew how to deal with men. He was in effect saying:
" I am offering you the hardest task in the world. I am offering

you something which will lacerate your body and tear out your heart. Are you big enough to accept it? " All the world knows Garibaldi's proclamation at the siege of Rome in 1849, when he appealed for recruits in these terms: " I offer neither pay, nor quarters, nor provisions; I offer hunger, thirst, forced marches, battles and death. Let him who loves his country in his heart, and not with his lips only, follow me." And join they did in their hundreds. When the Spaniards were conquering South America Pizarro presented his men with a choice. They might have the wealth of Peru with its dangers, or the comparative poverty of Panama with its safety. He drew a line in the sand with his sword and he said: " Comrades, on that side are toil, hunger, nakedness, storm, desertion and death; on this side is ease. There lies Peru with its riches; here lies Panama with its poverty. Choose, each man, what best becomes a brave Castilian. For my part, I go to the south." There was silence and hesitation; and then an old pilot and twelve soldiers stepped across to Pizarro's side. It was with them that the discovery and the conquest of Peru began.

Jesus offered, and still offers, not the way of ease, but the way of glory. He wants men who are prepared with open eyes to venture for his name.

THE WORK OF THE HOLY SPIRIT

John 16: 5–11

" I did not tell you these things at the beginning, because I was with you. But now I am going away to him who sent me, and none of you asks me: ' Where are you going? ' But grief has filled your hearts because I have spoken these things to you. But it is the truth I am telling you—it is to your interest that I should go away, for If I do not go away the Helper will not come to you. But when he has come, he will convict the world of sin, and convince it of righteousness and judgment; of sin, because they do not believe in me; of righteousness, because I go to my Father, and you no longer see me; of judgment, because the ruler of this world is judged."

THE disciples were bewildered and grief-stricken men. All they knew was that they were going to lose Jesus. But he told them that in the end this was all for the best, because, when he went away, the Holy Spirit, the Helper, would come. When he was in the body he could not be everywhere with them; it was always a case of greetings and farewells. When he was in the body, he could not reach the minds and hearts and consciences of men everywhere, he was confined by the limitations of place and time. But there are no limitations in the Spirit. Everywhere a man goes the Spirit is with him. The coming of the Spirit would be the fulfilment of the promise: " Lo, I am with you always, to the close of the age " (*Matthew* 28: 20). The Spirit would bring to men an uninterrupted fellowship for ever; and would bring to the Christian preacher a power and an effectiveness no matter where he preached.

We have here an almost perfect summary of the work of the Spirit. The word that John uses of the work of the Spirit is the word *elegchein*, translated *convince* by the Revised Standard Version. The trouble is that no one word can translate it adequately. It is used for the cross-examination of a witness, or a man on trial, or an opponent in an argument. It has always this idea of crossexamining a man until he sees and admits his errors, or acknowledges the force of some argument which he had not yet seen. It is, for instance, sometimes used by the Greeks for the action of conscience on a man's mind and heart. Clearly such cross-examination can do two things—it can *convict* a man of the crime he has committed or the wrong that he has done; or it can *convince* a man of the weakness of his own case and the strength of the case which he has opposed. In this passage we need *both* meanings, both *convict* and *convince*. Now let us go on to see what Jesus says the Holy Spirit will do.

(i) The Holy Spirit will *convict men of sin*. When the Jews crucified Jesus, they did not believe that they were sinning; they believed that they were serving God. But when the story of that crucifixion was later preached, they were pricked in their heart (*Acts* 2: 37). They suddenly had the terrible conviction that the crucifixion was the greatest crime in history and that their sin

had caused it. What is it that gives a man a sense of sin? What
is it that abases him in face of the Cross? In an Indian village a
missionary was telling the story of Christ by means of lantern
slides flung on the white-washed wall of a village house. When
the picture of the Cross was shown, an Indian stepped forward,
as if he could not help it: " Come down! " he cried. " I should
be hanging there—not you." Why should the sight of a man
crucified as a criminal in Palestine two thousand years ago tear
the hearts of people open throughout the centuries and still
today? *It is the work of the Holy Spirit.*

(ii) The Holy Spirit will *convince men of righteousness*. It
becomes clear what this means when we see that it is *Jesus
Christ's righteousness* of which men will be convinced. Jesus
was crucified as a criminal. He was tried; he was found guilty;
he was regarded by the Jews as an evil heretic, and by the
Romans as a dangerous character; he was given the punishment that the worst criminals had to suffer, branded as a felon
and an enemy of God. What changed that? What made men see
in this crucified figure the Son of God, as the centurion saw at
the Cross (*Matthew* 27: 54) and Paul on the Damascus Road
(*Acts* 9: 1–9)? It is amazing that men should put their trust for
all eternity in a crucified Jewish criminal. *It is the work of the
Holy Spirit.* It is he who convinces men of the sheer righteousness of Christ, backed by the fact that Jesus rose again and
went to his Father.

(iii) The Holy Spirit *convinces men of judgment*. On the
Cross evil stands condemned and defeated. What makes a man
feel certain that judgment lies ahead? *It is the work of the Holy
Spirit.* It is he who gives us the inner and unshakable conviction
that we shall all stand before the judgment seat of God.

(iv) There remains one thing which at the moment John does
not go on to mention. When we are convicted of our own sin,
when we are convinced of Christ's righteousness, when we are
convinced of judgment to come, what gives us the certainty that
in the Cross of Christ is our salvation and that with Christ we
are forgiven, and saved from judgment? *This, too, is the work
of the Holy Spirit.* It is he who convinces us and makes us sure

that in this crucified figure we can find our Saviour and our Lord. The Holy Spirit convicts us of our sin and convinces us of our Saviour.

THE SPIRIT OF TRUTH

John 16: 12–15

" I have many things to say to you, but you cannot bear them now. When the Spirit of Truth has come, he will lead you into all the truth. For he will not speak on his own authority and out of his own knowledge, but he will speak all that he will hear, and he will tell you of the things to come. He will glorify me, for he will take of the things which belong to me, and will tell you of them. All things that the Father has are mine. That is why I said that the Spirit will take of the things which belong to me, and tell them to you."

To Jesus the Holy Spirit is the Spirit of Truth, whose great work is to bring God's truth to men. We have a special name for this bringing of God's truth to men; we call it *revelation*, and no passage in the New Testament shows us what we might call the principles of revelation better than this one.

(i) *Revelation is bound to be a progressive process.* Many things Jesus knew he could not at that moment tell his disciples, because they were not yet able to receive them. It is only possible to tell a man as much as he can understand. We do not start with the binomial theorem when we wish to teach a boy algebra; we work up to it. We do not start with advanced theorems when we wish to teach a child geometry; we approach them gradually. We do not start with difficult passages when we teach a lad Latin or Greek; we start with the easy and the simple things. God's revelation to men is like that. He teaches men what they are able and fit to learn. This most important fact has certain consequences.

(*a*) It is the explanation of the parts of the Old Testament which sometimes worry and distress us. *At that stage* they were all of God's truth that men could grasp. Take an actual illustration—in the Old Testament there are many passages which call for the wiping out of men and women and children when an enemy city is taken. At the back of these passages there is the great thought that Israel must not risk the taint of any heathen and lower religion. To avoid that risk, those who do not worship the true God must be destroyed. That is to say, the Jews had *at that stage* grasped the fact that the purity of religion must be safeguarded; but they wished to preserve that purity by *destroying* the heathen. When Jesus came, men came to see that the way to preserve that purity is to *convert* the heathen. The people of the Old Testament times had grasped a great truth, but only one side of it. Revelation has to be that way; God can reveal only as much as a man can understand.

(*b*) It is the proof that there is no end to God's revelation. One of the mistakes men sometimes make is to identify God's revelation *solely* with the Bible. That would be to say that since about A.D. 120, when the latest book in the New Testament was written, God has ceased to speak. But God's Spirit is *always* active; he is *always* revealing himself. It is true that his supreme and unsurpassable revelation came in Jesus; but Jesus is not just a figure in a book, he is a living person and in him God's revelation goes on. God is still leading us into greater realization of what Jesus means. He is not a God who spoke up to A.D. 120 and is now silent. He is still revealing his truth to men.

(ii) God's revelation to men is a revelation of *all* truth. It is quite wrong to think of it as confined to what we might call theological truth. The theologians and the preachers are not the only people who are inspired. When a poet delivers to men a great message in words which defy time, he is inspired. When H. F. Lyte wrote the words of *Abide with me* he had no feeling of composing them; he wrote them as to dictation. A great musician is inspired. Handel, telling of how he wrote *The Hallelujah Chorus*, said: " I saw the heavens opened, and the Great White God sitting on the Throne." When a scientist discovers something which will help the world's toil and make life better for men, when a surgeon discovers a new technique

which will save men's lives and ease their pain, when someone
discovers a new treatment which will bring life and hope to
suffering humanity, that is a revelation from God. All truth is
God's truth, and the revelation of all truth is the work of the
Holy Spirit.

(iii) That which is revealed comes from God. He is alike the
possessor and the giver of all truth. Truth is not men's
discovery; it is God's gift. It is not something which we create;
it is something already waiting to be discovered. At the back of
all truth there is God.

(iv) Revelation is the taking of the things of Jesus and
revealing their significance to us. Part of the greatness of Jesus
is his inexhaustibleness. No man has ever grasped all that he
came to say. No man has fully worked out all the significance of
his teaching for life and for belief, for the individual and for the
world, for society and for the nation. Revelation is a continual
opening out of the meaning of Jesus.

There we have the crux of the matter. Revelation comes to
us, not from any book or creed, but from a living person. The
nearer we live to Jesus, the better we will know him. The more
we become like him, the more he will be able to tell us. To enjoy
his revelation we must accept his mastery.

SORROW TURNED TO JOY

John 16: 16–24

" In a little while you will not see me any more; and again in a
little while you will see me." Some of his disciples said to each
other: " What is the meaning of this that he is saying to us—' In a
little while you will not see me, and again in a little while you will
see me '? And what does he mean when he says: ' I am going to
my Father '? What does he mean when he talks about ' A little '?
We do not know what he means." Jesus knew that they wished to
ask him their questions, and he said to them: " You are discussing
among yourselves what I meant when I said: ' In a little while you

will not see me, and again in a little while you will see me.' This is
the truth I tell you—you will weep and you will lament, but the
world will rejoice. You will be grieved, but your grief will turn into
joy. When a woman bears a child she has grief, because her hour
has come. But, when the child is born, she does not remember her
pain because of her joy that a man is born into the world. So you
too for the present have grief. But I will see you again, and your
heart will rejoice, and no one will take your joy from you. In that
day you will not have any questions to ask me. This is the truth I
tell you—the Father will give you in my name whatever you will
ask him. Up till now you have asked nothing in my name. Ask,
and you will receive, that your joy may stand complete.

HERE Jesus is looking beyond the present to the new age which
is to come. When he does, he uses a conception deeply rooted in
Jewish thought. The Jews believed that all time was divided into
two ages—the present age and the age to come. The present age
was wholly bad and wholly under condemnation; the age to
come was the golden age of God. In between the two ages,
preceding the coming of the Messiah, who would bring in the
new age, there lay the Day of the Lord; and the Day of the Lord
was to be a terrible day, when the world would be shattered into
fragments before the golden age would dawn. The Jews were in
the habit of calling that terrible between-time " the birth travail
of the days of the Messiah."

The Old Testament and the literature written between the
Testaments are both full of pictures of this terrible between-
time. " Behold the Day of the Lord comes, cruel with wrath and
fierce anger, to make the earth a desolation and to destroy its
sinners from it " (*Isaiah* 13: 9). " Let all the inhabitants of the
land tremble; for the day of the Lord is coming, it is near, a day
of darkness and gloom, a day of clouds and thick darkness "
(*Joel* 2: 1, 2). " And honour shall be turned into shame, and
strength humiliated into contempt, and probity destroyed, and
beauty shall become ugliness " (2 *Baruch* 27). " The Day of the
Lord will come as a thief, and then the heavens will pass away
with a loud noise, and the elements will be dissolved with fire,
and the earth and the works that are upon it will be burned up "

(2 *Peter* 3: 10). Such was the picture of the birthpangs of the coming of the Messiah.

Jesus knew the scriptures and these pictures were in his mind and memory. And now he was saying to his disciples: " I am leaving you; but I am coming back; the day will come when my reign will begin and my kingdom will come; but before that you will have to go through terrible things, with pain like birthpangs upon you. But, if you faithfully endure, the blessings will be very precious." Then he went on to outline the life of the Christian who endures.

(i) Sorrow will turn to joy. There may be a time when it looks as if to be a Christian brings nothing but sorrow, and to be of the world brings nothing but joy. But the day will come when the roles are reversed. The world's careless joy will turn to sorrow; and the Christian's apparent sorrow will turn to joy. The Christian must always remember, when his faith costs him dear, that this is not the end of things and that sorrow will give way to joy.

(ii) There will be two precious things about this Christian joy. (*a*) It will never be taken away. It will be independent of the chances and changes of the world. It is the simple fact that in every generation people who were suffering terribly have spoken of sweet times with Christ. The joy the world gives is at the mercy of the world. The joy which Christ gives is independent of anything the world can do. (*b*) It will be complete. In life's greatest joy there is always something lacking. It may be that somehow there lingers some regret; that there is a cloud no bigger than a man's hand to mar it; that the memory that it cannot last is always at the back of our minds. In Christian joy, the joy of the presence of Christ, there is no tinge of imperfection. It is perfect and complete.

(iii) In Christian joy the pain which went before is forgotten. The mother forgets the pain in the wonder of the child. The martyr forgets the agony in the glory of heaven. As Browning wrote of the martyr's tablet on the wall:

" I was some time in being burned.
    At last a hand came through

> The flames and drew
> My soul to Christ whom now I see;
> Sergius a brother writes for me
> This testimony on the wall.
> For me—I have forgot it all."

If a man's fidelity costs him much, he will forget the cost in the joy of being for ever with Christ.

(iv) There will be fullness of knowledge. " In that day," said Jesus, " you will not need to aks me any questions any more." In this life there are always some unanswered questions and some unsolved problems. In the last analysis we must always walk by faith and not by sight; we must always be accepting what we cannot understand. It is only fragments of the truth that we can grasp and glimpses of God that we may see; but in the age to come with Christ there will be fullness of knowledge.

As Browning had it in *Abt Vogler*:

> " The evil is null, is nought, is silence implying sound;
>> What was good shall be good, with, for evil, so much good
>> more;
>> On the earth the broken arcs; in the heaven, a perfect round.
>
> All we have willed or hoped or dreamed of good shall exist;
>> Not its semblance, but itself; no beauty, nor good, nor power
> Whose voice has gone forth, but each survives for the melodist
>> When eternity affirms the conception of an hour.
> The high that proved too high, the heroic for earth too hard,
>> The passion that left the ground to lose itself in the sky,
> Are music sent up to God by the lover and the bard;
>> Enough that he heard it once we shall hear it by-and-by."

When we are fully with Christ the time of questions will be gone and the time of answers will have come.

(iv) There will be a new relationship with God. When we really and truly know God we are able to go to him and ask him for anything. We know that the door is open; we know that his name is Father; we know that his heart is love. We are like children who never doubt that their father delights to see them or that they can talk to him as they wish. In that relationship

Jesus says we may ask for anything. But let us think of it in human terms—the only terms we have. When a child loves and trusts his father, he knows quite well that sometimes his father will say no because his wisdom and his love know best. We can become so intimate with God that we may take everything to him, but always we must end by saying: " Thy will be done."

(v) That new relationship is made possible by Jesus; it exists *in his name*. It is because of him that our joy is indestructible and perfect, that our knowledge is complete, that the new way to the heart of God is open to us. All that we have, came to us through Jesus Christ. It is in his name that we ask and receive, that we approach and are welcomed.

THE DIRECT ACCESS

John 16: 25–28

" I have spoken these things to you in sayings that are hard to understand; but the hour is coming when I will no longer speak to you in sayings that are hard to understand, but I will tell you plainly about the Father. In that day you will ask in my name. I do not say that I will ask the Father for you, because the Father himself loves you, because you have loved me and have believed that I came forth from the Father. I came forth from the Father, and I came into the world; I am leaving the world again, and I am going to the Father."

THE Revised Standard Version has it that up till now Jesus has been speaking to his disciples in figures. The Greek is *paroimia*; it is the word used for Jesus's parables, but basically it means a saying that is hard to understand, a saying whose meaning is veiled to the casual listener, a saying which demands thought before its meaning can become clear. It can, for instance, be used for the pithy sayings of wise men with whose pregnant brevity the mind must grapple; it can be used for a riddle whose meaning a man must guess as best he can. Jesus is saying: " So far I have been giving you hints and indications; I have been giving you the truth with a veil on it; I have been saying things which you had to think your way through; but now I am going to speak the truth in all its stark clarity." Then he tells them plainly that he came from God, and that he is going back to God. Here is a tremendous claim—that he is none other than the Son of God and that the Cross is not for him a criminal's death, but the way back to God.

Then Jesus says something we must ever remember. His men can approach God direct, because God loves them; he does not need to take their requests to God; they can take their own. Here is the final proof of something which must never be forgotten. Often we tend to think in terms of an angry God and a gentle Jesus; what Jesus did is presented in a way which seems to mean that he changed the attitude of God to men, and made him a God of love instead of a God of judgment. But here Jesus is saying: " You can go to God, because he loves you," and he is saying that *before the Cross.* He did not die to change God into love; he died to tell us that God is love. He came, not because God so hated the world, but because he so *loved* the world. Jesus brought to men the love of God.

He tells them that his work is done. He came from the Father, and now, by way of the Cross, he goes back. And for every man the way is open to God. He does not need to take their prayers to God; they can take their own. The lover of Christ is the beloved of God.

CHRIST AND HIS GIFTS

John 16: 29–33

His disciples said: " See! now you are speaking clearly, and you are not speaking in hard sayings. Now we know that you know all things, and that you do not need that anyone should ask you anything. Because of this we believe that you came forth from God." Jesus answered them: " So you believe at this moment? See! the hour is coming—it has come—when each of you will be scattered to your own homes, and you will leave me alone. And

yet I am not alone, because the Father is with me. I have spoken
these things to you that you might have peace in me. In the world
you will have tribulation. But courage! I have conquered the
world."

THERE is a strange light here on how the disciples finally
surrendered to Jesus. They suddenly leapt into full belief
because they realized that Jesus did not need to ask any man
anything. What did they mean? Back in verses 17 and 18 we
find them puzzled by what Jesus had said. Beginning in verse 19
Jesus begins to answer their questions *without asking them
what they were.* In other words he could read their hearts like
an open book. That is why they believed in him. A traveller in
Scotland in the old days described two preachers whom he had
heard. Of one he said: " He showed me the glory of God." Of
the other he said: " He showed me my whole heart." Jesus
could do *both* of these things. It was·his knowledge of God and
his knowledge of the human heart which convinced the disciples
that he was the Son of God.

But Jesus was a realist. He told them that, in spite of their
belief, the hour was coming when they would desert him. Here
is perhaps the most extraordinary thing about Jesus. He knew
the weakness of his men; he knew their failure; he knew that
they would let him down in the moment of his direst need; *and
yet he still loved them*; and what is even more wonderful—*he
still trusted them.* He knew men at their worst and still loved
and trusted them. It is quite possible for a man to forgive
someone and, at the same time, to make it clear that he is never
prepared to trust that person again. But Jesus said: " I know
that in your weakness you will desert me; nevertheless I know
that you will still be conquerors." Never in all the world were
forgiveness and trust so combined. What a lesson is there! Jesus
teaches us how to forgive, and how to trust the man who was
guilty of failure.

There are four things about Jesus which this passage makes
very clear.

(i) *There is the loneliness of Jesus.* He was to be left alone by
men. And yet he was never alone, because he still had God. No

man ever stands alone for the right; he always stands with God.
No good man is ever completely forsaken, for he is never
forsaken by God.

(ii) *There is the forgiveness of Jesus.* Of that we have already
thought. He knew that his friends would abandon him, yet at
the moment he did not upbraid them, and afterwards he did not
hold it against them. He loved men in all their weakness; saw
them and loved them as they were. Love must be clear-sighted.
If we idolize a person and think him faultless, we are doomed to
disappointment. We must love him as he really is.

(iii) *There is the sympathy of Jesus.* One verse here at first
sight seems out of place: " I have said this to you, that in me
you may have peace." The point is this—if Jesus had not
foretold the weakness of the disciples, afterwards when they
realized how they had failed him, might well have been driven
to utter and absolute despair. It is as if he said: " I know what's
going to happen; you must not think that your disloyalty came
as a shock to me; I knew it was coming; and it does not make
any difference to my love. When you think about it afterwards,
don't despair." Here is divine pity and divine forgiveness. Jesus
was thinking, not of how men's sin would hurt him, but of how
it would hurt them. Sometimes it would make all the difference
if we thought, not of how much someone has hurt us, but of
how much the fact that they hurt us has driven them to regret
and the sorrow of an aching heart.

(iv) *There is the gift of Jesus*—courage and conquest. Very
soon something was going to be unanswerably proved to the
disciples. They were going to see that the world could do its
worst to Jesus and still not defeat him. And he says: " The
victory which I will win can be your victory too. The world did
its worst to me, and I emerged victorious. Life can do its worst
to you, and you too can emerge victorious. You too can possess
the courage and the conquest of the Cross."

THE GLORY OF THE CROSS

John 17: 1–5

When Jesus had spoken these words, he lifted up his eyes to
heaven, and said: " Father, the hour has come. Glorify the Son
that the Son may glorify you. Glorify him, just as you gave him
authority over mankind, that he may give eternal life to every one
whom you have given to him. It is eternal life to know you, who
are the only true God, and to know Jesus Christ, whom you sent. I
have glorified you upon earth, because I have finished the work
which you gave me to do; and now, Father, glorify me in your
own presence with the glory which I had with you before the
world began."

FOR Jesus life had a climax, and that was the Cross. To him the
Cross was the glory of life and the way to the glory of eternity.
" The hour has come," he said, " for the Son of Man to be
glorified " (*John* 12: 23). What did Jesus mean when he re-
peatedly spoke of the Cross as his glory and his glorification?
There is more than one amswer to that question.

(i) It is one of the facts of history that again and again it was
in death that the great ones found their glory. It was when they
died, and how they died, which showed people what and who
they really were. They may have been misunderstood, under-
valued, condemned as criminals in their lives, but their deaths
showed their true place in the scheme of things.

Abraham Lincoln had his enemies during his lifetime; but
even those who had criticized him saw his greatness when he
died. Someone came out of the room where Lincoln lay, after
the assassin's shot had killed him, saying: " Now he belongs to
the ages." Stanton, his war minister, who had always regarded
Lincoln as crude and uncouth and who had taken no pains to
conceal his contempt, looked down at his dead body with tears
in his eyes. " There lies," he said, " the greatest ruler of men the
world has ever seen."

Joan of Arc was burned as a witch and a heretic by the
English. Amidst the crowd there was an Englishman who had

sworn to add a faggot to the fire. " Would that my soul," he said, " were where the soul of that woman is!" One of. the secretaries of the King of England left the scene saying: " We are all lost because we have burned a saint."

When Montrose was executed, he was taken down the High Street of Edinburgh to the Mercat Cross. His enemies had encouraged the crowd to revile him and had actually provided them with ammunition to fling at him, but not one voice was raised to curse and not one hand was lifted. He had on his finest clothes, with ribbons on his shoes and fine white gloves on his hands. James Frazer, an eyewitness, said: " He stept along the street with so great state, and there appeared in his countenance so much beauty, majesty and gravity as amazed the beholder, and many of his enemies did acknowledge him to be the bravest subject in the world, and in him a gallantry that braced all that crowd." John Nicoll, the notary public, thought him more like a bridegroom than a criminal. An Englishman in the crowd, a government agent, wrote back to his superiors: " It is absolutely certain that he hath overcome more men by his death, in Scotland, than he would have done if he had lived. For I never saw a more sweeter carriage in a man in all my life."

Again and again a martyr's majesty has appeared in death. It was so with Jesus, for even the centurion at the foot of the Cross was left saying: " Truly this was the Son of God " (*Matthew* 27: 54). The Cross was the glory of Jesus because he was never more majestic than in his death. The Cross was his glory because its magnet drew men to him in a way that even his life had never done—and it is so yet.

THE GLORY OF THE CROSS

John 17: 1–5 (*continued*)

(ii) Further, the Cross was the glory of Jesus because it was the completion of his work. " I have accomplished the work," he said, " which you gave me to do." For him to have stopped short of the Cross would have been to leave his task uncompleted. Why should that be so? Jesus had come into this world to tell men about the love of God and to show it to them. If he had stopped short of the Cross, it would have been to say that God's love said: " Thus far and no farther." By going to the Cross Jesus showed that there was nothing that the love of God was not prepared to do and suffer for men, that there was literally no limit to it.

H. L. Gee tells of a war incident from Bristol. Attached to one of the Air Raid Precautions Stations there was a boy messenger called Derek Bellfall. He was sent with a message to another station on his bicycle. On his way back a bomb mortally wounded him. When they found him, he was still conscious. His last whispered words were: " Messenger Bellfall reporting—I have delivered my message."

A famous painting from the First World War showed an engineer fixing a field telephone line. He had just completed the line so that an essential message might come through, when he was shot. The picture shows him in the moment of death, and beneath it there is the one word, " Through! " He had given his life, that the message might get through.

That is exactly what Jesus did. He completed his task; he brought God's love to men. For him that meant the Cross; and the Cross was his glory because he finished the work God gave him to do; he made men for ever certain of God's love.

(iii) There is another question—how did the Cross glorify God? The only way to glorify God is to obey him. A child brings honour to his parents when he brings them obedience. A citizen brings honour to his country when he obeys it. A scholar brings honour to his teacher when he obeys his master's teaching. Jesus brought glory and honour to God by his perfect obedience to him. The gospel story makes it quite clear that Jesus could have escaped the Cross. Humanly speaking, he could have turned back and need never have gone to Jerusalem. As we look at Jesus in the last days, we are bound to say: " See how he loved God! See to what lengths his obedience would go! " He glorified God on the Cross by rendering the perfect obedience of perfect love.

(iv) But there is still more. Jesus prayed to God to glorify him and to glorify himself. *The Cross was not the end.* There was the Resurrection to follow. This was the vindication of Jesus. It was the proof that men could do their worst, and that Jesus could still triumph. It was as if God pointed at the Cross and said: " That is what *men* think of my Son," and then pointed at the resurrection and said: " That is what *I* think of my Son." The Cross was the worst that men could do to Jesus; but not all their worst could conquer him. The glory of the resurrection obliterated the shame of the Cross.

(v) For Jesus the Cross was the way back. " Glorify me," he prayed, " with the glory which I had before the world began." He was like a knight who left the king's court to perform some perilous and awful deed, and who, having performed it, came home in triumph to enjoy the victor's glory. Jesus came from God, and returned to him. The exploit between his coming forth and his going back was the Cross. For him, therefore, it was the gateway to glory; and, if he had refused to pass through it, there would have been no glory for him to enter into. For Jesus the Cross was his return to God.

ETERNAL LIFE

John 17: 1–5 (*continued*)

THERE is another important thought in this passage, for it contains the great New Testament definition of eternal life. It is eternal life to know God and to know Jesus Christ whom he has sent. Let us remind ourselves of what *eternal* means. In Greek it is *aiōnis*. This word has to do, not so much with duration of life, for life which went on for ever would not necessarily be a boon. Its main meaning is *quality* of life. There is only one person to whom the word *aiōnis* can properly be applied, and that is God. Eternal life is, therefore, nothing other than the life of God. To possess it, to enter into it, is to experience here and now something of the splendour, and the majesty, and the joy, and the peace, and the holiness which are characteristic of the life of God.

To know God is a characteristic thought of the Old Testament. Wisdom is " a tree of life to those who lay hold of her " (*Proverbs* 3: 18). " To know thy power," said the writer of *Wisdom*, " is the root of immortality " (*Wisdom* 5: 3). " By knowledge are the righteous delivered " (*Proverb* 11: 9). Habbakuk's dream of the golden age is that " the earth will be filled with the knowledge of the glory of God " (*Habbakuk* 2: 14). Hosea hears God's voice saying to him: " My people are destroyed for lack of knowledge " (*Hosea* 4: 6). A Rabbinic exposition asks what is the smallest section of scripture on which all the essentials of the law hang? It answers, *Proverbs* 3: 6, which literally means: " *Know* him, and he shall direct thy paths." Again there was a Rabbinic exposition which said that Amos had reduced all the many commandments of the Law to one, when he said: " Seek me, and live " (*Amos* 5: 4), for *seeking God* means seeking to *know* him. The Jewish teachers had long insisted that to know God is necessary to true life. What then does it mean to know God?

(i) Undoubtedly there is an element of intellectual knowledge. It means, at least in part, to know what God is like; and to know that does make the most tremendous difference to life. Take two examples. Heathen peoples in primitive countries believe in a horde of gods. Every tree, brook, hill, mountain, river, stone has its gods and its spirit; all these spirits are hostile to man; and primitive people are haunted by the gods; living in perpetual fear of offending one of them. Missionaries tell us that it is almost impossible to understand the sheer wave of relief which comes to these people when they discover that *there is only one God*. This new knowledge makes all the difference in the world. Further, it makes a tremendous difference to know that God is not stern and cruel, but love.

We know these things; but we could never have known them unless Jesus had come to tell them. We enter into a new life, we share something of the life of God himself, when, through the work of Jesus, we discover what God is like. It is eternal life to know what God is like.

(ii) But there is something else. The Old Testament regularly uses *know* for sexual knowledge. " Adam knew Eve his wife, and she conceived, and bore Cain " (*Genesis* 4: 1). Now the knowledge of husband and wife is the most intimate there can be. Husband and wife are no longer two; they are one flesh. The sexual act itself is not the important thing; the important thing is the intimacy of heart and mind and soul which in true love precede that act. To *know* God is therefore not merely to have intellectual knowledge of him; it is to have an intimate personal relationship with him, which is like the nearest and dearest relationship in life. Once again, without Jesus such intimacy with God would have been unthinkable and impossible. It is Jesus who taught men that God is not remote and unapproachable, but the Father whose name and nature are love.

To know God is to know what he is like, and to be on the most intimate terms of friendship with him; and neither of these things is possible without Jesus Christ.

THE WORK OF JESUS

John 17: 6–8

" I have shown forth your name to the men whom you gave me out of the world. They were yours and you gave them to me, and they have kept your word. Now they realize that everything you gave me comes from you, because I gave to them the words you gave to me, and they received them, and they truly know that I came forth from you, and they believe that you sent me."

JESUS gives us a definition of the work that he did. He says to God: " I have shown forth your name."

There are two great ideas here, both of which would be quite clear to those who heard this saying for the first time.

(i) There is an idea which is an essential and characteristic idea of the Old Testament. In the Old Testament *name* is used in a very special way. It does not mean simply the name by which a person is called; it means the whole character of the person in so far as it can be known. The Psalmist says: " Those who know thy name put their trust in thee " (*Psalm* 9: 10). Clearly that does not mean that those who know what God *is called* will trust him; it means that those who know what God *is like*, those who know his character and nature will be glad to put their trust in him.

The psalmist says: " Some boast of chariots, and some of horses; but we boast of the name of the Lord our God " (*Psalm* 20: 7). This means that he can trust God because he knows what he is like. The Psalmist says: " I will tell of thy name to my brethren " (*Psalm* 22: 22). This was a psalm which the Jews believed to be a prophecy of the Messiah and of the work that he would do; and it means that the Messiah's work would be to declare to his fellow-men what God is like. It is the vision of Isaiah that in the new age, " My people shall know my name " (*Isaiah* 52: 6). That is to say that in the golden days men will know fully and truly what God is like.

So when Jesus says: " I have shown forth your name," he is saying: " I have enabled men to see what the real nature of God is like." It is in fact another way of saying: " He who has seen me has seen the Father " (*John* 14: 9). It is Jesus's supreme claim that in him men see the mind, the character, the heart of God.

(ii) But there is another idea here. In later times when the Jews spoke of *the name of God* they meant the sacred four-letter symbol, the tetragrammaton as it is called, IHWH. That name was held to be so sacred that it was never pronounced, except by the High Priest when he went into the Holy of Holies on the Day of Atonement.

These four letters stand for the name Jahweh. We usually speak about Jehovah and the change in the vowels is due to the fact that the vowels of Jehovah are those of *Adonai*, which means *Lord*. In the Hebrew alphabet there were no vowels at all. Later the vowel sounds were shown by little signs put above

and below the consonants. The four letters IHWH were so
sacred that the vowels of Adonai were put below them, so that
when the reader came to IHWH he read, not Jahweh, but
Adonai. That is to say, in the time of Jesus the name of God
was so sacred that ordinary people were not even supposed to
know it, far less to speak it. God was the remote, invisible king,
whose name was not for ordinary men to speak. So Jesus is
saying: " I have told you God's name; that name which is so
sacred can be spoken now because of what I have done. I have
brought the remote, invisible God so close that even the
simplest people can speak to him and take his name upon their
lips."

It is Jesus's great claim that he showed to men the true
nature and the true character of God; and that he brought him
so close that the humblest Christian can take his unutterable
name upon his lips.

THE MEANING OF DISCIPLESHIP

John 17: 6–8 (*continued*)

THIS passage also sheds an illuminating light on the meaning of
discipleship.

(i) Discipleship is based on the realization that Jesus came
forth from God. The disciple is essentially a person who has
realized that Jesus is God's ambassador, and that in his words
we hear God's voice, and in his deeds we see God's action. The
disciple is one who sees God in Jesus and is aware that no one
in all the universe is one with God as Jesus is.

(ii) Discipleship issues in obedience. The disciple is one who
keeps God's word as he hears it in Jesus. He is one who has
accepted the mastery of Jesus. So long as we wish to do what
we like, we cannot be disciples; discipleship involves sub-
mission.

(iii) Discipleship is something which is destined. Jesus's men
were given to him by God. In God's plan they were destined for

discipleship. That does not mean that God destined some men to be disciples and some to refuse discipleship. Think of it this way. A parent dreams great dreams for his son; he works out a future for him; but the son can refuse that future and go his own way. A teacher thinks out a great future for a student; he sees that he has it in him to do great work for God and man; but the student can lazily or selfishly refuse the offered task. If we love someone we are always dreaming of his future and planning for greatness; but the dream and the plan can be frustrated. The Pharisees believed in fate, but they also believed in free-will. One of their great sayings was: " Everything is decreed except the fear of God." God has his plan, his dream, his destiny for every man; and our tremendous responsibility is that we can accept or reject it. As someone has said: " Fate is what we are compelled to do; destiny is what we are meant to do."

There is throughout this whole passage, and indeed throughout this whole chapter, a ringing confidence about the future in the voice of Jesus. He was with his men, the men God had given him; he thanked God for them; and he never doubted that they would carry on the work he had given them to do. Let us remember who and what they were. A great commentator said: " Eleven Galilaean peasants after three years' labour! But it is enough for Jesus, for in these eleven he beholds the pledge of the continuance of God's work upon earth." When Jesus left this world, he did not seem to have great grounds for hope. He seemed to have achieved so little and to have won so few, and it was the great and the orthodox and the religious of the day who had turned against him. But Jesus had that confidence which springs from God. He was not afraid of small beginnings. He was not pessimistic about the future. He seemed to say: " I have won only eleven very ordinary men; but give me these eleven ordinary men and I will change the world."

Jesus had two things—belief in God and belief in men. It is one of the most uplifting things in the world to think that Jesus put his trust in men like ourselves. We too must never be daunted by human weakness or by the small beginning. We too must go forward with confident belief in God and in men. Then

we will never be pessimists, because with these two beliefs the
possibilities of life are infinite.

JESUS'S PRAYER FOR HIS DISCIPLES

John 17: 9–19

" It is for them that I pray. It is not for the world that I pray, but
for those whom you have given me because they are yours. All that I
have is yours, and all that you have is mine. And through them
glory has been given to me. I am no longer in the world and they
are no longer in the world, and I go to you. Holy Father, keep
them in your name, which you gave to me, that they may be one,
as we are one. When I was with them I kept them in your name,
which you gave to me. I guarded them and none of them went lost,
except the one who was destined to be lost—and this happened
that the scriptures might be fulfilled. And now I come to you. I am
saying these things while I am still in the world that they may
have my joy completed in themselves. I gave them your word, and
the world hated then, because they are not of the world. I do not
ask that you should take them out of the world, but that you should
preserve them from the evil one. They are not of the world, just as
I am not of the world. Consecrate them by the truth; your word is
truth. As you send me into the world, I send them into the world.
And for their sakes I consecrate myself, that they too may be
consecrated by the truth."

HERE is a passage close-packed with truths so great that we can
grasp only fragments of them.

First of all, it tells us something about the disciple of Jesus.

(i) The disciple is given to Jesus by God. What does that
mean? It means that the Spirit of God moves our hearts to
respond to the appeal of Jesus.

(ii) Through the disciple, glory has come to Jesus. The
patient whom he has cured brings honour to a doctor; the
scholar whom he has taught brings honour to the teacher;
the athlete whom he has trained brings honour to his trainer.

The men whom Jesus has redeemed bring honour to him. The bad man made good is the honour of Jesus.

(iii) The disciple is the man who is commissioned to a task. As God sent out Jesus, so Jesus sends out his disciples. Here is the explanation of a puzzling thing in this passage. Jesus begins by saying that he does not pray for the world; and yet he came because God so loved the world. But, as we have seen, in John's gospel *the world* stands for " human society organizing itself without God." What Jesus does for the world is to send out his disciples into it, in order to lead it back to God and to make it aware of God. He prays for his men in order that they may be such as to win the world for him.

Further, this passage tells us that Jesus offered his men two things.

(i) He offered them his *joy*. All he was saying to them was designed to bring them joy.

(ii) He also offered them *warning*. He told them that they were different from the world, and that they could not expect anything else but hatred from it. Their values and standards were different from the world's. But there is a joy in battling against the storm and struggling against the tide; it is by facing the hostility of the world that we enter into the Christian joy.

Still further, in this passage Jesus makes the greatest claim he ever made. He prays to God and says: " All that I have is yours, and all that you have is mine." The first part of that sentence is natural and easy to understand, for all things belong to God, and again and again Jesus had said so. But the second part of this sentence is the astonishing claim—" All that you have is mine." Luther said: " This no creature can say with reference to God." Never did Jesus so vividly lay down his oneness with God. He is so one with him that he exercises his very power and prerogatives.

JESUS'S PRAYER FOR HIS DISCIPLES

John 17: 9–19 (*continued*)

THE great interest of this passage is that it tells us of the things for which Jesus prayed for his disciples.

(i) The first essential is to note that Jesus did not pray that his disciples should be taken out of this world. He never prayed that they might find escape; he prayed that they might find victory. The kind of Christianity which buries itself in a monastery or a convent would not have seemed Christianity to Jesus at all. The kind of Christianity which finds its essence in prayer and meditation and in a life withdrawn from the world, would have seemed to him a sadly truncated version of the faith he died to bring. He insisted that it was in the rough and tumble of life that a man must live out his Christianity.

Of course there is need of prayer and meditation and quiet times, when we shut the door upon the world to be alone with God, but all these things are not the end of life, but means to the end; and the end is to demonstrate the Christian life in the ordinary work of the world. Christianity was never meant to withdraw a man from life, but to equip him better for it. It does not offer us release from problems, but a way to solve them. It does not offer us an easy peace, but a triumphant warfare. It does not offer us a life in which troubles are escaped and evaded, but a life in which troubles are faced and conquered. However much it may be true that the Christian is not of the world, it remains true that it is within the world that his Christianity must be lived out. He must never desire to abandon the world, but always desire to win it.

(ii) Jesus prayed for the unity of his disciples. Where there are divisions, where there is exclusiveness, where there is competition between the Churches, the cause of Christianity is harmed and the prayer of Jesus frustrated. The gospel cannot truly be preached in any congregation which is not one united band of brothers. The world cannot be evangelized by com

peting Churches. Jesus prayed that his disciples might be as
fully one as he and the Father are one; and there is no prayer of
his which has been so hindered from being answered by
individual Christians and by the Churches than this.

(iii) Jesus prayed that God would protect his disciples from
the attacks of the Evil One. The Bible is not a speculative book;
it does not discuss the origin of evil; but it is quite certain that
in this world there is a power of evil which is in opposition to
the power of God. It is uplifting to feel that God is the sentinel
who stands over our lives to guard us from the assaults of evil.
The fact that we fall so often is due to the fact that we try to
meet life in our own strength and forget to seek the help and to
remember the presence of our protecting God.

(iv) Jesus prayed that his disciples might be consecrated by
the truth. The word for to *consecrate* is *hagiazein* which comes
from the adjective *hagios*. In the Authorized Version *hagios* is
usually translated *holy* but its basic meaning is *different* or
separate. So then *hagiazein* has two ideas in it.

(*a*) It means *to set apart for a special task*. When God called
Jeremiah, he said to him: " Before I formed you in the womb I
knew you; and before you were born I consecrated you; I
appointed you a prophet to the nations " (*Jeremiah* 1: 5). Even
before his birth God had set Jeremiah apart for a special task.
When God was instituting the priesthood in Israel he told
Moses to *ordain* the sons of Aaron and to *consecrate* them that
they might serve in the office of the priests (*Exodus* 28: 41).
Aaron's sons were to be set apart for a special office and a
special duty.

(*b*) But *hagiazein* means not only to set apart for some
special office and task, it also means *to equip a man with the
qualities of mind and heart and character which are necessary
for that task*. If a man is to serve God, he must have something
of God's goodness and God's wisdom in him. He who would
serve the holy God must himself be holy too. And so God does
not only choose a man for his special service, and set him apart
for it, he also equips a man with the qualities he needs to carry
it out.

We must always remember that God has chosen us out and dedicated us for his special service. That special service is that we should love and obey him and should bring others to do the same. And God has not left us to carry out that great task in our own strength, but out of his grace he fits us for our task, if we place our lives in his hands.

A GLIMPSE OF THE FUTURE

John 17: 20, 21

" It is not only for these that I pray, but also for those who are going to believe in their word of testimony to me. And my prayer is that they may all be one, even as you, Father, are in me, and I in you, so that they may be in us, so that the world may believe that you sent me."

GRADUALLY in this section Jesus's prayer has been going out to the ends of the earth. First, he prayed for himself as the Cross faced him. Second, he prayed for his disciples, and for God's keeping power for them. Now his prayers take a sweep into the distant future, and he prays for those who in distant lands and far-off ages will also enter the Christian faith.

Here two great characteristics of Jesus are full displayed. First, we see his complete faith and his radiant certainty. At that moment his followers were few, but even with the Cross facing him, his confidence was unshaken, and he was praying for those who would come to believe in his name. This passage should be specially precious to us, for it is Jesus's prayer for us. Second, we see his confidence in his men. He knew that they did not fully understand him; he knew that in a very short time they were going to abandon him in his hour of sorest need. Yet to these very same men he looked with complete confidence to spread his name throughout the world. Jesus never lost his faith in God or his confidence in men.

What was his prayer for the Church which was to be? It was that all its members would be one as he and his Father are one.

What was that unity for which Jesus prayed? It was not a unity of administration or organization; it was not in any sense an ecclesiastical unity. *It was a unity of personal relationship.* We have already seen that the union between Jesus and God was one of love and obedience. It was a unity of love for which Jesus prayed, a unity in which men loved each other because they loved him, a unity based entirely on the relationship between heart and heart.

Christians will never organize their Churches all in the same way. They will never worship God all in the same way. They will never even all believe precisely the same things. But Christian unity transcends all these differences and joins men together in love. The cause of Christian unity at the present time, and indeed all through history, has been injured and hindered, because men loved their own ecclesiastical organiza tions, their own creeds, their own ritual, more than they loved each other. If we really loved each other and really loved Christ, no Church would exclude any man who was Christ's disciple. Only love implanted in men's hearts by God can tear down the barriers which they have erected between each other and between their Churches.

Further, as Jesus saw it and prayed for it, it was to be precisely that unity which convinced the world of the truth of Christianity and of the place of Christ. It is more natural for men to be divided than to be united. It is more human for men to fly apart than to come together. Real unity between all Christians would be a " supernatural fact which would require a supernatural explanation." It is the tragic fact that it is just that united front that the Church has never shown to men. Faced by the disunity of Christians, the world cannot see the supreme value of the Christian faith. It is our individual duty to demonstrate that unity of love with our fellow men which is the answer to Christ's prayer. The rank and file of the Churches can do and must do what the leaders of the Church refuse officially to do.

THE GIFT AND THE PROMISE OF GLORY

John 17: 22–26

" And I have given them the glory which you gave me, that they may be one as we are one. I am in them, and you are in me, so that their unity with us and with each other may stand consummated and complete. I pray for this that the world may realize that you sent me, and that you loved them as you loved me. Father, it is my will that those whom you have given me should be with me where I am going, that they may see my glory which you gave me, because you loved me before the foundation of the world. Righteous Father, the world did not know you, but I knew you, and these realized that you sent me. I have told them what you are like, and I will go on telling them, that the love with which you loved me may be in them, and that I may be in them.

BENGEL, an old commentator, exclaimed as he began to comment on this passage: " O how great is the Christians' glory! " And indeed it is.

First, Jesus said that he had given his disciples the glory which his Father had given him. We must fully understand what that means. What was the glory of Jesus? There were three ways in which he talked of it.

(*a*) The Cross was his glory. Jesus did not speak of being crucified; he spoke of being glorified. Therefore, first and foremost, a Christian's glory is the cross that he must bear. It is an honour to suffer for Jesus Christ. We must never think of our cross as our penalty; we must think of it as our glory. The harder the task a knight was given, the greater he considered its glory. The harder the task we give a student, or a craftsman, or a surgeon, the more we honour him. In effect, we say that we believe that nobody but he could attempt that task at all. So when it is hard to be a Christian, we must regard it as our glory given to us by God.

(*b*) *Jesus's perfect obedience to the will of God was his glory. We find our glory, not in doing as we like, but in doing as God wills. When we try to do as we like—as many of us have*

done—we find nothing but sorrow and disaster both for our-
selves and for others. We find the real glory of life in doing
God's will; the greater the obedience, the greater the glory.

(c) Jesus's glory lay in the fact that, from his life, men
recognized his special relationship with God. They saw that no
one could live as he did unless he was uniquely near to God. As
with Christ, it is our glory when men see in us the reflection of
God.

Second, Jesus said that it was his will that his disciples
should see his glory in the heavenly places. It is the Christian's
conviction that he will share *all* the experiences of Christ. If he
has to share Christ's Cross, he will also share his glory. " The
saying is sure: If we have died with him, we shall also live with
him; if we endure, we shall also reign with him " (2 *Timothy* 2:
11, 12). Here in this world at best we see dimly in a mirror, but
then we shall see face to face (1 *Corinthians* 13: 12). The joy we
have now is only a faint foretaste of the joy which is to come. It
is Christ's promise that if we share his glory and his sufferings
on earth, we shall share his glory and his triumph when life on
this earth is ended. What greater promise could there be than
that?

From this prayer Jesus was to go straight out to the betrayal,
the trial and the Cross. He was not to speak to his disciples
again. It is a wonderful and a precious thing to remember that
before these terrible hours his last words were not of despair but
of glory.

THE ARREST IN THE GARDEN

John 18: 1–11

When Jesus had said these things he went out with his disciples
across the Kedron Valley to a place where there was a garden,
into which he and his disciples entered; and Judas, his betrayer,
knew the place for Jesus often met with his disciples there. So
Judas took a company of soldiers, together with officers from the
chief priests and Pharisees, and went there with lanterns and

torches and weapons. Jesus knew the things which were going to happen to him, so he came out and said: " Who are you looking for? " They answered: " Jesus of Nazareth." Jesus said to them: " I am he." And Judas, his betrayer, stood there with them. When he said to them: " I am he," they stepped back and fell on the ground. So Jesus again asked them: " Who are you looking for? " They said: " Jesus of Nazareth." Jesus said: " I told you that I am he. If it is I for whom you are looking, let these go, so that the word which scripture said may be fulfilled—I have lost none of those whom you gave me." Now Simon Peter had a sword and he drew it; and he struck the high priest's servant and cut off his right ear. The servant's name was Malchus. Jesus said to Peter: " Put your sword in its sheath. Shall I not drink the cup which my Father gave me? "

WHEN the last meal was finished and when Jesus's talk and prayer with his disciples were ended, he and his friends left the upper room. They were bound for the Garden of Gethsemane. They would leave by the gate, go down the steep valley and cross the channel of the brook Kedron. There a symbolic thing must have happened. All the Passover lambs were killed in the Temple, and the blood of the lambs was poured on the altar as an offering to God. The number of lambs slain for the Passover was immense. On one occasion, thirty years later than the time of Jesus, a census was taken and the number was 256,000. We may imagine what the Temple courts were like when the blood of all these lambs was dashed on to the altar. From the altar there was a channel down to the brook Kedron, and through that channel the blood of the Passover lambs drained away. When Jesus crossed the brook Kedron it would still be red with the blood of the lambs which had been sacrificed; and as he did so, the thought of his own sacrifice would surely be vivid in his mind.

Having crossed the channel of the Kedron, they came to the Mount of Olives. On its slopes lay the little garden of Gethsemane, which means the oil-press, the press where the oil was extracted from the olives which grew on the hill. Many well-to-do people had their private gardens there. Space in Jerusalem was too limited for private gardens, for it was built on the top of

a hill. Further, there were ceremonial prohibitions which for
bade the use of manure on the soil of the sacred city. That was
why the wealthy people had their private gardens outside the
city on the slopes of the Mount of Olives.

They show pilgrims to this day a little garden on the hillside.
It is lovingly tended by the Franciscan friars, and in it there are
eight old olive trees of such girth that they seem, as H. V.
Morton says, more like rocks than trees. They are very old; it is
known that they go back to a time before the Moslem conquest
of Palestine. It is scarcely possible that they go back to the time
of Jesus himself; but certainly the little paths criss-crossing the
Mount of Olives were trodden by the feet of Jesus.

So to this garden Jesus went. Some wealthy citizen—an
anonymous friend of Jesus whose name will never be known—
must have given him the key of the gate and the right to use it
when he was in Jerusalem. Often Jesus and his disciples had
gone there for peace and quiet. Judas knew that he would find
Jesus there and it was there that he had decided it would be
easiest to engineer the arrest.

There is something astonishing about the force which came
out to arrest Jesus. John said that there was a company of
soldiers, together with officers from the chief priests and
Pharisees. The *officers* would be the Temple police. The Temple
authorities had a kind of private police force to keep good
order, and the Sanhedrin had its police officers to carry out its
decrees. The officers, therefore, were the Jewish police force. But
there was a band of Roman soldiers there too. The word is
speira. Now that word, if it is correctly used, can have three
meanings. It is the Greek word for a Roman cohort and a
cohort had six hundred men. If it was a cohort of auxiliary
soldiers, a *speira* had one thousand men, two hundred and forty
cavalry and seven hundred and sixty infantry. Sometimes,
much more rarely, the word is used for the detachment of men
called a maniple which was made up of two hundred men.

Even if we take this word to mean the smallest force, the
maniple, what an expedition to send out against an unarmed
Galilaean carpenter! At the Passover time there were always

extra soldiers in Jerusalem, quartered in the Tower of Antonia which overlooked the Temple, and men would be available. But what a compliment to the power of Jesus! When the authorities decided to arrest him, they sent what was almost an army to do it.

THE ARREST IN THE GARDEN

John 18: 1–11 (*continued*)

FEW scenes in scripture so show us the qualities of Jesus as does the arrest in the garden.

(i) It shows us his courage. At Passover time it was full moon and the night was almost like daylight. Yet the enemies of Jesus had come with lamps and torches. Why? They did not need them to see the way. They must have thought that they would have to search among the trees and in the hillside nooks and crannies to find Jesus. So far from hiding, when they arrived, Jesus stepped out. " Who are you looking for? " he demanded. " Jesus of Nazareth," they said. Back came the answer: " I am he." The man they had thought they would have to search for as he skulked in the trees and the caves was standing before them with glorious defiance. Here is the courage of the man who will face things out. During the Spanish Civil War a city was besieged. There were some who wished to surrender, but a leader arose. " It is better," he said, " to die on our feet than to live on our knees."

(ii) It shows us his authority. There he was, one single, lonely, unarmed figure; there they were, hundreds of them, armed and equipped. Yet face to face with him, they retreated and fell to the ground. There flowed from Jesus an authority which in all his loneliness made him stronger than the might of his enemies.

(iii) It shows us that Jesus chose to die. Here again it is clear that he could have escaped death if he had so wished. He could have walked through them and gone his way. But he did not. He even helped his enemies to arrest him. He chose to die.

(iv) It shows his protective love. It was not for himself that he took thought; it was for his friends. " Here I am," he said. " It is I whom you want. Take me, and let them go." Among the many immortal stories of the Second World War that of Alfred Sadd, missionary of Tarrawa, stands out. When the Japanese came to his island, he was lined up with twenty other men, mostly New Zealand soldiers who had been part of the garrison. The Japanese laid a Union Jack on the ground and ordered Sadd to walk over it. He approached the flag and, as he came to it, he turned off to the right. They ordered him again to trample on it; this time he turned off to the left. The third time he was compelled to go up to the flag; and he gathered it in his arms and kissed it. When the Japanese took them all out to be shot, many were so young that they were heavy-hearted, but Alfred Sadd cheered them up. They stood in a line, he in the middle, but presently he went out and stood in front of them and spoke words of cheer. When he had finished, he went back but still stood a little in front of them, so that he would be the first to die. Alfred Sadd thought more of others' troubles than his own. Jesus's protecting love surrounded his disciples even in Gethsemane.

(v) It shows his utter obedience. " Shall I not drink," he said, " the cup that God has given me to drink? " This was God's will, and that was enough. Jesus was himself faithful unto death.

There is a figure in this story to whom we must do justice, and that is Peter. He, one man, drew his sword against hundreds. As Macaulay had it:

> " How can man die better
> Than facing fearful odds? "

Peter was soon to deny his master, but at that moment he was prepared to take on hundreds all alone for the sake of Christ. We may talk of the cowardice and the failure of Peter; but we must never forget the sublime courage of this moment.

JESUS BEFORE ANNAS

John 18: 12–14, 19–24

> The company of soldiers and their commander and the officers of the Jews took Jesus, and bound him, and led him first of all to Annas. He was the father-in-law of Caiaphas who was High Priest in that year. It was Caiaphas who had advised the Jews that it was better that one man should die for the people. . . . The High Priest questioned Jesus about his disciples and about his teaching. Jesus answered him: I spoke openly in the world. I taught at all times in the synagogue and in the precincts of the Temple, where all the Jews assemble, and I spoke nothing in secret. Why do you ask me questions? Ask those who heard me what I said to them. See! These know what I have said." When he had said these things, one of the officers who was standing by, dealt Jesus a blow. " Do you answer the High Priest like this? " he said. Jesus answered: " If I have spoken ill, produce evidence about the ill; if I have spoken well, why do you strike me? " So Annas sent him bound to Caiaphas the High Priest.

FOR the sake of keeping the narrative continuous we take together the two passages which deal with the trial before Annas; and we will do the same with the two passages which deal with the tragedy of Peter.

Only John tells us that Jesus was brought first of all to Annas. Annas was a notorious character. Edersheim writes of him: " No figure is better known in contemporary Jewish history than that of Annas; no person deemed more fortunate or successful, but none also more generally execrated than the late High Priest." Annas was the power behind the throne in Jerusalem. He himself had been High Priest from A.D. 6 to 15. Four of his sons had also held the high priesthood and Caiaphas was his son-in-law. That very fact is itself suggestive and illuminating. There had been a time, when the Jews were free, when the High Priest had held office for life; but when the Roman governors came, the office became a matter for contention and intrigue and bribery and corruption. It now went to the greatest sycophant and the highest bidder, to the man who was most willing to toe the line with the Roman governor. The High Priest was the arch-collaborator, the man who brought comfort and ease and prestige and power not with bribes only but with close co-operation with his country's masters. The family of Annas was immensely rich and one by one they had intrigued and bribed their way into office, while Annas remained the power behind it all.

Even the way in which Annas made his money was most probably disgraceful. In the Court of the Gentiles there were the sellers of victims for the sacrifices, those sellers whom Jesus had driven out. They were not traders; they were extortioners. Every victim offered in the Temple had to be without spot and blemish. There were inspectors to see that it was so. If a victim was bought outside the Temple it was certain that a flaw would be found. The worshipper was then directed to buy at the Temple booths where the victims had already been examined and where there was no risk of rejection. That would have been convenient and helpful but for one thing. Outside the Temple a pair of doves could cost as little as 4p; inside they could cost as much as 75p. The whole business was sheer exploitation; and the shops where the Temple victims were sold were called The Bazaars of Annas. They were the property of the family of Annas; it was by the exploitation of the worshippers, by trading on the sacred sacrifices that Annas had amassed a fortune. The Jews themselves hated the household of Annas. There is a passage in the *Talmud* which says: " Woe to the house of Annas! Woe to their serpent's hiss! They are High Priests; their sons are keepers of the treasury; their sons-in-law are guardians of the Temple; and their servants beat the people with staves." Annas and his household were notorious.

Now we can see why Annas arranged that Jesus should be brought first to him. Jesus was the man who had attacked Annas's vested interest; he had cleared the Temple of the sellers of victims and had hit Annas where it hurt—in his pocket. Annas wanted to be the first to gloat over the capture of this disturbing Galilaean.

The examination before Annas was a mockery of justice. It was an essential regulation of the Jewish law that a prisoner must be asked no question which would incriminate him. Maimonides, the great Jewish medieval scholar, lays it down: " Our true law does not inflict the penalty of death upon a sinner by his own confession." Annas violated the principles of Jewish justice when he questioned Jesus. It was precisely of this that Jesus reminded him. Jesus said: " Don't ask me questions. Ask those who heard me." He was, in effect, saying: " Take your evidence about me in the proper and legal way. Examine your witnesses, which you have every right to do; stop examining me, which you have no right to do." When Jesus said that, one of the officers hit him a slap across the face. He said, in effect, " Are you trying to teach the High Priest how to conduct a trial? " Jesus's answer was: " If I have said or taught anything illegal, witnesses should be called. I have only stated the law. Why hit me for that? "

Jesus never had any hope of justice. The self-interest of Annas and his colleagues had been touched; and Jesus was condemned before he was tried. When a man is engaged on an evil way, his only desire is to eliminate anyone who opposes him. If he cannot do it by fair means, he is compelled to resort to foul.

THE HERO AND THE COWARD

John 18: 15–18, 25–27

Simon Peter was following Jesus with another disciple. That disciple was known to the High Priest, and he went in with Jesus into the courtyard of the High Priest's house. Peter was standing at the door outside. The other disciple, who was known to the High Priest came out and spoke to the door-keeper, and brought Peter in. The maid-servant, who kept the door, said to Peter: " You are not one of this man's disciples, are you? " He said: " I am not." The servants and the officers stood beside a charcoal brazier they had kindled, because it was cold, and they were warming themselves; and Peter too was standing with them warming himself. . . . Simon Peter was standing warming himself. They said to him: " Surely you too are one of his disciples? " He denied it, and said: " I am not." One of the servants of the High Priest, a relation of the man whose ear Peter had cut off, said: " Did I not see you in the garden with him? " Again Peter denied it, and immediately cockcrow sounded.

WHEN the other disciples forsook Jesus and fled, Peter refused to do so. He followed Jesus, even after his arrest, because he could not tear himself away. So he came to the house of Caiaphas, the High Priest; and he was in the company of another disciple who had the right of entry to the house, because he was known to the High Priest.

There have been many speculations about who this other disciple was. Some have thought that he was simply some unknown disciple whose name we can never know. Some have connected him with either Nicodemus or Joseph of Arimathaea who were both members of the Sanhedrin, and must both have known the High Priest well. One very interesting suggestion is that he was Judas Iscariot. Judas must have had much coming and going to arrange the betrayal and would be well known both to the maid-servant who answered the door and to the High Priest himself. The one thing that seems to invalidate this theory is that, after the scene in the garden, Judas's part in the betrayal must have been quite clear; and it is almost incredible that Peter would have had anything more to do with him. The traditional view is that the unnamed disciple was John himself; and the tradition is so strong that it is difficult to set it aside. The question becomes, in that case, How could John from Galilee be known, apparently intimately, to the High Priest?

Two suggestions have been made to explain this.

(*a*) In later days a man called Polycrates wrote about the Fourth Gospel. He never doubted that John wrote the gospel and that he was the beloved disciple, but he says a very curious thing about him. He says that John was by birth a priest, and that he wore the *petalos*, which was the narrow gold band, or *ziz*, inscribed with the words, " Holiness unto the Lord," which the High Priest wore upon his forehead. If that were so, John would be actually of the High Priest's kin; but it is difficult to believe that he could be of the priestly line, for the gospels so clearly show him as a Galilaean fisherman.

(*b*) The second explanation is easier to accept. It is clear that John's father had a very flourishing fishing business because he could afford to employ hired servants (*Mark* 1: 20). One of the great Galilaean industries was salt fish. Fresh fish was a great luxury because there was no way of transporting fish in such a way that it would remain fresh. On the other hand, salt fish was a staple article of diet. It has been supposed that John's father was in the salt fish trade, and that he actually supplied the household of the High Priest. If that were so, John would be well-known to the High Priest and to his servants, because often it would be he who would bring the supplies. There is some kind of support in legend for this theory. H. V. Morton tells us of visiting in the back streets of Jerusalem a little building which was presently an Arab coffee house. In it were certain stones and arches which once had been part of a very early Christian church, believed to have stood on the site of a house which belonged to Zebedee, John's father. The family, so the Franciscans believe, were fish merchants in Galilee with a branch office in Jerusalem and supplied the household of Caiaphas the High Priest with salt fish, which was why John had entry into the High Priest's house.

However these things may be, Peter was brought into the courtyard of the High Priest's house and there he three times denied his Lord.

There is this very interesting thing. Jesus had said that Peter would deny him three times before the cock crew. There are difficulties about that. According to Jewish ritual law, it was not lawful to keep cocks in the holy city, although we cannot be sure whether that law was kept or not. Further, it is never possible to be sure that a cock will crow. But the Romans had a certain military practice. The night was divided into four watches—6 p.m. to 9 p.m., 9 p.m. to 12 midnight, 12 midnight to 3 a.m., and 3 a.m. to 6 a.m. After the third watch the guard

was changed and to mark the changing of the guard there was a
trumpet call at 3 a.m. That trumpet call was called in latin
gallicinium and in Greek *alektorophōnia*, which both mean
cockcrow. It may well be that Jesus said to Peter: " Before the
trumpet sounds the cockcrow you will deny me three times."
Everyone in Jerusalem must have known that trumpet call at 3
a.m. When sounded through the city that night Peter remembered.

THE HERO AND THE COWARD

John 18: 15–18, 25–27 (*continued*)

So in the courtyard of the High Priest's house Peter denied his
Lord. No man has ever been so unjustly treated as Peter by
preachers and commentators. Always what is stressed is his
failure and his shame. But there are other things we must
remember

(i) We must remember that all the other disciples, except
John, if he is the unnamed disciple, had forsaken Jesus and fled.
Think what Peter had done. He alone drew his sword against
fearful odds in the garden; he alone followed out to see the end.
The first thing to remember about Peter is not his failure, but
the courage which kept him near to Jesus when everyone else
had run away. His failure could have happened only to a man
of superlative courage. True, he failed; but he failed in a
situation which none of the other disciples even dared to face.
He failed, not because he was a coward, but because he was
brave.

(ii) We must remember how much Peter loved Jesus. The
others had abandoned Jesus; Peter alone stood by him. He
loved Jesus so much that he could not leave him. True, he
failed; but he failed in circumstances which only a faithful lover
of Jesus would ever have encountered.

(iii) We must remember how Peter redeemed himself. Things
could not have been easy for him. The story of his denial would

soon get about, for people love a malicious tale. It may well be, as legend has it, that people imitated the crow of the cock when he passed. But Peter had the courage and the tenacity of purpose to redeem himself, to start from failure and attain to greatness.

The essence of the matter was that it was the real Peter who protested his loyalty in the upper room; it was the real Peter who drew his lonely sword in the moonlight of the garden; it was the real Peter who followed Jesus, because he could not allow his Lord to go alone; it was *not* the real Peter who cracked beneath the tension and denied his Lord. *And that is just what Jesus could see.* A tremendous thing about Jesus is that beneath all our failures he sees the real man. He understands. He loves us in spite of what we do because he loves us, not for what we are, but what we have it in us to be. The forgiving love of Jesus is so great that he sees our real personality, not in our faithfulness, but in our loyalty, not in our defeat by sin, but in our teaching after goodness, even when we are defeated.

JESUS AND PILATE

John 18: 28–19: 16

They brought Jesus from Caiaphas to the governor's headquarters. It was early in the morning and they themselves did not enter into the headquarters, in case they should be defiled; but they wished to avoid defilement because they wished to eat the Passover. So Pilate came out to them and said: " What charge do you bring against this man? " They answered him: " If he had not been an evildoer, we would not have handed him over to you." Pilate said to them: " You take him, and judge him according to your laws." The Jews said to Pilate: " It is not permitted to us to put anyone to death." This happened that there might be fulfilled the word of Jesus, which he spoke in indication of the kind of death he was going to die. So Pilate went again into his headquarters, and called Jesus, and said to him: " Are you the

King of the Jews? " Jesus answered: " Are you saying this because you have discovered it yourself? Or did others tell it to you about me? " Pilate answered: " Am I a Jew? Your own countrymen and the chief priests handed you over to me. What have you done? " Jesus answered: " My kingdom is not of this world. If my kingdom was of this world, my servants would have fought to prevent me being handed over to the Jews. But, as it is, my kingdom does not have its source here." So Pilate said to him: " So you are a king then? " Jesus said: " It is you who are saying that I am a king. The reason why I was born and came into the world is that I should bear witness to the truth. Every one who is of the truth hears my voice." " What is truth? " Pilate said to him.

When he had said this, he again went out to the Jews and said to them: " I find no fault in him. You have a custom that I should release one person to you at the Passover time. Do you wish me to release the King of the Jews for you? " They shouted: " Not this man, but Barabbas." And Barabbas was a brigand.

Then Pilate took Jesus and scourged him; and the soldiers plaited a crown of thorns, and put it on his head. And they put a purple robe on him; and they kept coming to him and saying: " Hail! King of the Jews! " And they dealt him repeated blows. Pilate came out again and said to them: " See! I bring him out to you, because I want you to know that I find no fault in him." So Jesus came out, wearing the crown of thorns and the purple robe. And Pilate said to them: " See! The Man! " So, when the chief priests and officers saw him, they shouted: " Crucify him! Crucify him! " Pilate said to them: " You take. him, and crucify him! For I find no fault in him." The Jews answered him: " We have a law, and by that law he ought to die, because he made himself out to be the Son of God." When Pilate heard this saying, he was still more alarmed.

He went into his headquarters again, and said to Jesus: " Where do you come from? " Jesus gave him no answer. Pilate said to him: " Do you refuse to speak to me? Are you not aware that I have authority to release you, and authority to crucify you? " Jesus answered him: " You would have no authority against me whatsoever, unless it had been given to you from above. That is why he who betrayed me to you is guilty of the greater sin." From this moment Pilate tried every way to release him; but the Jews kept insistently shouting: " If you release this

man, you are not Caesar's friend. Every man who makes himself a
king is an opponent of Caesar." So when Pilate heard these
words, he brought Jesus out. He took his seat on his judgment seat,
in the place that is called the Pavement—in Hebrew, Gabbatha.
It was the day of the preparation for the Passover. It was
about twelve o'clock midday. He said to the Jews: " See! Your
king! " They shouted: " Away with him! Away with him! Crucify
him! " Pilate said to them: " Shall I crucify your king? " The chief
priests answered: " We have no king but Caesar." Then he
handed him over to them to be crucified.

THIS is the most dramatic account of the trial of Jesús in the
New Testament, and to have cut it into small sections would
have been to lose the drama. It has to be read as one; but now
that we have read it as one, we shall take several days to study
it. The drama of this passage lies in the clash and interplay of
personalities. It will therefore be best to study it, not section by
section, but in the light of the actors within it.

We begin by looking at the *Jews*. In the time of Jesus the
Jews were subject to the Romans. The Romans allowed them a
good deal of self-government, but they had not the right to
carry out the death penalty. The *ius gladii*, as it was called,
the right of the sword, belonged only to the Romans. As the
Talmud records: " Forty years before the destruction of the
Temple, judgment in matters of life and death was taken away
from Israel." The first Roman governor of Palestine was named
Coponius, and Josephus, telling of his appointment as governor, says that he was sent as procurator " having the power of
life and death put into his hands by Caesar." (Josephus, *Wars
of the Jews*, 2, 8, 1). Josephus also tells of a certain priest called
Ananus who determined to execute certain of his enemies. Jews
of more prudent mind protested against his decision on the
grounds that he had no right either to take it or carry it out.
Ananus was not allowed to carry his decision into practice and
was deposed from office for even thinking of doing so.
(Josephus, *Antiquities of the Jews*, 20, 9, 1). It is true that
sometimes, as, for instance, in the case of Stephen, the Jews did
take the law into their own hands; but legally they had no right

to inflict the death penalty on anyone. That was why they had to bring Jesus to Pilate before he could be crucified.

If the Jews had themselves been able to carry out the death penalty, it would have been by stoning. The Law lays it down: " And he who blasphemes the name of the Lord, shall be put to death, all the congregation shall stone him " (*Leviticus* 24: 16). In such a case the witnesses whose word proved the crime had to be the first to fling the stones. " The hand of the witnesses shall be first against him to put him to death, and afterward the hand of all the people " (*Deuteronomy* 17: 7). That is the point of verse 32. That verse says that all this was happening that there might be fulfilled the word of Jesus in indication of the kind of death he was going to die. He had said that when he was *lifted up*, that is, when he was *crucified*, he would draw all men to him (*John* 12: 32). If that prophecy of Jesus was to be fulfilled, he must be *crucified*, not *stoned*; and therefore, even apart from the fact that Roman law would not allow the Jews to carry out the death penalty, Jesus had to die a Roman death, because he had to be *lifted up*.

The Jews from start to finish were seeking to use Pilate for their purposes. They could not kill Jesus themselves, so they were determined that the Romans would kill him for them.

JESUS AND PILATE

John 18: 28–19: 16 (*continued*)

BUT there were more things about the Jews than that.

(i) They began by hating Jesus; but they finished in a very hysteria of hatred, howling like wolves, with faces twisted in bitterness: " Crucify him! Crucify him! " In the end they reached such an insanity of hatred that they were impervious to reason and to mercy and even to the claims of common humanity. Nothing in this world warps a man's judgment as hatred does. Once a man allows himself to hate, he can neither think nor see straight, nor listen without distortion. Hatred is a terrible thing because it takes a man's senses away.

(ii) The hatred of the Jews made them lose all sense of proportion. They were so careful of ceremonial and ritual cleanness that they would not enter Pilate's headquarters, and yet they were busy doing everything possible to crucify the Son of God. To eat the Passover, a Jew had to be absolutely ceremonially clean. Now, if they had gone into Pilate's head-quarters, they would have incurred uncleanness in a double way. First, the scribal law said: " The dwelling-places of Gentiles are unclean." Second, the passover was the Feast of Unleavened Bread. Part of the preparation for it was a cere-monial search for leaven, and the banishing of every particle of leaven from every house because it was the symbol of evil. To go into Pilate's headquarters would have been to go into a place where leaven might be found; and to go into such a place when the Passover was being prepared was to render oneself unclean. But even if the Jews had entered a Gentile house which contained leaven, they would have been unclean only until evening. Then they would have had to undergo ceremonial bathing after which they would have been clean.

Now see what the Jews were doing. They were carrying out the details of the ceremonial law with meticulous care; and at the same time they were hounding to the Cross the Son of God. That is just the kind of thing that men are always liable to do. Many a church member fusses about the sheerest trifles, and breaks God's law of love and of forgiveness and of service every day. There is even many a church in which the details of vestments, furnishings, ritual, ceremonial are attended to with the most detailed care, and where the spirit of love and fellowship are conspicuous only by their absence. One of the most tragic things in the world is how the human mind can lose its sense of proportion and its ability to put first things first.

(ii) The Jews did not hesitate to twist their charge against Jesus. In their own private examination the charge they had formulated was one of blasphemy (*Matthew* 26: 65). They knew well that Pilate would not proceed on a charge like that. He would have said it was their own private religious quarrel and they could settle is as they liked without coming to him. In the end what the Jews produced was a charge of rebellion and political insurrection. They accused Jesus of claiming to be a king, although they knew that their accusation was a lie. Hatred is a terrible thing and does not hesitate to twist the truth.

(iv) In order to compass the death of Jesus the Jews denied every principle they had. The most astonishing thing they said that day was: " We have no king but Caesar." Samuel's word to the people was that God alone was their king (1 *Samuel* 12: 12). When the crown was offered to Gideon, his answer was: " I will not rule over you, and my son will not rule over you: the Lord will rule over you " (*Judges* 8: 23). When the Romans had first come into Palestine, they had taken a census in order to arrange the normal taxation to which subject people were liable. And there had been the most bloody rebellion, because the Jews insisted that God alone was their king, and to him alone they would pay tribute. When the Jewish leader said: " We have no king but Caesar," it was the most astonishing *volte-face* in history. The very statement must have taken Pilate's breath away, and he must have looked at them in half-bewildered, half-cynical amusement. The Jews were prepared to abandon every principle they had in order to eliminate Jesus.

It is a terrible picture. The hatred of the Jews turned them into a maddened mob of shrieking, frenzied fanatics. In their hatred they forgot all mercy, all sense of proportion, all justice, all their principles, even God. Never in history was the insanity of hatred so vividly shown.

JESUS AND PILATE

John 18: 28—19: 16 (*continued*)

Now we turn to the second personality in this story—*Pilate*. Throughout the trial his conduct is well-nigh incomprehensible. It is abundantly clear, it could not be clearer, that Pilate knew that the charges of the Jews were a series of lies, that he knew that Jesus was completely innocent, that he was deeply impressed with him, and that he did not wish to condemn him to death—and yet he did. First, he tried to refuse to deal with the case; then he tried to release Jesus on the grounds that at the Passover a criminal was always released; then he tried to compromise by scourging Jesus; then he made a last appeal. But he refused all through to put his foot down and tell the Jews that he would have nothing to do with their evil machinations. We will never even begin to understand Pilate unless we understand his history, which is set out for us partly in the writings of Josephus and partly in the writings of Philo.

To understand the part that Pilate played in this drama we must go back a long way. To begin with, what was a Roman governor doing in Judaea at all?

In 4 B.C. Herod the Great died. He had been king of the whole of Palestine. For all his faults he was in many ways a good king, and he had been very friendly with the Romans. In his will he divided up his kingdom between three of his sons. Antipas received Galilee and Peraea; Philip received Batanea, Auranitis and Trachonitis, the wild unpopulated regions of the north-east; and Archelaus, who at the time was only eighteen years old, received Idumaea, Judaea and Samaria. The Romans approved this distribution of the kingdom, and ratified it.

Antipas and Philip governed quietly and well; but Archelaus governed with such extortion and tyranny that the Jews themselves requested the Romans to remove him, and to appoint a governor. The likelihood is that they expected to be incorporated into the large province of Syria; and had that been so, the province was so large that they would very probably have been left pretty much to carry on the way they were. All Roman provinces were divided into two classes. Those which required troops stationed in them were in the direct control of the Emperor and were imperial provinces; those which did not require troops but were peaceful and trouble-free, were in the direct control of the senate and were senatorial provinces.

Palestine was obviously a troubled land; it needed troops and therefore it was in the control of the Emperor. Really great provinces were governed either by a proconsul or a legate; Syria was like that. Smaller provinces of the second class, were governed by a procurator. He was in full control of the military and judicial administration of the province. He visited every part of the province at least once a year and heard cases and complaints. He superintended the ingathering of taxes but had no authority to increase them. He was paid a salary from the treasury and was strictly forbidden to accept either presents or bribes; and, if he exceeded his duties, the people of his province had power to report him to the Emperor.

It was a procurator that Augustus appointed to control the affairs of Palestine, and the first one took over in A.D. 6. Pilate took over in A.D. 26 and remained in office until A.D. 35. Palestine was a province bristling with problems, one which required a firm and a strong and a wise hand. We do not know Pilate's previous history, but we do know that he must have had the reputation of being a good administrator or he would never have been given the responsible position of governing Palestine. It had to be kept in order, for, as a glance at the map will show, it was the bridge between Egypt and Syria.

But as governor Pilate was a failure. He seemed to begin with a complete contempt and a complete lack of sympathy for the Jews. Three famous, or infamous, incidents marked his career.

The first occurred on his first visit to Jerusalem. Jerusalem was not the capital of the province; its headquarters were at Caesarea. But the procurator paid many visits to Jerusalem, and, when he did, he stayed in the old palace of the Herods in the west part of the city. When he came to Jerusalem, he always came with a detachment of soldiers. The soldiers had their standards; and on the top of the standard there was a little bust in metal of the reigning Emperor. The Emperor was regarded as a god, and to the Jew that little bust on the standards was a graven image.

All previous Roman governors, in deference to the religious scruples of the Jews, had removed that image before they entered the city. Pilate refused to do so. The Jews besought him

to do so. Pilate was adamant; he would not pander to the
superstitions of the Jews. He went back to Caesarea. The Jews
followed him. They dogged his footsteps for five days. They
were humble, but determined in their requests. Finally he told
them to meet him in the amphitheatre. He surrounded them
with armed soldiers, and informed them that if they did not stop
their requests they would be killed there and then. The Jews
bared their necks and bade the soldiers strike. Not even Pilate
could massacre defenceless men like that. He was beaten and
compelled to agree that the images should thereafter be removed from the standards. That was how Pilate began, and it
was a bad beginning.

The second incident was this. The Jerusalem water supply
was inadequate. Pilate determined to build a new aqueduct.
Where was the money to come from? He raided the Temple
treasury which contained millions. It is very unlikely that
Pilate took money that was deposited for the sacrifices and the
Temple service. Much more likely, he took money which was
entitled *Korban,* and which came from sources which made it
impossible to use for sacred purposes. His aqueduct was much
needed; it was a worthy and a great undertaking; the water
supply would even be of great benefit to the Temple which
needed much cleansing with its continual sacrifices. But the
people resented it; they rioted and surged through the streets.
Pilate mingled his soldiers with them in plain clothes, with
concealed weapons. At a given signal they attacked the mob
and many a Jew was clubbed or stabbed to death. Once again
Pilate was unpopular—and he was rendered liable to be
reported to the Emperor.

The third incident turned out even worse for Pilate. As we
have seen, when he was in Jerusalem, he stayed in the ancient
palace of the Herods. He had certain shields made; and on them
he had inscribed the name of Tiberius the Emperor. These
shields were what is known as votive shields; they were devoted
to the honour and the memory of the Emperor. Now the
Emperor was regarded as a god; so here was the name of a
strange god inscribed and displayed for reverence in the holy

city. The people were enraged; the greatest men, even his closest
supporters, besought Pilate to remove them. He refused. The
Jews reported the matter to Tiberius the Emperor, and he
ordered Pilate to remove them.

It is relevant to note how Pilate ended up. This last incident
happened after Jesus had been crucified, in the year A.D. 35.
There was a revolt in Samaria. It was not very serious but
Pilate crushed it with sadistic ferocity and a plethora of
executions. The Samaritans had always been regarded as loyal
citizens of Rome and the legate of Syria intervened. Tiberius
ordered Pilate back to Rome. When he was on the way,
Tiberius died; so far as we know, Pilate never came to
judgment; and from that moment he vanishes from history.

It is clear why Pilate acted as he did. The Jews blackmailed
him into crucifying Jesus. They said: " If you let this man go,
you are not Caesar's friend." This was, in effect: " Your record
is not too good; you were reported once before; if you do not
give us our way, we will report you again to the Emperor, and
you will be dismissed." On that day in Jerusalem, Pilate's past
rose up and haunted him. He was blackmailed into assenting to
the death of Christ, because his previous mistakes had made it
impossible for him both to defy the Jews and to keep his post.
Somehow one cannot help being sorry for Pilate. He wanted to
do the right thing; but he had not the courage to defy the Jews
and do it. He crucified Jesus in order to keep his job.

JESUS AND PILATE

John 18: 28–19: 16 (*continued*)

WE have seen Pilate's history; let us now look at his conduct
during his trial of Jesus. He did not wish to condemn Jesus,
because he knew that he was innocent; and yet he was caught in
the mesh of his own past.

(i) Pilate began by trying to put the responsibility on to
someone else. He said to the Jews: " You take this man and

judge him according to your laws." He tried to evade the
responsibility of dealing with Jesus; but that is precisely what
no one can do. No one can deal with Jesus for us; we must deal
with him ourselves.

(ii) Pilate went on to try to find a way of escape from the
entanglement in which he found himself. He tried to use the
custom of releasing a prisoner at the Passover in order to
engineer the release of Jesus. He tried to evade dealing directly
with Jesus himself; but again that is precisely what no one can
do. There is no escape from a personal decision in regard to
Jesus; we must ourselves decide what we will do with him,
accept him or reject him.

(iii) Pilate went on to see what compromise could do. He
ordered Jesus to be scourged. It must have been in Pilate's mind
that a scourging might satisfy, or at least blunt the edge of,
Jewish hostility. He felt that he might avoid having to give the
verdict of the cross by giving the verdict of scourging. Once
again, that is what no man can do. No man can compromise
with Jesus; no man can serve two masters. We are either for
Jesus or against him.

(iv) Pilate went on to try what appeal could do. He led Jesus
out broken by the scourging and showed him to the people. He
asked them: " Shall I crucify your king? " He tried to swing the
balance by this appeal to emotion and to pity. But no man can
hope that appeal to others can take the place of his own
personal decision; and it was Pilate's place to make his own
decision. No man can evade a personal verdict and a personal
decision in regard to Jesus Christ.

In the end Pilate admitted defeat. He abandoned Jesus to the
mob, because he had not the courage to take the right decision
and to do the right thing.

But there are still more side-lights here on the character of
Pilate.

(i) There is a hint of Pilate's ingrained attitude of contempt.
he asked Jesus if he was a king. Jesus asked whether he asked
this on the basis of what he himself had discovered, or on the
basis of information indirectly received. Pilate's answer was:

" Am I a Jew? How do you expect me to know anything about Jewish affairs? " He was too proud to involve himself in what he regarded as Jewish squabbles and superstitions. And that pride was exactly what made him a bad governor. No one can govern a people if he makes no attempt to understand them and to enter into their thoughts and minds.

(ii) There is a kind of superstitious curiosity about Pilate. He wished to know whence Jesus came—and it was more than Jesus's native place that he was thinking of. When he heard that Jesus had claimed to be the Son of God, he was still more disturbed. Pilate was superstitious rather than religious, fearing that there might be something in it. He was afraid to come to a decision in Jesus's favour because of the Jews; he was equally afraid to come to a decision against him, because he had the lurking suspicion that God might be in this.

(iii) But at the heart of Pilate was a wistful longing. When Jesus said that he had come to witness to the truth, Pilate's answer was: " What is truth? " There are many ways in which a man might ask that question. He might ask it in cynical and sardonic humour. Bacon immortalized Pilate's answer, when he wrote: " What is truth? said jesting Pilate; and would not stay for an answer." But it was not in cynical humour that Pilate asked this question; nor was it the question of a man who did not care. Here was the chink in his armour. He asked the question wistfully and wearily.

Pilate by this world's standards was a successful man. He had come almost to the top of the Roman civil service; he was governor-general of a Roman province; but there was something missing. Here in the presence of this simple, disturbing hated Galilaean, Pilate felt that for him the truth was still a mystery—and that now he had got himself into a situation where there was no chance to learn it. It may be he jested, but it was the jest of despair. Philip Gibbs somewhere tells of listening to a debate between T. S. Eliot, Margaret Irwin, C. Day Lewis and other distinguished people on the subject, " Is this life worth living? " " True, they jested," he said, " but they jested like jesters knocking at the door of death."

Pilate was like that. Into his life there came Jesus, and suddenly he saw what he had missed. That day he might have found all that he had missed; but he had not the courage to defy the world in spite of his past, and to take his stand with Christ and a future which was glorious.

JESUS AND PILATE

John 18: 28–19: 16 (*continued*)

WE have thought of the picture of the crowd in this trial of Jesus and we have thought of the picture of Pilate. Now we must come to the central character in the drama—Jesus himself. He is depicted before us with a series of master-strokes.

(i) First and foremost, no one can read this story without seeing the sheer majesty of Jesus. There is no sense that he is upon trial. When a man faces him, it is not Jesus who is on trial; it is the man. Pilate may have treated many Jewish things with arrogant contempt, but he did not so treat Jesus. We cannot help feeling that it is Jesus who is in control and Pilate who is bewildered and floundering in a situation which he cannot understand. The majesty of Jesus never shone more radiantly than in the hour when he was on trial before men.

(ii) Jesus speaks with utter directness to us of his kingdom; it is not, he says, of this earth. The atmosphere in Jerusalem was always explosive; during the Passover it was sheer dynamite. The Romans well knew that, and during the Passover time they always drafted extra troops into Jerusalem. But Pilate never at any time had more than three thousand men under his command. Some would be in Caesarea, his headquarters; some would be on garrison duty in Samaria; there cannot really have been more than a few hundred on duty in Jerusalem. If Jesus had wished to raise the standard of rebellion and to fight it out, he could have done it easily enough. But he makes it quite clear that he claims to be a king and equally clear that his kingdom is not based on force but is a kingdom in the hearts of men. He would never deny that he aimed at conquest, but it was the conquest of love.

(iii) Jesus tells us why he came into the world. He came to witness to the truth; he came to tell men the truth about God, the truth about themselves, and the truth about life. As Emerson had it:

> " When half-gods go,
>   The gods arrive."

The days of guessings and gropings and half-truths were gone. He came to tell men the truth. That is one of the great reasons why we must either accept or refuse Christ. There is no half-way house about the truth. A man either accepts it, or rejects it; and Christ is the truth.

(iv) We see the physical courage of Jesus. Pilate had him scourged. When a man was scourged he was tied to a whipping-post in such a way that his back was fully exposed. The lash was a long leathern thong, studded at intervals with pellets of lead and sharpened pieces of bone. It literally tore a man's back into strips. Few remained conscious throughout the ordeal; some died; and many went raving mad. Jesus stood that. And after it, Pilate led him out to the crowd and said: " See! The man! " Here is one of John's double meanings. It must have been Pilate's first intention to awaken the pity of the Jews. " Look! " he said. " Look at this poor, bruised, bleeding creature! Look at this wretchedness! Can you possibly wish to hound a creature like this to an utterly unnecessary death? " But we can almost hear the tone of his voice change as he says it, and see the wonder dawn in his eyes. And instead of saying it half-contemptuously, to awaken pity, he says it with an admiration that will not be repressed. The word that Pilate used is *ho anthrōpos*, which is the normal Greek for a human being; but not so long afterwards the Greek thinkers were using that very term for *the heavenly man*, the ideal man, the pattern of manhood. It is always true that whatever else we say or do not say about Jesus, his sheer heroism is without parallel. Here indeed is a man.

JESUS AND PILATE

John 18: 28–19: 16 (*continued*)

(v) Once again we see here in the trial of Jesus the spontane-ousness of his death and the supreme control of God. Pilate warned Jesus that he had power to release him or to crucify him. Jesus answered that Pilate had no power at all, except what had been given him by God. The crucifixion of Jesus never, from beginning to end, reads like the story of a man caught up in an inexorable web of circumstances over which he had no control; it never reads like the story of a man who was hounded to his death; it is the story of a man whose last days were a triumphant procession towards the goal of the Cross.

(vi) And here also is the terrible picture of the silence of Jesus. There was a time when he had no answer to give to Pilate. There were other times when Jesus was silent. He was silent before the High Priest (*Matthew* 26: 63; *Mark* 14: 61). He was silent before Herod (*Luke* 23: 9). He was silent when the charges against him were made to Pilate by the Jewish authorities (*Matthew* 27: 14; *Mark* 15: 5). We have sometimes the experience, when talking to other people, of finding that argument and discussion are no longer possible, because we and they have no common ground. It is almost as if we spoke another language. That happens when men do in fact speak another mental and spiritual language. It is a terrible day when Jesus is silent to a man. There can be nothing more terrible than for a man's mind to be so shut by his pride and his self-will, that there is nothing Jesus can say to him that will make any difference.

(vii) Finally, it is just possible that in this trial scene there is a strange, dramatic climax, which is a magnificent example of John's dramatic irony.

The scene comes to an end by saying that Pilate brought Jesus out; as we have translated it, and as the Authorized Version and Revised Standard translate it, Pilate came out to the place that was called the Pavement of Gabbatha—which may mean the tessellated pavement of marble mosaic—and sat upon the judgment seat. This was the *bēma*, on which the magistrate sat to give his official decisions. Now the verb for *to sit* is *kathizein*, and that may be either intransitive or transitive; it may mean either to sit down oneself, or to seat another. Just possibly it means here that Pilate with one last mocking gesture brought Jesus out, clad in the terrible finery of the old purple robe and with his forehead girt with the crown of thorns and the drops of blood the thorns had wakened, and set *him* in the judgment seat, and with a wave of his hand said: " Am I to crucify your king? " The apocryphal Gospel of Peter says that in the mockery, they set Jesus on the seat of judgment and said: " Judge justly, King of Israel." Justin Martyr too says that " they set Jesus on the judgment seat, and said, ' Give judgment for us'." It may be that Pilate jestingly caricatured Jesus as judge. If that is so, what dramatic irony is there. That which was a mockery was the truth; and one day those who had mocked Jesus as judge would meet him as judge—and would remember.

So in this dramatic trial scene we see the immutable majesty, the undaunted courage and the serene acceptance of the Cross of Jesus. Never was he so regal as when men did their worst to humiliate him.

JESUS AND PILATE

John 18: 28–19: 16 (*continued*)

WE have looked at the main personalities in the trial of Jesus—the Jews with their hatred, Pilate with his haunting past, and Jesus in the serenity of his regal majesty. But certain other people were on the outskirts of the scene.

(i) There were the soldiers. When Jesus was given into their hands to be scourged, they amused themselves with their crude horse-play. He was a king? Well then, let him have a robe and crown. So they put an old purple robe on him and a crown of thorns round his brow; and they slapped him on the face. They were playing a game that ancient people commonly played. Philo in his work *On Flaccus* tells of a very similar thing that the mob at Alexandria did. " There was a madman named Carabas, afflicted not with the savage and beastlike sort of madness—for this form is undisguisable both for sufferers and bystanders—but with the quiet and milder kind. He used to spend his days and nights naked in the streets, sheltering from neither heat nor frost, a plaything of children and idle lads. They joined in driving the wretch to the gymnasium, and, setting him aloft so that he could be seen by everyone, they flattened a strip of bark for a fillet and put it on his head, and wrapped a floor-rug round his body for a mantle, and for sceptre someone catching sight of a small piece of the native papyrus that had been thrown on the road handed it to him. And when he had assumed the insignia of kingship as in theatrical mimes, and had been arrayed in the character of king, young men bearing staffs on their shoulders took their stance on either side in place of spearmen, mimic lancers. Then others approached, some as if to greet him, others as though to plead their causes, others as though to petition him about public matters. Then from the surrounding multitudes rang forth an outlandish shout of ' Marin,' the name by which it is said that kings are called in Syria." It is a poignant thing that the soldiers treated Jesus as a ribald crowd might treat an idiot boy.

And yet of all the people involved in the trial of Jesus, the soldiers were least to blame, for they did not know what they were doing. Most likely they had come up from Caesarea and did not know what it was all about. Jesus to them was only a chance criminal.

Here is another example of the dramatic irony of John. The soldiers made a caricature of Jesus as king, while in actual fact he was the only king. Beneath the jest there was eternal truth.

JESUS AND PILATE

John 18: 28–19: 16 (*continued*)

(ii) Last of all there was Barabbas whose episode John tells very briefly indeed. Of the custom of freeing a prisoner at Passover we know nothing more than the gospels tell us. The other gospels to some extent fill out John's brief picture and when we put all our information together we find that Barabbas was a notable prisoner, a brigand, who had taken part in a certain insurrection in the city and had committed murder (*Matthew* 27: 15–26; *Mark* 15: 6–15; *Luke* 23: 17–25; *Acts* 3: 14).

The name Barabbas is interesting. There are two possibilities as to its derivation. It may be compounded of Bar Abba which would mean " son of the father," or it may be compounded of Bar Rabban, which would mean " son of the Rabbi." It is not impossible that Barabbas was the son of some Rabbi, a scion of some noble family who had gone wrong; and it may well be that, criminal though he was, he was popular with the people as a kind of Robin Hood character. It is certainly true that we must not think of Barabbas as a sneak thief, or a petty pilferer, or a burglar. He was a *lēstēs*, which means a *brigand*. Either he was one of the warrior brigands who infested the Jericho road, the kind of man into whose hands the traveller in the parable fell; or, perhaps even more probable, he was one of the Zealots who had sworn to rid Palestine of the Romans, even if it meant a career of murder, robbery, assassination and crime. Barabbas was no petty criminal. A man of violence he might be, but his violence was the kind which might well have a romance and a glamour about it and make him the popular hero of the crowd and the despair of the law at one and the same time.

There is a still more interesting thing about *Barabbas*. It is a second name and there must have been a first name, just as, for instance, Peter had been Simon bar-Jonah, Simon the son of Jonah. Now there are certain ancient Greek manuscripts, and certain Syrian and Armenian translations of the New Testament which actually give the name of Barabbas as *Jesus*. That is by no means impossible, because in those days *Jesus* was a common name, being the Greek form of *Joshua*. If so, the choice of the crowd was even more dramatic, for they were shouting: " Not Jesus the Nazarene, but Jesus Barabbas."

The choice of the mob has been the eternal choice. Barabbas was the man of force and blood, the man who chose to reach his end by violent means. Jesus was the man of love and of gentleness, whose kingdom was in the hearts of men. It is the tragic fact of history that all through the ages men have chosen the way of Barabbas and refused the way of Jesus.

What happened to Barabbas no man knows; but John Oxenham in one of his books has an imaginary picture of him. At first Barabbas could think of nothing but his freedom; then he began to look at the man who had died that he might live. Something about Jesus fascinated him and he followed him out to see the end. As he saw Jesus bearing his Cross, one thought burned into his mind: " I should have been carrying that Cross, not he. He saved me! " And as he saw Jesus hanging on Calvary, the only thing of which he could think was: " I should have been hanging there, not he. He saved me! " It may be so, or it may not be so; but certainly Barabbas was one of the sinners Jesus died to save.

THE WAY TO THE CROSS

John 19: 17–22

So they took Jesus, and he, carrying his Cross for himself, went out to the place that is called the Place of a Skull, which is called in Hebrew Golgotha. They crucified him there, and with him they crucified two others, one on either side, and Jesus in the middle. Pilate wrote a title, and put it on the Cross. On it was written: " Jesus of Nazareth, the King of the Jews." Many of the Jews read this title, because the place where Jesus was crucified was near the city; and it was written in Hebrew, in Latin and in Greek. So the chief priests repeatedly said to Pilate: " Do not write, ' The King of the Jews.' But write, ' He said I am the King of the Jews.' " Pilate answered: " What I have written, I have written."

THERE was no more terrible death than death by crucifixion. Even the Romans themselves regarded it with a shudder of horror. Cicero declared that it was " the most cruel and horrifying death." Tacitus said that it was a " despicable death." It was originally a Persian method of execution. It may have been used because, to the Persians, the earth was sacred, and they wished to avoid defiling it with the body of an evil-doer. So they nailed him to a cross and left him to die there, looking to the vultures and the carrion crows to complete the work. The Carthaginians took over crucifixion from the Persians; and the Romans learned it from the Carthaginians.

Crucifixion was never used as a method of execution in the homeland, but only in the provinces, and there only in the case of slaves. It was unthinkable that a Roman citizen should die such a death. Cicero says: " It is a crime for a Roman citizen to be bound; it is a worse crime for him to be beaten; it is well nigh parricide for him to be killed; what am I to say if he be killed on a cross? A nefarious action such as that is incapable of description by any word, for there is none fit to describe it." It was that death, the most dreaded in the ancient world, the death of slaves and criminals, that Jesus died.

The routine of crucifixion was always the same. When the case had been heard and the criminal condemned, the judge uttered the fateful sentence: " *Ibis ad crucem*," " You will go to the cross." The verdict was carried out there and then. The condemned man was placed in the centre of a quaternion, a company of four Roman soldiers. His own cross was placed upon his shoulders. Scourging always preceded crucifixion and it is to be remembered how terrible scourging was. Often the criminal had to be lashed and goaded along the road, to keep him on his feet, as he staggered to the place of crucifixion. Before him walked an officer with a placard on which was written the crime for which he was to die and he was led through as many streets as possible on the way to execution.

There was a double reason for that. There was the grim reason that as many as possible should see and take warning from his fate. But there was a merciful reason. The placard was carried before the condemned man and the long route was chosen, so that if anyone could still bear witness in his favour, he might come forward and do so. In such a case, the procession was halted and the case retried.

In Jerusalem the place of execution was called *The Place of a Skull*, in Hebrew, *Golgotha*. (Calvary is the Latin for the Place of a Skull.) It must have been outside the city walls, for it was not lawful to crucify a man within the boundaries of the city. Where it was we do not certainly know.

More than one reason has been put forward for the strange, grim name, The Place of a Skull. There is a legend that it was so called because the skull of Adam was buried there. There is a suggestion that it was because it was littered with the skulls of crucified criminals. That is not likely. By Roman law a criminal must hang upon his cross until he died from hunger and thirst and exposure, a torture which sometimes lasted for days; but by Jewish law the body must be taken down and buried by nightfall. In Roman law the criminal's body was not buried but simply thrown away for the vultures and the crows and the pariah dogs to dispose of; but that would have been quite illegal under Jewish law and no Jewish place would be littered with skulls. It is much more likely that the place received its name because it was on a hill shaped like a skull. In any event it was a grim name for a place where grim things were done.

So Jesus went out, bruised and bleeding, his flesh torn to ribbons by the scourging, carrying his own Cross to the place where he was to die.

THE WAY TO THE CROSS

John 19: 17–22 (*continued*)

IN this passage there are two further things we must note. The inscription on Jesus's Cross was in Hebrew, in Latin and in

Greek. These were the three great languages of the ancient world and they stood for three great nations. In the economy of God every nation has something to teach the world; and these three stood for three great contributions to the world and to world history. Greece taught the world beauty of form and of thought; Rome taught the world law and good government; the Hebrews taught the world religion and the worship of the true God. The consummation of all these things is seen in Jesus. In him was the supreme beauty and the highest thought of God. In him was the law of God and the kingdom of God. In him was the very image of God. All the world's seekings and strivings found their consummation in him. It was symbolic that the three great languages of the world should call him king.

There is no doubt that Pilate put this inscription on the Cross of Jesus to irritate and annoy the Jews. They had just said that they had no king but Caesar; they had just absolutely refused to have Jesus as their king. And Pilate, by way of a grim jest, put this inscription on his Cross. The Jewish leaders repeatedly asked him to remove it; and Pilate refused. " What I have written," he said, " I have written." Here is Pilate the inflexible, the man who will not yield an inch. So very short a time before, this same man had been weakly vacillating as to whether to crucify Jesus or to let him go; and in the end had allowed himself to be bullied and blackmailed into giving the Jews their will. Adamant about the inscription, he had been weak about the crucifixion.

It is one of the paradoxical things in life that we can be stubborn about things which do not matter and weak about things of supreme importance. If Pilate had only withstood the blackmailing tactics of the Jews and had refused to be coerced into giving them their will with Jesus, he might have gone down in history as one of its great, strong men. But because he yielded on the important thing and stood firm on the unimportant, his name is a name of shame. Pilate was the man who took a stand on the wrong things and too late.

THE GAMBLERS AT THE CROSS

John 19: 23, 24

> When the soldiers had crucified Jesus, they took his clothes, and
> they divided them into four parts, a part for each soldier; and
> they took his tunic. It was a tunic which had no seam, woven
> throughout in one piece from the top. They said to each other:
> " Don't let's cut it up, but let us cast lots for it, and settle that way
> who will have it." This happened that the passage of scripture
> which says, " They divided my clothes among themselves, and
> they cast lots for my raiment," might be fulfilled. So, then, that is
> what the soldiers did.

WE have already seen that a criminal was escorted to the place
of execution by a quaternion of four soldiers. One of the per-
quisites of these soldiers was the clothes of the victim. Every
Jew wore five articles of apparel—his shoes, his turban, his
girdle, his tunic, and his outer robe. There were four soldiers,
and there were five articles. They diced for them, each had his
pick and the inner tunic was left. It was seamless, woven all in
one piece. To have cut it into four pieces would have been to
render it useless, and so they diced again to see who would
possess it. There are many things in this vivid picture.

(i) Studdert Kennedy has a poem based on it. The soldiers
were gamblers; and so in a sense was Jesus. He staked
everything on his utter fidelity to God; he staked everything on
the Cross. This was his last and greatest appeal to men, his last
and greatest act of obedience towards God.

> " And, sitting down, they watched him there,
> The soldiers did;
> There, while they played at dice,
> He made his sacrifice,
> And died upon his Cross to rid
> God's world of sin.
> He was a gambler, too, my Christ.
> He took his life and threw
> It for a world redeemed.

> And ere the agony was done,
> Before the westering sun went down,
> Crowning that day with its crimson crown,
> He knew that he had won."

There is a sense in which every Christian is a gambler, for every Christian must venture for his name.

(ii) No picture so shows the indifference of the world to Christ. There on the Cross Jesus was dying in agony; and there at the foot of the Cross the soldiers threw their dice as if it did not matter. An artist painted Christ standing with nail-pierced hands outstretched in a modern city, while the crowds surge by. Not one of them is even sparing him a look, except only a young hospital nurse; and beneath the picture there is the question: " Is it nothing to you all you who pass by? " (*Lamentations* 1: 12). The tragedy is not the hostility of the world to Christ; the tragedy is the world's indifference which treats the love of God as if it did not matter.

(iii) There are two further points which we must note in this picture. There is a legend that Mary herself had woven the seamless tunic and given it as a last gift to her son when he went out into the world. If that be true—and it may well be, for it was a custom of Jewish mothers to do just that—there is a double poignancy in the picture of these insensitive soldiers gambling for the tunic of Jesus which was his mother's gift.

(iv) But there is something half-hidden here. Jesus's tunic is described as being without seam, woven in one piece from top to bottom. That is the precise description of the linen tunic which the High Priest wore. Let us remember that the function of the priest was to be the liaison between God and man. The Latin for priest is *pontifex*, which means *bridge-builder*, and the priest was to build a bridge between God and man. No one ever did that as Jesus did. He is the perfect High Priest through whom men come to God. Again and again we have seen that there are two meanings in so many of John's statements, a meaning which lies on the surface, and a deeper inner meaning. When John tells us of the seamless tunic of Jesus it is not just a description of the kind of clothes that Jesus wore; it is something which tells us that Jesus is the perfect priest, opening the perfect way for all men to the presence of God.

(v) Lastly we note that in this incident John finds a fulfilment of Old Testament prophecy. He reads back into it the saying of the Psalmist: " They divide my garments among them, and for my raiment they cast lots " (*Psalm* 22: 18).

A SON'S LOVE

John 19: 25–27

> But his mother, and his mother's sister, and Mary the wife of Clopas, and Mary from Magdala, stood near the Cross of Jesus. So Jesus saw his mother, and he saw the disciple whom he loved standing by, and he said to his mother: " Woman! See! Your son." Then he said to the disciple: " See! Your mother! " And from that hour the disciple took her into his own home.

IN the end Jesus was not absolutely alone. At his Cross there were these four women who loved him. Some commentators explain their presence there by saying that in those days women were so unimportant that no one ever took any notice of women disciples, and that therefore these women were running no risk at all by being near the Cross of Jesus. That surely is a poor and unworthy explanation. It was always a dangerous thing to be an associate of a man whom the Roman government believed to be so dangerous that he deserved a Cross. It is always a dangerous thing to demonstrate one's love for someone whom the orthodox regard as a heretic. The presence of these women at the Cross was not due to the fact that they were so unimportant that no one would notice them; their presence was due to the fact that perfect love casts out fear.

They are a strange company. Of one, Mary the wife of Clopas, we know nothing; but we know something of the other three.

(i) There was Mary, Jesus's mother. Maybe she could not understand, but she could love. Her presence there was the most natural thing in the world for a mother. Jesus might be a criminal in the eyes of the law, but he was her son. As Kipling had it:

> " If I were hanged on the highest hill,
>   *Mother o' mine, O mother o' mine!*
> I know whose love would follow me still,
>   *Mother o' mine, O mother o' mine!*
>
> If I were drowned in the deepest sea,
>   *Mother o' mine, O mother o' mine!*
> I know whose tears would come down to me,
>   *Mother o' mine, O mother o' mine!*
>
> If I were damned of body and soul,
> I know whose prayers would make me whole,
>   *Mother o' mine, O mother o' mine!* "

The eternal love of motherhood is in Mary at the Cross.

(ii) There was Jesus's mother's sister. In John she is not named, but a study of the parallel passages (*Mark* 15: 40; *Matthew* 27: 56) makes it quite clear that she was Salome, the mother of James and John. The strange thing about her is that she had received from Jesus a very definite and stern rebuff. Once she had come to Jesus to ask him to give her sons the chief place in his kingdom (*Matthew* 20: 20), and Jesus had taught her how wrong such ambitious thoughts were. Salome was the woman he had rebuked—and yet she was there at the Cross. Her presence says much for her and for Jesus. It shows that she had the humility to accept rebuke and to love on with undiminished devotion; it shows that he could rebuke in such a way that his love shone through the rebuke. Salome's presence is a lesson to us on how to give and how to receive a rebuke

(ii) There was Mary from Magdala. All we know about her is that out of her Jesus cast seven devils (*Mark* 16: 9; *Luke* 8: 2). She could never forget what Jesus had done for her. His love had rescued her, and her love was such that it could never die. It was Mary's motto, written on her heart: " I will not forget what he has done for me."

But in this passage there is something which is surely one of the loveliest things in all the gospel story. When Jesus saw his mother, he could not but think of the days ahead. He could not commit her to the care of his brothers, for they did not believe in him yet (*John* 7: 5). And, after all, John had a double qualification for the service Jesus entrusted to him—he was Jesus's cousin, being Salome's son, and he was the disciple whom Jesus loved. So Jesus committed Mary to John's care and John to Mary's, so that they should comfort each other's loneliness when he was gone.

There is something infinitely moving in the fact that Jesus in the agony of the Cross, when the salvation of the world hung in the balance, thought of the loneliness of his mother in the days ahead. He never forgot the duties that lay to his hand. He was Mary's eldest son, and even in the moment of his cosmic battle, he did not forget the simple things that lay near home. To the end of the day, even on the Cross, Jesus was thinking more of the sorrows of others than of his own.

THE TRIUMPHANT ENDING

John 19: 28–30

> After that, when Jesus knew that everything was completed, he said, in order that the scripture might be fulfilled: " I thirst." There was a vessel standing there full of vinegar. So they put a sponge soaked in vinegar on a hyssop reed, and put it to his mouth. When he had received the vinegar, Jesus said; " It is finished." And he leaned his head back, and gave up his spirit.

IN this passage John brings us face to face with two things about Jesus.

(i) He brings us face to face with his human suffering; when Jesus was on the Cross, he knew the agony of thirst. When John was writing his gospel, round about A.D. 100, a certain tendency had arisen in religious and philosophical thought, called gnosticism. One of its great tenets was that spirit was altogether good and matter altogether evil. Certain conclusions followed. One was that God, who was pure spirit, could never take upon himself a body, because that was matter, and matter was evil. They therefore taught that Jesus never had a real body. They said that he was only a phantom. They said, for instance, that when Jesus walked, his feet left no prints on the ground, because he was pure spirit in a phantom body.

They went on to argue that God could never really suffer, and that therefore Jesus never really suffered but went through the whole experience of the Cross without any real pain. When the Gnostics thought like that, they believed they were honouring God and honouring Jesus; but they were really destroying Jesus. If he was ever to redeem man, he must become man. He had to become what we are in order to make us what he is. That is why John stresses the fact that Jesus felt thirst; he wished to show that he was really human and really underwent the agony of the Cross. John goes out of his way to stress the real humanity and the real suffering of Jesus.

(ii) But, equally, he brings us face to face with the triumph of Jesus. When we compare the four gospels we find a most illuminating thing. The other three do not tell us that Jesus said, " It is finished." But they do tell us that he died with a great shout upon his lips (*Matthew* 27: 50; *Mark* 15: 37; *Luke* 23: 46). On the other hand, John does not speak of the great cry, but does say that Jesus's last words were, " It is finished." The explanation is that the great shout and the words, " It is finished," are one and the same thing. " It is finished " is one word in Greek—*tetelestai*—and Jesus died with a shout of triumph on his lips. He did not say, " It is finished," in weary defeat; he said it as one who shouts for joy because the victory is won. He seemed to be broken on the Cross, but he knew that his victory was won.

The last sentence of this passage makes the thing even clearer. John says that Jesus leaned back his head and gave up his spirit. John uses the word which might be used for settling back upon a pillow. For Jesus the strife was over and the battle was won; and even on the Cross he knew the joy of victory and the rest of the man who has completed his task and can lean back, content and at peace.

Two further things we must notice in this passage, John traces back Jesus's cry, " I thirst," to the fulfilment of a verse in the Old Testament. He is thinking of *Psalm* 69: 21. " They gave me poison for food, and for my thirst they gave me vinegar to drink."

The second thing is another of John's hidden things. He tells us that it was on a hyssop reed that they put the sponge containing the vinegar. Now a hyssop reed is an unlikely thing to use for such a purpose, for it was only a stalk, like strong grass, and at the most two feet long. So unlikely is it that some scholars have thought that it is a mistake for a very similar word which means a *lance* or a *spear*. But it was *hyssop* which John wrote and *hyssop* which John meant. When we go centuries back to the first Passover when the children of Israel left their slavery in Egypt, we remember how the angel of death was to walk abroad that night and to slay every first born son of the Egyptians. We remember how the Israelites were to slay the Passover lamb and were to smear the doorposts of their houses with its blood so that the avenging angel of death would *pass over* their houses. And the ancient instruction was: " Take a *bunch of hyssop* and dip it in the blood which is in the basin, and touch the lintel and the two doorposts with the blood which is in the basin " (*Exodus* 12: 22). It was the blood of the Passover lamb which saved the people of God; it was the blood of Jesus which was to save the world from sin. The very mention of *hyssop* would take the thoughts of any Jew back to the saving blood of the Passover lamb; and this was John's way of saying that Jesus was the great Passover Lamb of God whose death was to save the whole world from sin.

THE WATER AND THE BLOOD

John 19: 31–37

Since it was the day of preparation, so that the bodies should not remain on the cross on the Sabbath (for that Sabbath was a very important day) the Jews asked Pilate to break their limbs, and to have the bodies removed. So the soldiers came, and they broke the limbs of the first criminal, and of the other who had been crucified with him. When they came to Jesus, and when they saw that he was already dead, they did not break his limbs. But one of the soldiers pierced his side with a spear, and immediately water and blood came forth. And he who saw it is a witness to this, and his word is true. And he knows that he is speaking the truth, that you also may believe. These things happened that the passage of scripture which says: " His bone shall not be broken," should be fulfilled. And again another passage says: " They shall see him whom they have pierced."

IN one thing the Jews were more merciful than the Romans. When the Romans carried out crucifixion under their own customs, the victim was simply left to die on the cross. He might hang for days in the heat of the midday sun and the cold of the night, tortured by thirst and tortured also by the gnats and the flies crawling in the weals on his torn back. Often men died raving mad on their crosses. Nor did the Romans bury the bodies of crucified criminals. They simply took them down and let the vultures and the crows and the dogs feed upon them.

The Jewish law was different. It laid it down: " If a man has committed a crime punishable by death, and he is put to death, and you hang him on a tree, his body shall not remain all night upon the tree, but you shall bury him the same day " (*Deuteronomy* 21: 22, 23). The *Mishnah*, the Jewish scribal law, laid down: " Everyone who allows the dead to remain overnight transgresses a positive command." The Sanhedrin actually was charged to have two burying places ready for those who had suffered the death penalty and were not to be buried in the burying place of their fathers. On this occasion it was even

more important that the bodies should not be allowed to hang
on the crosses overnight, because the next day was the Sabbath,
and the very special Sabbath of the Passover.

A grim method was used to despatch criminals who lingered
on. Their limbs were smashed with a mallet. That was done to
the criminals who were crucified with Jesus, but mercifully he
was spared that, for he was already dead. John sees that sparing
of Jesus as a symbol of another Old Testament passage. It was
laid down of the Passover lamb that not a bone of it should be
broken (*Numbers* 9: 12). Once again John is seeing Jesus as the
Passover Lamb who delivers his people from death.

Finally there follows a strange incident. When the soldiers
saw that Jesus was already dead they did not break his limbs
with the mallet; but one of them—it must have been to make
doubly sure that Jesus was dead—thrust a spear into his side.
And there flowed out water and blood. John attaches special
importance to that. He sees in it a fulfilment of the prophecy in
Zechariah 12: 10: " They look on him whom they have
pierced." And he goes out of his way to say that this is an
eye-witness account of what actually happened, and that he
personally guarantees that it is true.

First of all, let us ask what actually happened. We cannot be
sure but it may well be that Jesus died literally of a broken
heart. Normally, of course, the body of a dead man will not
bleed. It is suggested that what happened was that Jesus's
experiences, physical and emotional, were so terrible that his
heart was ruptured. When that happened the blood of the heart
mingled with the fluid of the pericardium which surrounds the
heart. The spear of the soldier pierced the pericardium and the
mingled fluid and blood came forth. It would be a poignant
thing to believe that Jesus, in the literal sense of the term, died
of a broken heart.

Even so, why does John stress it so much? He does so for
two reasons.

(i) To him it was the final, unanswerable proof that Jesus was
a real man with a real body. Here was the answer to the
gnostics with their ideas of phantoms and spirits and an unreal

manhood. Here was proof that Jesus was bone of our bone and flesh of our flesh.

√ (ii) But to John this was more than a proof of the manhood of Jesus. It was a symbol of the two great sacraments of the Church. There is one sacrament which is based on water—baptism; and there is one which is based on blood—the Lord's Supper with its cup of blood-red wine. The water of baptism is the sign of the cleansing grace of God in Jesus Christ; the wine of the Lord's Supper is the symbol of the blood which was shed to save men from their sins. The water and the blood which flowed from the side of Christ were to John the sign of the cleansing water of baptism and the cleansing blood commemorated and experienced in the Lord's Supper. As Toplady wrote:

> " Rock of ages, cleft for me,
> Let me hide myself in thee;
> Let the water and the blood,
> From thy riven side which flowed,
> Be of sin the double cure,
> Cleanse me from its guilt and power."

THE LAST GIFTS TO JESUS

John 19: 38–42

After that, Joseph from Arimathaea, who because of fear of the Jews was a secret disciple of Jesus, asked Pilate to be allowed to take away Jesus's body, and Pilate gave him permission to do so. So he came and took his body away. Nicodemus, who first came to Jesus by night, came too, bringing a mixture of myrrh and aloes, about a hundred pounds in weight. So they took Jesus's body and they wrapped it in linen clothes with spices, as it is the Jewish custom to lay a body in the tomb. There was a garden in the place where he was crucified; and in the garden there was a new tomb in which no one had ever been laid. So they laid Jesus there, because it was the day of preparation for the Sabbath, because the tomb was near at hand.

So Jesus died, and what had to be done now must be done quickly, for the Sabbath was almost begun and on the Sabbath no work could be done. The friends of Jesus were poor and could not have given him a fitting burial; but two people came forward.

Joseph of Arimathaea was one. He had always been a disciple of Jesus; he was a great man and a member of the Sanhedrin, and up to now he had kept his discipleship secret for he was afraid to make it known. Nicodemus was the other. It was the Jewish custom to wrap the bodies of the dead in linen clothes and to put sweet spices between the folds of the linen. Nicodemus brought enough spices for the burial of a king. So Joseph gave to Jesus a tomb; and Nicodemus gave him the clothes to wear within the tomb.

There is both tragedy and glory here.

(i) There is tragedy. Both Nicodemus and Joseph were members of the Sanhedrin, but they were secret disciples of Jesus. Either they had absented themselves from the meeting of the Sanhedrin which examined him and formulated the charge against him, or they had sat silent through it all. What a difference it would have made to Jesus, if, among these condemning, hectoring voices, one voice had been raised in his support. What a difference it would have made to see loyalty on one face amidst that sea of bleak, envenomed faces. But Nicodemus and Joseph were afraid.

We so often leave our tributes until people are dead. How much greater would loyalty in life have been than a new tomb and a shroud fit for a king. One flower in life is worth all the wreaths in the world in death; one word of love and praise and thanks in life is worth all the panegyrics in the world when life is gone.

(ii) But there is glory here, too. The death of Jesus had done for Joseph and Nicodemus what not even his life could do. No sooner had Jesus died on the Cross than Joseph forgot his fear and bearded the Roman governer with a request for the body. No sooner had Jesus died on the Cross than Nicodemus was there to bring a tribute that all men could see. The cowardice, the hesitation, the prudent concealment were gone. Those who had been afraid when Jesus was alive declared for him in a way that everyone could see as soon as he was dead. Jesus had not been dead an hour when his own prophecy came true: " I when I be lifted up from the earth will draw all men to myself " (*John* 12: 32). It may be that the silence of Nicodemus or his absence from the Sanhedrin brought sorrow to Jesus; but it is certain that he knew of the way in which they cast their fear aside after the Cross, and it is certain that already his heart was glad, for already the power of the Cross had begun to operate, and already it was drawing all men to him. The power of the Cross was even then turning the coward into the hero, and the waverer into the man who took an irrevocable decision for Christ.

BEWILDERED LOVE

John 20: 1–10

> On the first day of the week, very early in the morning, while it was still dark, Mary from Magdala came to the tomb; and she saw the stone taken away from the tomb. So she ran and came to Simon Peter, and to the other disciple whom Jesus loved, and she said to them: " They have taken the Lord away from the tomb, and we do not know where they have laid him." So Peter went out with the other disciple, and they set out for the tomb. The two were running together. The other disciple ran on ahead faster than Peter, and he was the first to come to the tomb. He stooped down and he saw the linen clothes lying there, but he did not go in. Then Simon Peter came, following him, and he went into the tomb. He saw the linen clothes lying there and he saw the napkin, which had been upon Jesus's head, not lying with the rest of the linen clothes, but lying apart from them, still in its folds, by itself. So then, the other disciple, who had arrived first at the tomb, went in too, and he saw, and believed. For as yet they did not realize the meaning of scripture, that Jesus should rise from the dead. So the disciples went back to their lodgings.

No one ever loved Jesus so much as Mary Magdalene. He had done something for her that no one else could ever do, and she could never forget. Tradition has always had it that Mary was a scarlet sinner, whom Jesus reclaimed and forgave and purified. Henry Kingsley has a lovely poem about her.

> " Magdalen at Michael's gate
>   Tirled at the pin;
> On Joseph's thorn sang the blackbird,
>   ' Let her in!   Let her in! '
>
> ' Hast thou seen the wounds? ' said Michael,
>   ' Knowest thou thy sin? '
> ' It is evening, evening,' sang the blackbird,
>   ' Let her in!   Let her in! '
>
> ' Yes, I have seen the wounds,
>   And I know my sin.'
> ' She knows it well, well, well,' sang the blackbird.
>   ' Let her in!   Let her in! '
>
> ' Thou bringest no offerings,' said Michael,
>   ' Nought save sin.'
> And the blackbird sang, ' She is sorry, sorry, sorry.
>   ' Let her in!   Let her in! '
>
> When he had sung himself to sleep,
>   And night did begin,
> One came and opened Michael's gate,
>   And Magdalen went in."

Mary had sinned much and she loved much; and love was all she had to bring.

It was the custom in Palestine to visit the tomb of a loved one for three days after the body had been laid to rest. It was believed that for three days the spirit of the dead person hovered round the tomb; but then it departed because the body had become unrecognizable through decay. Jesus's friends could not come to the tomb on the Sabbath, because to make the journey then would have been to break the law. Sabbath is, of course, our Saturday, so it was on Sunday morning that Mary came to the tomb. She came very early. The word used for *early* is *prōi* which was the technical word for the last of the four watches into which the night was divided, that which ran from 3 a.m. to 6 a.m. It was still grey dark when Mary came, because she could no longer stay away.

When she arrived at the tomb she was amazed and shocked. Tombs in ancient times were not commonly closed by doors. In front of the opening was a groove in the ground; and in the groove ran a stone, circular like a cartwheel; and the stone was wheeled into position to close the opening. Further Matthew tells us that the authorities had actually sealed the stone to make sure that no one would move it (*Matthew* 27: 66). Mary was astonished to find it removed. Two things may have entered her mind. She may have thought that the Jews had taken away Jesus's body; that, not satisfied with killing him on a cross, they were inflicting further indignities on him. But there were ghoulish creatures who made it their business to rob tombs; and Mary may have thought that this had happened here.

It was a situation Mary felt that she could not face herself; so she returned to the city to seek out Peter and John. Mary is the supreme instance of one who went on loving and believing even when she could not understand; and that is the love and the belief which in the end finds glory.

THE GREAT DISCOVERY

John 20: 1–10 (*continued*)

ONE of the illuminating things in this story is that Peter was still the acknowledged leader of the apostolic band. It was to him that Mary went. In spite of his denial of Jesus—and a story like that would not be long in being broadcast—Peter was still the leader. We often talk of Peter's weakness and instability, but there must have been something outstanding about a man who could face his fellow-men after that disastrous crash into cowardice; there must have been something about a man whom others were prepared to accept as leader even after that. His moment's weakness must never blind us to the moral strength and stature of Peter, and to the fact that he was a born leader.

So, then, it was to Peter and John that Mary went; and they immediately set out for the tomb. They went at a run; and John, who must have been a younger man than Peter since he lived on until the end of the century, outstripped Peter in this breathless race. When they came to the tomb, John looked in but went no farther. Peter with typical impulsiveness not only looked in, but went in. For the moment Peter was only amazed at the empty tomb; but things began to happen in John's mind. If someone had removed Jesus's body, if tomb-robbers had been at work, why should they leave the grave-clothes?

Then something else struck him—the grave-clothes were not dishevelled and disarranged. They were lying there *still in their folds*—that is what the Greek means—the clothes for the body where the body had been; the napkin where the head had lain. The whole point of the description is that the grave-clothes did not look as if they had been put off or taken off; they were lying there in their regular folds as if the body of Jesus had simply evaporated out of them. The sight suddenly penetrated to John's mind; he realized what had happened—and he believed. It was not what he had read in scripture which convinced him that Jesus had risen; it was what he saw with his own eyes.

The part that love plays in this story is extraordinary. It was Mary, who loved Jesus so much, who was first at the tomb. It was John, the disciple whom Jesus loved and who loved Jesus, who was first to believe in the Resurrection. That must always be John's great glory. He was the first man to understand and to believe. Love gave him eyes to read the signs and a mind to understand.

Here we have the great law of life. In any kind of work it is true that we cannot really interpret the thought of another person, unless between us and him there is a bond of sympathy. It is at once clear, for instance, when the conductor of an orchestra is in sympathy with the music of the composer whose work he is conducting. Love is the great interpreter. Love can grasp the truth when intellect is left groping and uncertain. Love can realize the meaning of a thing when research is blind. Once a young artist brought a picture of Jesus to Dorè for his verdict. Dorè was slow to give it; but at last he did so in one sentence. " You don't love him, or you would paint him better." We can neither understand Jesus nor help others to understand him, unless we take our hearts to him as well as our minds.

THE GREAT RECOGNITION

John 20: 11–18

> But Mary stood weeping outside at the tomb. As she wept she stooped down, and looked into the tomb, and she saw two angels sitting there in white robes, one at the head, and the other at the feet of the place where Jesus's body had been lying. They said to her: " Woman, why are you crying? " She said to them: " Because they have taken my Lord away, and I do not know where they have laid him." When she had said this, she turned round, and saw Jesus standing there, and did not know that it was Jesus. Jesus said to her: " Woman, why are you crying? Who are you looking for? " She, thinking that he was the gardener, said to him: " Sir, if you are the man who has removed him, tell me where you have laid him, and I will take him away." Jesus said to her: " Mary! " She turned, and said to him in Hebrew, " Rabbouni! " which means, " Master! " Jesus said to her: " Do not touch me! For I have not yet ascended to the Father. But go to my brethren, and say to them that I am going to ascend to my Father and your Father, to my God and your God." Mary of Magdala came to the disciples, telling them: " I have seen the Lord," and telling them what he had said to her.

SOMEONE has called this story the greatest recognition scene in all literature. To Mary belongs the glory of being the first person to see the Risen Christ. The whole story is scattered with indications of her love. She had come back to the tomb; she had taken her message to Peter and John, and then must have been left behind in their race to the tomb so that by the

time she got there, they were gone. So she stood there weeping.
There is no need to seek for elaborate reasons why Mary did
not know Jesus. The simple and the poignant fact is that she
could not see him through her tears.

Her whole conversation with the person she thought to be the
gardener shows her love. " If you are the man who has removed
him, tell me where you have laid him." She never mentioned the
name of Jesus; she thought everyone must know of whom she
was thinking; her mind was so full of him that there was not
anyone else for her in all the world. " I will take him away."
How was her woman's strength to do that? Where was she
going to take him? She had not even thought of these problems.
Her one desire was to weep her love over Jesus's dead body. As
soon as she had answered the person she took to be the
gardener, she must have turned again to the tomb and so turned
her back on Jesus. Then came his single word, " Mary! " and
her single answer, " Master! " (*Rabbouni* is simply an Aramaic
form of *Rabbi*; there is no difference between the words).

So we see there were two very simple and yet very profound
reasons why Mary did not recognize Jesus.

(i) She could not recognize him because of her tears. They
blinded her eyes so that she could not see. When we lose a dear
one, there is always sorrow in our hearts and tears shed or
unshed in our eyes. But one thing we must always remember—at such a time our sorrow is in essence selfish. It is of our
loneliness, our loss, our desolation, that we are thinking. We
cannot be weeping for one who has gone to be the guest of God;
it is for ourselves we weep. That is natural and inevitable. At
the same time, we must never allow our tears to blind us to the
glory of heaven. Tears there must be, but through the tears we
should glimpse the glory.

(ii) She could not recognize Jesus becasuse she insisted on
facing in the wrong direction. She could not take her eyes off
the tomb and so had her back to him. Again it is often so with
us. At such a time our eyes are upon the cold earth of the grave;
but we must wrench our eyes away from that. That is not where
our loved ones are; their worn-out bodies may be there; but the

real person is in the heavenly places in the fellowship of Jesus face to face, and in the glory of God.

When sorrow comes, we must never let tears blind our eyes to glory; and we must never fasten our eyes upon the grave and forget the heavens. Alan Walker in *Everybody's Calvary* tells of officiating at a funeral for people to whom the service was only a form, and who had neither Christian faith nor Christian connection. " When the service was over a young woman looked into the grave, and said brokenly: ' Goodbye, father.' It is the end for those who have no Christian hope." But for us at such a time, it is literally " Adieu! " " To God! " and it is literally " Until we meet again."

SHARING THE GOOD NEWS

John 20: 11–18 (*continued*)

THERE is one very real difficulty in this passage. When the recognition scene is complete, at first sight, at all events, Jesus said to Mary: " Touch me not, for I have not yet ascended to the Father." Just a few verses later we find him *inviting* Thomas to touch him (*John* 20: 27). In Luke we read of him inviting the terrified disciples: " See my hands and my feet, that it is I myself; handle me and see; for a spirit has not flesh and bones, as you see that I have " (*Luke* 24: 39). In Matthew's story we read that " they came up and took hold of his feet and worshipped him " (*Matthew* 28: 9). Even the form of John's statement is difficult. He makes Jesus say: " Do not hold me, for I have not yet ascended to the Father," as if to say that he could be touched after he had ascended. No explanation of this is fully satisfying.

(i) The whole matter has been given a spiritual significance. It has been argued that the only real contact with Jesus does in fact come after his Ascension; that it is not the physical touch of hand to hand that is important, but the contact which comes through faith with the Risen and Ever-living Lord. That is certainly true and precious but it does not seem to be the meaning of the passage here.

(ii) It is suggested that the Greek is really a mistranslation of an Aramaic original. Jesus of course would speak in Aramaic, and not in Greek; and what John gives us is a translation into Greek of what Jesus said. It is suggested that what Jesus really said was: " Hold me not; but before I ascend to my Father go to my brethren and say to them . . ." It would be as if Jesus said: " Do not spend so long in worshipping me in the joy of your new discovery. Go and tell the good news to the rest of the disciples." It may well be that here we have the explanation. The Greek imperative is a *present* imperative, and strictly speaking ought to mean: " Stop touching me." It may be that Jesus was saying to Mary: " don't go on clutching me selfishly to yourself. In a short time I am going back to my Father. I want to meet my disciples as often as possible before then. Go and tell them the good news that none of the time that we and they should have together may be wasted." That would make excellent sense, and that in fact is what Mary did.

(iii) There is one further possibility. In the other three gospels, the *fear* of those who suddenly recognized Jesus is always stressed. In *Matthew* 28: 10 Jesus's words are: " Do not be *afraid*." In *Mark* 16: 8 the story finishes: " For they were *afraid*." In *Luke* 24: 5 it is said that they were "*frightened*." In John's story as it stands there is no mention of this awe-stricken fear. Now, sometimes the eyes of the scribes who copied the manuscripts made mistakes, for the manuscripts were not easy to read. Some scholars think that what John originally wrote was not *MĔ APTOU*, Do not touch me, but, *MĔ PTOOU*, Do not be afraid. (The verb PTOEIN means *to flutter with fear*.) In that case Jesus was saying to Mary: " Don't be afraid; I haven't gone to my Father yet; I am still here with you."

No explanation of this saying of Jesus is altogether satisfying, but perhaps the second is the best of the three which we have considered.

Whatever happened, Jesus sent Mary back to the disciples with the message that what he had so often told them was now about to happen—he was on his way to his father; and Mary came with the news, " I have seen the Lord."

In that message of Mary there is the very essence of Christianity, for a Christian is essentially one who can say: " I have seen the Lord." Christianity does not mean knowing about Jesus; it means knowing him. It does not mean arguing about him; it means meeting him. It means the certainty of experience that Jesus is alive.

THE COMMISSION OF CHRIST

John 20: 19–23

> Late on that day, the first day of the week, when for fear of the Jews the doors had been locked in the place where the disciples were, Jesus came and stood in the midst of them, and said: " Peace be to you." And when he had said this he showed them his hands and his side. So the disciples rejoiced because they had seen the Lord. Jesus again said to them: " Peace to you. Even as the Father sent me, so I send you." When he had said this, he breathed on them and said to them: " Receive the Holy Spirit. If you remit the sins of any, they are remitted; if you retain them they are retained."

It is most likely that the disciples continued to meet in the upper room where the Last Supper had been held. But they met in something very like terror. They knew the envenomed bitterness of the Jews who had compassed the death of Jesus, and they were afraid that their turn would come next. So they were meeting in terror, listening fearfully for every step on the stair and for every knock at the door, lest the emissaries of the Sanhedrin should come to arrest them too. As they sat there, Jesus was suddenly in their midst. He gave them the normal everyday eastern greeting: " Peace be to you." It means far more than: " May you be saved from trouble." It means: " May God give you every good thing." Then Jesus gave the disciples the commission which the Church must never forget.

(i) He said that as God had sent him forth, so he sent them forth. Here is what Westcott called "The Charter of the Church." It means three things.

(a) It means that Jesus Christ needs the Church which is exactly what Paul meant when he called the Church " the body of Christ " (*Ephesians* 1: 23; 1 *Corinthians* 12: 12). Jesus had come with a message for all men and now he was going back to his Father. His message could never be taken to all men, unless the Church took it. The Church was to be a mouth to speak for Jesus, feet to run upon his errands, hands to do his work. Therefore, the first thing this means is that *Jesus is dependent on his Church.*

(b) It means that the Church needs Jesus. A person who is to be sent out needs someone to send him; he needs a message to take; he needs a power and an authority to back his message; he needs someone to whom he may turn when he is in doubt and in difficulty. Without Jesus, the Church has no message; without him she has no power; without him she has no one to turn to when up against it; without him she has nothing to enlighten her mind, to strengthen her arm, and to encourage her heart. This means that *the Church is dependent on Jesus.*

(c) There remains still another thing. The sending out of the Church by Jesus is parallel to the sending out of Jesus by God. But no one can read the story of the Fourth Gospel without seeing that the relationship between Jesus and God was continually dependent on Jesus's perfect obedience and perfect love. Jesus could be God's messenger only because he rendered to God that perfect obedience and love. It follows that the Church is fit to be the messenger and the instrument of Christ only when she perfectly loves him and perfectly obeys him. The Church must never be out to propagate *her* message; she must be out to propagate the message of Christ. She must never be out to follow man-made policies; she must be out to follow the will of Christ. The Church fails whenever she tries to solve some problem in her own wisdom and strength, and leaves out of account the will and guidance of Jesus Christ.

(ii) Jesus breathed on his disciples and gave them the Holy

Spirit. There is no doubt that, when John spoke in this way, he was thinking back to the old story of the creation of man. There the writer says: " And the Lord God formed man of dust from the ground, and breathed into his nostrils the breath of life; and man became a living being " (*Genesis* 2: 7). This was the same picture as Ezekiel saw in the valley of dead, dry bones, when he heard God say to the wind: " Come from the four winds, O breath, and breath upon these slain that they may live " (*Ezekiel* 37: 9). The coming of the Holy Spirit is like the wakening of life from the dead. When he comes upon the Church she is recreated for her task.

(iii) Jesus said to the disciples: " If you remit the sins of anyone, they are remitted; if you retain them, they are retained." This is a saying whose true meaning we must be careful to understand. One thing is certain—no man can forgive any other man's sins. But another thing is equally certain—it is the great privilege of the Church to convey the message of God's forgiveness to men. Suppose someone brings us a message from another, our assessment of the value of that message will depend on how well the bringer of the message knows the sender. If someone proposes to interpret another's thought to us, we know that the value of his interpretation depends on his closeness to the other.

The apostles had the best of all rights to bring Jesus's message to men, because they knew him best. If they knew that a person was really penitent, they could with absolute certainty proclaim to him the forgiveness of Christ. But equally, if they knew that there was no penitence in his heart or that he was trading on the love and the mercy of God, they could tell him that until his heart was altered there was no forgiveness for him. This sentence does not mean that the power to forgive sins was ever entrusted to any man or men; it means that the power to proclaim that forgiveness was so entrusted; along with the power to warn that forgiveness is not open to the impenitent. This sentence lays down the duty of the Church to convey forgiveness to the penitent in heart and to warn the impenitent that they are forfeiting the mercy of God.

THE DOUBTER CONVINCED

John 20: 24–29

But Thomas, who is called Didymus, one of the Twelve, was not with them when Jesus came. The other disciples told him: " We have seen the Lord." He said to them: " Unless I see the print of the nails in his hands, and put my finger in the print of the nails, and unless I put my hand into his side, I will not believe." Eight days later the disciples were again in the room, and Thomas was with them. When the doors were locked, Jesus came and stood in the midst of them, and said: " Peace be to you." Then he said to Thomas: " Stretch out your finger here, and look at my hands; stretch out your hand and put it into my side; and show yourself not faithless but believing." Thomas answered: " My Lord and my God! " Jesus said to him: " You have believed because you have seen me. Blessed are those who have not seen and who have believed."

To Thomas the Cross was only what he had expected. When Jesus had proposed going to Bethany, after the news of Lazarus's illness had come, Thomas's reaction had been: " Let us also go, that we may die with him " (*John* 11: 16). Thomas never lacked courage, but he was the natural pessimist. There can never be any doubt that he loved Jesus. He loved him enough to be willing to go to Jerusalem and die with him when the other disciples were hesitant and afraid. What he had expected had happened, and when it came, for all that he had expected it, he was broken-hearted, so broken-hearted that he could not meet the eyes of men, but must be alone with his grief.

King George the Fifth used to say that one of his rules of life was: " If I have to suffer, let me be like a well-bred animal, and let me go and suffer alone." Thomas had to face his suffering and his sorrow alone. So it happened that, when Jesus came back again, Thomas was not there; and the news that he had come back seemed to him far too good to be true, and he refused to believe it. Belligerent in his pessimism, he said that he would never believe that Jesus had risen from the dead until he had seen and handled the print of the nails in his hands and thrust his hand into the wound the spear had made in Jesus's side. (There is no mention of any wound-print in Jesus's feet because in crucifixion the feet were usually not nailed, but only loosely bound to the cross.)

Another week elapsed and Jesus came back again; and this time Thomas was there. And Jesus knew Thomas's heart. He repeated Thomas's own words, and invited him to make the test that he had demanded. And Thomas's heart ran out in love and devotion, and all he could say was: " My Lord and my God! " Jesus said to him: " Thomas, you needed the eyes of sight to make you believe; but the days will come when men will see with the eye of faith and believe."

The character of Thomas stands out clear before us.

(i) He made one mistake. He withdrew from the Christian fellowship. He sought loneliness rather than togetherness. And because he was not there with his fellow Christians he missed the first coming of Jesus. We miss a great deal when we separate ourselves from the Christian fellowship and try to be alone. Things can happen to us within the fellowship of Christ's Church which will not happen when we are alone. When sorrow comes and sadness envelops us, we often tend to shut ourselves up and refuse to meet people. That is the very time when, in spite of our sorrow, we should seek the fellowship of Christ's people, for it is there that we are likeliest of all to meet him face to face.

(ii) But Thomas had two great virtues. He absolutely refused to say that he understood what he did not understand, or that he believed what he did not believe. There is an uncompromising honesty about him. He would never still his doubts by pretending that they did not exist. He was not the kind of man who would rattle off a creed without understanding what it was all about. Thomas had to be sure—and he was quite right. Tennyson wrote:

> " There lives more faith in honest doubt,
> Believe me, than in half the creeds."

There is more ultimate faith in the man who insists on being sure than in the man who glibly repeats things which he has never thought out, and which he may not really believe. It is doubt like that which in the end arrives at certainty.

(ii) Thomas's other great virtue was that when he was sure, he went the whole way. " My Lord and my God! " said he. There was no halfway house about Thomas. He was not airing his doubts just for the sake of mental acrobatics; he doubted in order to become sure; and when he did, his surrender to certainty was complete. And when a man fights his way through his doubts to the conviction that Jesus Christ is Lord, he has attained to a certainty that the man who unthinkingly accepts things can never reach.

THOMAS IN THE AFTER DAYS

John 20: 24–29

WE do not know for sure what happened to Thomas in the after days; but there is an apocryphal book called *The Acts of Thomas* which purports to give his history. It is of course only legend, but there may well be some history beneath the legend; and certainly in it Thomas is true to character. Here is part of the story which it tells.

After the death of Jesus the disciples divided up the world among them, so that each might go to some country to preach the gospel. India fell by lot to Thomas. (The Thomist Church in South India does trace its origin to him.) At first he refused to go, saying that he was not strong enough for the long journey. He said: " I am an Hebrew man; how can I go amongst the Indians and preach the truth? " Jesus appeared to him by night and said: " Fear not, Thomas, go thou unto India and preach the word there, for my grace is with thee." But Thomas still stubbornly refused. " Whither thou wouldest send me, send me," he said, " but elsewhere, for unto the Indians I will not go."

It so happened that there had come a certain merchant from

India to Jerusalem called Abbanes. He had been sent by King Gundaphorus to find a skilled carpenter and to bring him back to India, and Thomas was a carpenter. Jesus came up to Abbanes in the market-place and said to him: " Wouldest thou buy a carpenter? " Abbanes said: " Yes." Jesus said, " I have a slave that is a carpenter, and I desire to sell him," and he pointed at Thomas in the distance. So they agreed on a price and Thomas was sold, and the agreement ran: " I, Jesus, the son of Joseph the carpenter, acknowledge that I have sold my slave, Thomas by name, unto thee Abbanes, a merchant of Gundaphorus, king of the Indians." When the deed was drawn up Jesus found Thomas and took him to Abbanes. Abbanes said: " Is this your master? " Thomas said: " Indeed he is." Abbanes said: " I have bought thee from him." And Thomas said nothing. But in the morning he rose early and prayed, and after his prayer he said to Jesus: " I will go whither thou wilt, Lord Jesus, thy will be done." It is the same old Thomas, slow to be sure, slow to surrender; but once his surrender is made, it is complete.

The story goes on to tell how Gundaphorus commanded Thomas to build a palace, and Thomas said that he was well able to do so. The king gave him money in plenty to buy materials and to hire workmen, but Thomas gave it all away to the poor. Always he told the king that the palace was rising steadily. The king was suspicious. In the end he sent for Thomas: " Hast thou built me the palace? " he demanded. Thomas answered: " Yes." " When, then, shall we go and see it? " asked the king. Thomas answered: " Thou canst not see it now, but when thou departest this life, then thou shalt see it." At first the king was very angry and Thomas was in danger of his life; but in the end the king too was won for Christ, and so Thomas brought Christianity to India.

There is something very lovable and very admirable about Thomas. Faith was never an easy thing for him; obedience never came readily to him. He was the man who had to be sure; he was the man who had to count the cost. But once he was sure, and once he had counted the cost, he was the man who went to the ultimate limit of faith and obedience. A faith like Thomas's is better than any glib profession; and an obedience like his is better than an easy acquiescence which agrees to do a thing without counting the cost and then goes back upon its word.

THE AIM OF THE GOSPEL

John 20: 30, 31

> Jesus did many other signs in the presence of his disciples which have not been written in this book. These have been written that you may believe that Jesus is the Anointed One, the Son of God, and that believing you may have life in his name.

It is quite clear that as the gospel was originally planned, it comes to an end with this verse. Chapter 21 is to be regarded as an appendix and an afterthought.

No passage in the gospels better sums up the aim of the writers than this.

(i) It is quite clear that the gospels never set out to give a full account of the life of Jesus. They do not follow him from day to day but are selective. They give us, not an exhaustive account of everything that Jesus said or did, but a selection which shows what he was like and the kind of things he was always doing.

(ii) It is also clear that the gospels were not meant to be biographies of Jesus, but appeals to take him as Saviour, Master and Lord. Their aim was, not to give information, but to give life. It was to paint such a picture of Jesus that the reader would be bound to see that the person who could speak and teach and act and heal like this could be none other than the Son of God; and that in that belief he might find the secret of real life.

When we approach the gospels as history and biography, we approach them in the wrong spirit. We must read them, not primarily as historians seeking information, but as men and women seeking God.

John 21

ON any view the twenty-first chapter of John is a strange one. The gospel comes to an end with chapter twenty; and then seems to begin again in chapter twenty-one. Unless there had been certain very special things that he wanted to say, the man who put the gospel into its final form would never have added this chapter. We know that in John's gospel there are often two meanings, one which lies on the surface, and a deeper one which lies beneath. So, then, as we study this chapter, we will try to find out why it is so strangely added after the gospel seemed to have come to an end.

THE RISEN LORD

John 21: 1–14

After these things Jesus again showed himself to the disciples by the Sea of Tiberias. This was the way in which he showed himself. Simon Peter, and Thomas, who is called Didymus, and Nathanael, who came from Cana in Galilee, and the sons of Zebedee, and two other disciples, were together. Simon Peter said to them: " I am going to fish." They said to him: " We, too, are coming with you." They went out, and went on board the boat, and that night they caught nothing. When early morning had come, Jesus stood on the seashore. But the disciples did not know that it was Jesus. So Jesus said to them: " Lads, have you got any fish? " They answered: " No." He said to them: " Cast your net on the right hand side of the ship, and you will find a catch." So they cast the net, and now they could not haul it in for the great number of the fishes. The disciple whom Jesus loved said to Peter: " It is the Lord." So, when Simon Peter heard that it was the Lord, he put on his tunic (for he was stripped for work) and jumped into the sea. The other disciples came to shore in the boat (for they were not far from the land, only about a hundred yards) dragging the net full of fishes. When they had disembarked on land, they saw a charcoal fire set there, and fish on it, and bread. Jesus said to them: " Bring some of the fish you have just caught." So Simon Peter went on board and hauled the net to land, full of large fishes, one hundred and fifty-three of them; and, although there were so many of them, the net was not broken. Jesus said to them: " come and have breakfast." None of the disciples dared to ask him: " Who are you? " because they knew that it was the Lord. Jesus came and took bread and gave it to them, and he gave them the fish in the same way. This was the third time Jesus showed himself to the disciples after he had been raised from among the dead.

IT was certainly someone who knew the fishermen of the Sea of Galilee who wrote this story. Night-time was the best for fishing. W. M. Thomson in *The Land and the Book* describes night fishing: " There are certain kinds of fishing always carried on at night. It is a beautiful sight. With blazing torch, the boat glides over the flashing sea, and the men stand gazing keenly into it until their prey is sighted, when, quick as lightning, they fling their net or fly their spear; and often you see the tired fishermen come sullenly into harbour in the morning, having toiled all night in vain."

The catch here is not described as a miracle, and it is not meant to be taken as one. The description is of something which still frequently happens on the lake. Remember that the boat was only about a hundred yards from land. H. V. Morton describes how he saw two men fishing on the shores of the lake. One had waded out from the shore and was casting a bell net into the water. " But time after time the net came up empty. It was a beautiful sight to see him casting. Each time the neatly folded net belled out in the air and fell so precisely on the water that the small lead weights hit the lake at the same moment making a thin circular splash. While he was waiting for another cast, Abdul shouted to him from the bank to fling to the left, which he instantly did. This time he was successful. . . . Then he drew up the net and we could see the fish struggling in it. . . . It happens very often that the man with the hand-net must rely on the advice of someone on shore, who tells him to cast either to the left or the right, because in the clear water he can often see a shoal of fish invisible to the man in the water." Jesus was acting as guide to his fishermen friends, just as people still do today.

It may be that it was because it was the grey dark that they did not recognize Jesus. But the eyes of the disciple whom Jesus loved were sharp. He knew it was the Lord; and when Peter realized who it was he leaped into the water. He was not actually naked. He was girt with a loin cloth as the fisher always was when he plied his trade. Now it was the Jewish law that to offer greeting was a religious act, and to carry out a religious act a man must be clothed; so Peter, before he set out to come to Jesus, put on his fisherman's tunic, for he wished to be the first to greet his Lord.

THE REALITY OF THE RESURRECTION

John 21: 1–14 (*continued*)

Now we come to the first great reason why this strange chapter was added to the already finished gospel. It was to demonstrate once and for all *the reality of the Resurrection.* There were many who said that the appearances of the Risen Christ were nothing more than visions which the disciples had. Many would admit the reality of the visions but insist that they were still only visions. Some would go further and say that they were not visions but hallucinations. The gospels go far out of their way to insist that the Risen Christ was not a vision, not an hallucination, not even a spirit, but a real person. They insist that the tomb was empty and that the Risen Christ had a real body which still bore the marks of the nails and the spear thrust in his side.

But this story goes a step further. A vision or a spirit would not be likely to point out a shoal of fish to a party of fishermen. A vision or a spirit would not be likely to kindle a charcoal fire on the seashore. A vision or a spirit would not be likely to cook a meal and to share it out. And yet, as this story has it, the Risen Christ did all these things. When John tells how Jesus came back to his disciples when the doors were shut, he says: " He showed them his hands and his side " (*John* 20: 20).

Ignatius, when writing to the Church at Smyrna, relates an even more definite tradition about that. He says: " I know and believe that he was in the flesh even after the resurrection, and when he came to Peter and his company, he said to them: ' Take, handle me, and see that I am not a bodiless demon.' And straightway they touched him, and they believed, for they were firmly convinced of his flesh and blood. . . . And after his resurrection he ate and drank with them as one in the flesh."

The first and simplest aim of this story is to make quite clear the reality of the resurrection. The Risen Lord was not a vision, nor the figment of someone's excited imagination, nor the appearance of a spirit or a ghost; it was Jesus who had conquered death and come back.

THE UNIVERSALITY OF THE CHURCH

John 21: 1–14 (*continued*)

THERE is a second great truth symbolized here. In the Fourth Gospel everything is meaningful, and it is therefore hardly possible that John gives the definite number one hundred and fifty-three for the fishes without meaning something by it. It has indeed been suggested that the fishes were counted simply because the catch had to be shared out between the various partners and the crew of the boat, and that the number was recorded simply because it was so exceptionally large. But when we remember John's way of putting hidden meanings in his gospel for those who have eyes to see, we must think that there is more to it than that.

Many ingenious suggestions have been made.

(i) Cyril of Alexandria said that the number 153 is made up of three things. First, there is 100; and that represents " the fullness of the Gentiles." 100, he says, is the fullest number. The shepherd's full flock is 100 (*Matthew* 18: 12). The seed's full fertility is 100-fold. So the 100 stands for the fullness of the Gentiles who will be gathered in to Christ. Second, there is the

50; and the 50 stands for the remnant of Israel who will be gathered in. Third, there is the 3; and the 3 stands for the Trinity to whose glory all things are done.

(ii) Augustine has another ingenious explanation. he says that 10 is the number of the Law, for there are ten commandments; 7 is the number of grace, for the gifts of the Spirit are sevenfold.

> " Thou the anointing Spirit art,
> Who dost thy sevenfold gifts impart."

Now 7+10 makes 17; and 153 is the sum of all the figures, 1+2+3+4 . . ., up to 17. Thus 153 stands for all those who either by Law or by grace have been moved to come to Jesus Christ.

(iii) The simplest of the explanations is that given by Jerome. He said that in the sea there are 153 different kinds of fishes; and that the catch is one which includes every kind of fish; and that therefore the number symbolizes the fact that some day all men of all nations will be gathered together to Jesus Christ.

We may note a further point. This great catch of fishes was gathered into the net, and the net held them all and was not broken. The net stands for the Church; and there is room in the Church for all men of all nations. Even if they all come in, she is big enough to hold them all.

Here John is telling us in his own vivid yet subtle way of the universality of the Church. There is no kind of exclusiveness in her, no kind of colour bar or selectiveness. The embrace of the Church is as universal as the love of God in Jesus Christ. It will lead us on to the next great reason why this chapter was added to the gospel if we note that it was Peter who drew the net to land (*John* 21: 11).

THE SHEPHERD OF CHRIST'S SHEEP

John 21: 15–19

When they had breakfasted, Jesus said to Simon Peter: " Simon, son of Jonas, do you love me more than these? " He said to him:

" Yes, Lord; you know that I love you." He said to him: " Be a shepherd to my lambs." Again he said to him a second time: " Simon, son of Jonas, do you love me? " He said to him: " Yes, Lord. You know that I love you." He said to him: " Be a shepherd to my sheep." He said to him the third time: " Simon, son of Jonas, do you love me? " Peter was vexed when he said to him the third time: " Do you love me? " So he said to him: " Lord, you know all things. You know that I love you." Jesus said to him: " Feed my sheep. This is the truth I tell you—when you were young, you fastened your girdle around you and you went where you wished. But when you grow old, you will stretch out your arms, and another will gird you, and will carry you to a place not of your own choosing." He said this to show by what kind of death Peter was going to glorify God. When he had said this, he said to Peter: " Follow me! "

HERE is a scene which must have been printed for ever on the mind of Peter.

(i) First we must note the question which Jesus asked Peter: " Simon, son of Jonas, do you love me more than these? " As far as the language goes that can mean two things equally well.

(a) It may be that Jesus swept his hand round the boat and its nets and equipment and the catch of fishes, and said to Peter: " Simon, do you love me more than these things? Are you prepared to give them all up, to abandon all hope of a successful career, to give up a steady job and a reasonable comfort, in order to give yourself for ever to my people and to my work? " This may have been a challenge to Peter to take the final decision to give all his life to the preaching of the gospel and the caring for Christ's folk.

(b) It may be that Jesus looked at the rest of the little group of the disciples, and said to Peter: " Simon, do you love me more than your fellow-disciples do? " It may be that Jesus was looking back to a night when Peter said: " Though they all fall away because of you, I will never fall away " (*Matthew* 26: 33). It may be that he was gently reminding Peter how once he had thought that he alone could be true and how his courage had failed. It is more likely that the second meaning is right, because in his answer Peter does not make comparisons any more; he is content simply to say: " You know that I love you."

(ii) Jesus asked this question three times; and there was a reason for that. It was three times that peter denied his Lord, and it was three times that his Lord gave him the chance to affirm his love. Jesus, in his gracious forgiveness, gave Peter the chance to wipe out the memory of the threefold denial by a threefold declaration of love.

(iii) We must note what love brought Peter. (a) It brought him a task. " If you love me," Jesus said, " then give your life to shepherding the sheep and the lambs of my flock." We can prove that we love Jesus only by loving others. Love is the greatest privilege in the world, but it brings the greatest responsibility. (b) It brought Peter a cross. Jesus said to him: " When you are young you can choose where you will go; but the day will come when they will stretch out your hands on a cross, and you will be taken on a way you did not choose." The day came when, in Rome, Peter did die for his Lord; he, too, went to the Cross, and he asked to be nailed to it head downwards, for he said that he was not worthy to die as his Lord had died. Love brought Peter a task, and it brought him a cross. Love always involves responsibility, and it always involves sacrifice. We do not really love Christ unless we are prepared to face his task and take up his Cross.

It was not for nothing that John recorded this incident. He recorded it to show Peter as the great shepherd of Christ's people. It may be, indeed it was inevitable, that people would draw comparisons in the early Church. Some would say that John was the great one, for his flights of thought went higher than those of any other man. Some would say that Paul was the great one, for he fared to the ends of the earth for Christ. but this chapter says that Peter, too, had his place. He might not write and think like John; he might not voyage and adventure like Paul; but he had the great honour, and the lovely task, of being the shepherd of the sheep of Christ. And here is where we can follow in the steps of Peter. We may not be able to think like John; we may not be able to go out to the ends of the earth like Paul; but each of us can guard some one else from going astray, and each of us can feed the lambs of Christ with the food of the word of God.

THE WITNESS TO CHRIST

John 21: 20-24

Peter turned and saw the disciple whom Jesus loved following, the disciple who at their meal reclined on Jesus's breast and said: " Lord, who is it who is to betray you? " When Peter saw this disciple, he said to Jesus: " Lord, what is going to happen to this man? " Jesus said to him: " If I wish him to remain till I come, what has that to do with you? Your job is to follow me." So this report went out to the brethren, that this disciple would not die. But Jesus did not say to him that he would not die. What he did say was: " If I wish him to remain till I come, what has that got to do with you? " This is the disciple who bears witness to these things, and who has written these things, and we know that his witness is true.

THIS passage makes it quite clear that John must have lived to a very old age; he must have lived on until the report went round that he was going to go on living until Jesus came again. Now, just as the previous passage assigned to Peter his place in the scheme of things, this one assigns to John his place. It was his function to be pre-eminently the witness to Christ. Again, people in the early Church must have made their comparisons. They must have pointed out how Paul went away to the ends of the earth. They must have pointed out how Peter went here and there shepherding his people. And then they may have wondered what was the function of John who had lived on in Ephesus until he was so old that he was past all activity. Here is the answer: Paul might be the pioneer of Christ, Peter might be the shepherd of Christ, but John was the witness of Christ. He was the man who was able to say: " I saw these things, and I know that they are true."

To this day the final argument for Christianity is Christian experience. To this day the Christian is the man who can say: " I know Jesus Christ, and I know that these things are true."

So, at the end, this gospel takes two of the great figures of the Church, Peter and John. To each Jesus had given his function. It was Peter's to shepherd the sheep of Christ, and in the end to die for him. It was John's to witness to the story of Christ, and to live to a great old age and to come to the end in peace. That did not make them rivals in honour and prestige, nor make the one greater or less than the other; it made them both servants of Christ.

Let a man serve Christ where Christ has set him. As Jesus said to Peter: " Never mind the task that is given to someone else. Your job is to follow me." That is what he still says to each one of us. Our glory is never in comparison with other men; our glory is the service of Christ in whatever capacity he has allotted to us.

THE LIMITLESS CHRIST

John 21: 25

> There are many other things that Jesus did, and if they were written down one by one, I think that not even the world itself would be big enough to hold the written volumes.

IN this last chapter the writer of the Fourth Gospel has set before the Church for whom he wrote certain great truths. He has reminded them of the reality of the Resurrection; he has reminded them of the universality of the Church; he has reminded them that Peter and John are not competitors in honour, but that Peter is the great shepherd and John the great witness. Now he comes to the end; and he comes there thinking once again of the splendour of Jesus Christ. Whatever we know of Christ, we have only grasped a fragment of him. Whatever the wonders we have experienced, they are as nothing to the wonders which we may yet experience. Human categories are powerless to describe Christ, and human books are inadequate to hold him. And so John ends with the innumerable triumphs, the inexhaustible power, and the limitless grace of Jesus Christ.

———————

NOTE ON THE STORY OF THE WOMAN TAKEN IN ADULTERY

John 8: 2–11

To many this is one of the loveliest and the most precious stories in the gospels; and yet it has great difficulties attaching to it.

The older the manuscripts of the New Testament are, the more valuable they are. They were all copied by hand, and obviously the nearer they are to the original writings the more likely they are to be correct. We call these very early manuscripts the Uncial manuscripts, because they are written in capital letters; and we base the text of the New Testament on the earliest ones, which date from the fourth to the sixth century. The fact is that out of all these early manuscripts this story occurs only in one, and that is not one of the best. Six of them omit it completely. Two leave a blank space where it should come. It is not till we come to the late Greek manuscripts and the medieval manuscripts that we find this story, and even then it is often marked to show that it is doubtful.

Another source of our knowledge of the text of the New Testament is what are called the versions; that is, the translations into languages other than Greek. This story is not included in the early Syriac version, nor in the Coptic or Egyptian version, nor in some of the early Latin versions.

Again, none of the early fathers seems to know anything about it. Certainly they never mention it or comment on it. Origen, Chrysostom, Theodore of Mopsuestia, Cyril of Alexandria on the Greek side do not mention it. The first Greek commentator to remark on it is Euthymius Zigabenus whose date is A.D. 1118, and even he says that it is not in the best manuscripts.

Where, then, did this incident come from? Jerome certainly knew it in the fourth century, for he included it in the Vulgate. We know that Augustine and Ambrose both knew it, for they comment on it. We know that it is in all the later manuscripts.

It is to be noted that its position varies a great deal. In some manuscripts it is put at the end of the fourth gospel; and in some it is inserted after *Luke* 21: 38.

But we can trace it even further back. It is quoted in a third century book called *The Apostolic Constitutions*, where it is given as a warning to bishops who are too strict. Eusebius, the Church historian, says that Papias tells a story " of a woman who was accused of many sins before the Lord," and Papias lived not very long after A.D. 100.

Here, then, are the facts. This story can be traced as far back as very early in the second century. When Jerome produced the Vulgate he, without question, included it. The later manuscripts and the medieval manuscripts all have it. And yet none of the great manuscripts includes it. None of the great Greek fathers of the Church ever mentions it. But some of the great Latin fathers did know it, and speak of it.

What is the explanation? We need not be afraid that we shall have to let this lovely story go; for it is guarantee enough of its genuineness that we can trace it back to almost A.D. 100. But we do need some explanation of the fact that none of the great manuscripts includes it. Moffatt, Weymouth and Rieu print it in brackets; and the Revised Standard Version prints it in small type at the foot of the page.

Augustine gives us a hint. He says that this story was removed from the text of the gospel because " some were of slight faith," and " to avoid scandal." We cannot tell for certain, but it would seem that in the very early days the people who edited the text of the New Testament thought that this was a dangerous story, a justification for a light view of adultery, and therefore omitted it. After all, the Christian Church was a little island in a sea of paganism. Its members were so apt to relapse into a way of life where chastity was unknown; and were for ever open to pagan infection. But as time went on the danger grew less, or was less feared, and the story, which had always circulated by word of mouth and which one manuscript retained, came back.

It is not likely that it is now in the place where it ought to be. It was probably inserted here to illustrate Jesus's saying in *John* 8: 15: " I judge no man." In spite of the doubt that the modern translations cast on it, and in spite of the fact that the early manuscripts do not include it, we may be sure that this is a real story about Jesus, although one so gracious that for long men were afraid to tell it.

NOTE ON THE DATE OF THE CRUCIFIXION

THERE is one great problem in the fourth gospel which we did not take note of at all when we were studying it. Here we can note it only very briefly, for it is really an unsolved problem on which the literature is immense.

It is quite certain that the fourth gospel and the other three give different dates for the Crucifixion, and take different views of what the last meal together was.

In the Synoptic gospels it is clear that the Last Supper was the Passover and that Jesus was crucified on Passover Day. It must be remembered that the Jewish day began at 6 p.m. on what to us is the day before. The Passover fell on 15th Nisan; but 15th Nisan began on what to us is 14th Nisan at 6 p.m. Mark seems to be quite clear; he says: " And on the first day of unleavened bread, when they sacrificed the passover, his disciples said unto him, Where will you have us go and prepare for you to eat the passover? " Jesus gives them instructions. Then Mark goes on: " And they prepared the passover, and when it was evening he came with the twelve." (*Mark* 14: 12–17.) Undoubtedly Mark wished to show the Last Supper as a Passover meal and that Jesus was crucified on Passover day; and Matthew and Luke follow Mark.

On the other hand John is quite clear that Jesus was crucified on the day *before* the passover. He begins his story of the last meal: " Now before the feast of the Passover . . ." (*John* 13: 1). When Judas left the upper room, they thought he had

gone to *prepare* for the Passover (*John* 13: 29). The Jews
would not enter the judgment hall lest they should become unclean and be prevented from eating the Passover (*John* 18: 28).
The judgment is during the *preparation* for the Passover (*John*
19: 14).

There is here a contradiction for which there is no compromise solution. Either the Synoptic gospels are correct or John
is. Scholars are much divided. But it seems most likely that the
Synoptics are correct. John was always looking for hidden
meanings. In his story Jesus is crucified as somewhere near
the *sixth hour* (*John* 19: 14). *It was just then that in the Temple the Passover lambs were being killed.* By far the likeliest
thing is that John dated things in order that Jesus would be
crucified at exactly the same time as the Passover lambs
were being killed, so that he might be seen as the great Passover Lamb who saved his people and took away the sins of
the world. It seems that the Synoptic gospels are right in *fact*,
while John is right in *truth*; and John was always more interested in eternal truth than in mere historic fact.

There is no full explanation of this obvious discrepancy; but
this seems to us the best.

FURTHER READING

C. Kingsley Barrett, *The Gospel According to Saint John* (*G*)

J. H. Bernard, *St John* (ICC; *G*)

E. C. Hoskyns (ed. F. M. Davey), *The Fourth Gospel* (*E*)

R. H. Lightfoot, *St John's Gospel: A Commentary* (*E*)

G. H. C. Macgregor, *The Gospel of John* (MC; *E*)

J. N. Saunders (ed. B. A. Mastin), *The Gospel According to Saint John* (ACB; *E*)

R. V. G. Tasker, *The Gospel According to Saint John* (TC; *E*)

B. F. Westcott, *The Gospel According to Saint John* (*E*)
  The Speaker's Commentary (MmC; *G*)

Abbreviations

ACB : A. and C. Black New Testament Commentary
ICC : International Critical Commentary
MC : Moffatt Commentary
MmC: Macmillan Commentary
TC : Tyndale Commentary

E : English Text
G : Greek Text

THE DAILY STUDY BIBLE

Published in 17 Volumes